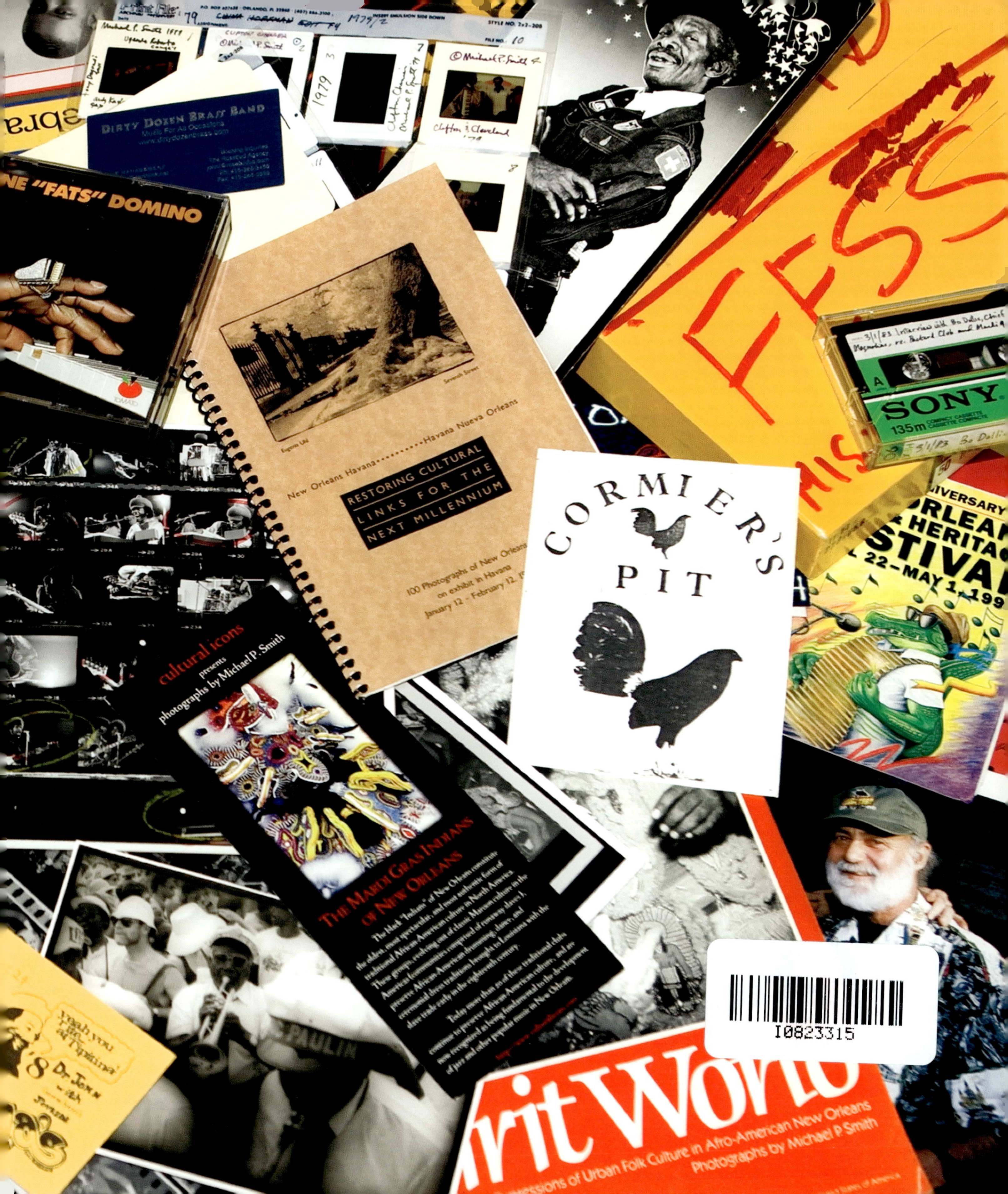

Dirty Dozen Brass Band
Music For All Occasions
www.dirtydozenbrass.com
"FATS" DOMINO
New Orleans Havana ........ Havana Nueva Orleans
RESTORING CULTURAL LINKS FOR THE NEXT MILLENNIUM
100 Photographs of New Orleans on exhibit in Havana
CORMIER'S PIT
cultural icons presents photographs by Michael P. Smith
The Mardi Gras Indians of New Orleans
SONY
135m
Photographs by Michael P. Smith
I0823315

# IN THE SPIRIT

## The Photography of
## Michael P. Smith
## from The Historic New Orleans Collection

WITH ESSAYS BY | JOHN H. LAWRENCE & JUDE SOLOMON
DAN CAMERON
JASON BERRY

EDITED BY | ERIN GREENWALD

PUBLISHED ON THE OCCASION OF THE EXHIBITION
*IN THE SPIRIT: THE PHOTOGRAPHY OF MICHAEL P. SMITH FROM THE HISTORIC NEW ORLEANS COLLECTION*

BEYOND THE MUSIC
THE HISTORIC NEW ORLEANS COLLECTION
MARCH 11–SEPTEMBER 13, 2009

TWENTY-FIVE JAZZ FESTS
CONTEMPORARY ARTS CENTER, NEW ORLEANS
APRIL 17–JULY 12, 2009

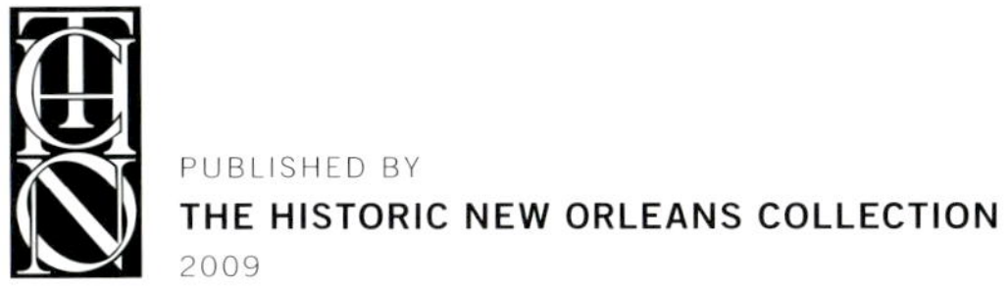

PUBLISHED BY
**THE HISTORIC NEW ORLEANS COLLECTION**
2009

The Historic New Orleans Collection is a museum, research center, and publisher dedicated to the study and preservation of the history of New Orleans and the Gulf South region. The Collection is operated by the Kemper and Leila Williams Foundation, a Louisiana nonprofit corporation.

*Library of Congress Cataloging-in-Publication Data*

Historic New Orleans Collection.

In the spirit : the photography of Michael P. Smith from the Historic New Orleans Collection / with essays by John H. Lawrence ... [et al.] ; edited by Erin Greenwald. -- 1st ed.

p. cm.

ISBN-13: 978-0-917860-54-6 (pbk. : alk. paper)

ISBN-10: 0-917860-54-3 (pbk. : alk. paper)

1. Photography, Artistic—Exhibitions. 2. Smith, Michael P. (Michael Proctor), 1937-2008—Exhibitions. 3. African Americans—Louisiana—New Orleans—Social life and customs—20th century—Pictorial works—Exhibitions. 4. New Orleans (La.)—Social life and customs—20th century—Pictorial works—Exhibitions. 5. Historic New Orleans Collection—Exhibitions. I. Smith, Michael P. (Michael Proctor), 1937-2008. II. Lawrence, John H. III. Greenwald, Erin. IV. Title.

TR647.S575 2009

770.9763'35--dc22

2008055304

CIP


533 Royal Street
New Orleans, Louisiana 70130
www.hnoc.org

First edition. 4,000 copies

Printed by Harvey-Hauser, New Orleans, Louisiana

FRONT COVER ILLUSTRATION:
*Funeral of Emile Victor Clay* (detail), image by Michael P. Smith, 1996; ©The Historic New Orleans Collection

BACK COVER ILLUSTRATION:
*Doug Kershaw*, image by Michael P. Smith, 1978; ©The Historic New Orleans Collection

# CONTENTS

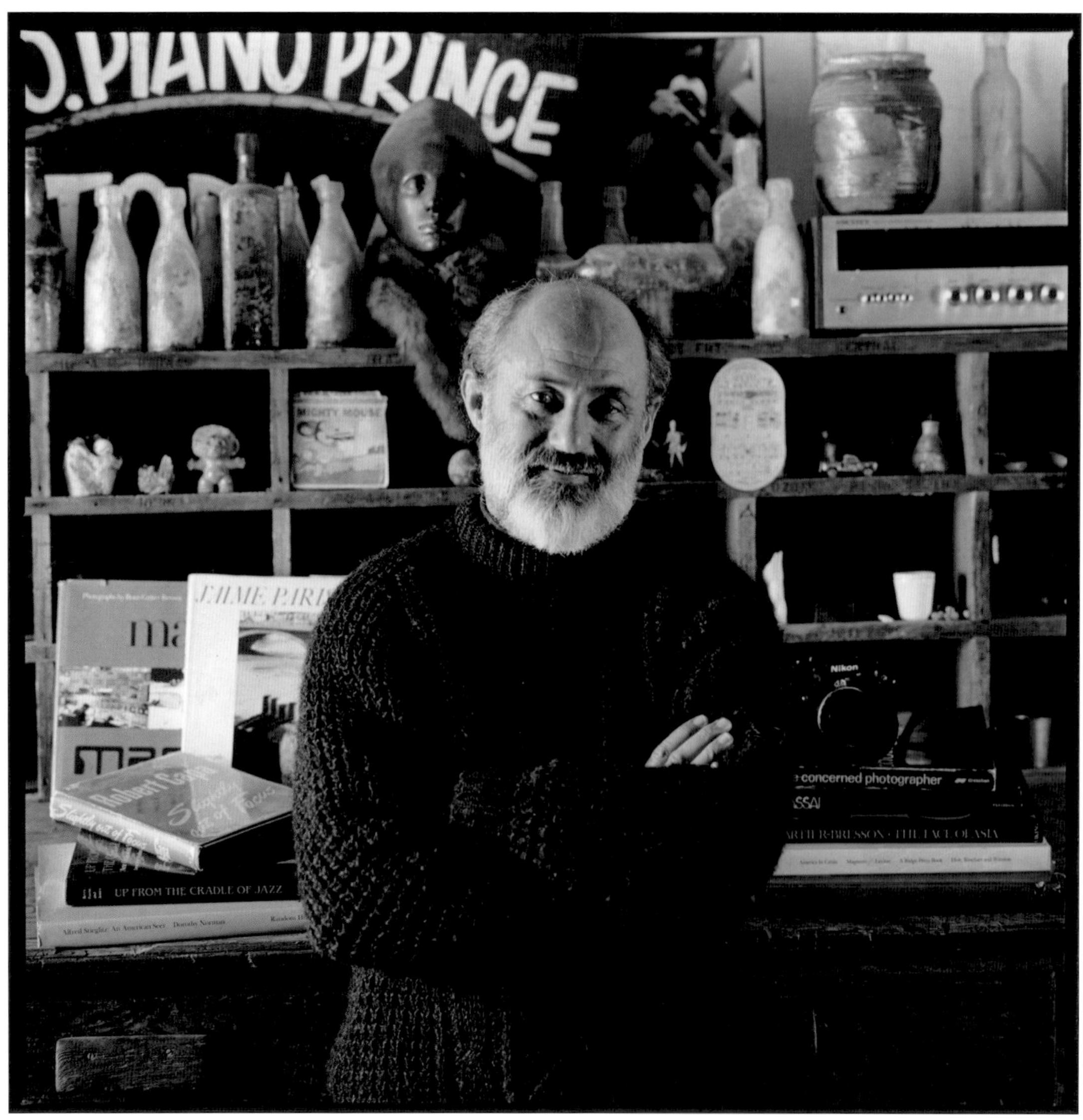


**MICHAEL P. SMITH** | BY TOM JIMISON; 1990

# INTRODUCTION

In the spring of 2007, The Historic New Orleans Collection acquired the archive of photographer Michael P. Smith, ensuring both its long-term preservation and ultimate public access. Its contents visually describe and contextualize a large swath of New Orleans's late-20th-century musical landscape: musicians, religious leaders, and citizens, along with the physical locations where these groups came together. In an overall sense, many of Smith's photographs present the multitude of regularly occurring but uniquely presented events that flow throughout the city's annual calendar.

Through photographs, field recordings, journals, correspondence, printed ephemera, and other documents, Smith's professional and personal interests offer an extended gaze into the world of spiritual churches, Mardi Gras Indians, and traditional jazz funerals, as well as the New Orleans Jazz and Heritage Festival, which Smith photographed without interruption from 1970 to 2004. The essays of Jason Berry, Dan Cameron, and John Lawrence and Jude Solomon serve to place these events both within the context of Smith's overall career and the materials of the archive.

The trove of Michael P. Smith archival material now housed at The Historic New Orleans Collection provides the basis for two exhibitions under the single title *In the Spirit: The Photography of Michael P. Smith from The Historic New Orleans Collection*. The exhibition at The Historic New Orleans Collection, subtitled *Beyond the Music,* focuses on the breadth of Smith's nearly forty-year career. *Twenty-Five Jazz Fests* at the Contemporary Arts Center, New Orleans, spotlights Smith's photographs of performers at the world-renowned New Orleans Jazz and Heritage Festival. This catalogue and the accompanying exhibitions mark the inaugural public presentation of the Michael P. Smith Archive.

## BEYOND THE MUSIC: AN ARCHIVE AND A LIFE

For many, the study of the past is an endeavor marked by a seemingly endless procession of dates and numbers: Ten Commandments; 1776; 1,000 days; Seven Years' War. But to examine the story of an individual life, it is not only a misrepresentation but a cruelty to reduce that life to numbers, since numbers are rarely effective in relaying the essence of a creative career. Nonetheless, those numbers associated with the life of Michael P. Smith (1937–2008) are telling, suggesting the breadth and depth of a very active thirty-six-year career: over 4,000 rolls of 35mm black-and-white film negatives (along with their contact sheets), nearly 1,500 rolls of 35mm transparencies, some 150 sheet-film negatives, and 1,500 photographic prints (color and black-and-white) in various sizes. Add to these five books devoted to his photographs and dozens of recording industry album and CD covers reproducing his work, and the contours of his life's work begin to take shape. Enlarging and deepening the understanding of this artist are approximately forty-three linear feet of letters, publications, printed ephemera, tape recordings, articles, notes, and journals that can be seen as the residue of Smith's full and passionate pursuit of life. Uncountable but no less important are other quantities associated with Smith's existence: lives affected, people enlightened, and cultures described through his defining images and ceaseless inquiry.

Smith was keenly aware of the history he was recording—first relying exclusively on still-film, and beginning in 1983 supplementing film with taped audio recordings. Given the breadth of his pursuits, he sought the organizational system best suited to preserve his labors. The necessary, but seemingly tedious, concerns about storage systems for negatives, slides, prints, and ephemera intrigued him. But the preservation of south Louisiana's "cultural wetlands"—a term Smith coined to describe the neighborhoods and social structures that permitted New Orleans's vibrant urban culture to flourish—was paramount.

Smith saw each photograph as the end of a process—not just an optical, mechanical, and chemical process of fashioning an image from experience, but a cultural process as well. Smith's interest in, knowledge of, and research into the subjects he photographed made him parts detective, folklorist, and cultural anthropologist, and gave him a profound ability to capture the essence of what he observed in photographs. He was also a spokesman for the traditions and people he respected. His advocacy on behalf of the region's folkways took shape not only through his photographs but also through his participation in scholarly conferences in the United States and abroad, and through his public defense of local customs before governmental bodies when legislative action or "progress" threatened cultural continuity. He was very much a part of the web of individuals who supported, promoted, and watched over unique elements of New Orleans's cultural fabric.

Smith's career was not limited to his photographic pursuits. He was a founding member of Tipitina's when it opened (in the space formerly occupied by the 501 Club) in early 1977. This now-legendary music hall showcased the best of tradition-based New Orleans music. In 1986, Smith served as a director of the Professor Longhair Foundation, dedicated to the work of New Orleans musician Henry Roeland Byrd, and in 1983 founded the New Orleans Urban Folklife Society, a not-for-profit entity created to preserve and nurture the Crescent City's traditional music and cultural heritage.

Those peering past the curtain to the world captured in Smith's photographs are often interested in specific topics: spiritual churches, traditional jazz funeral processions, outings of social aid and pleasure clubs and their second line parades, Mardi Gras Indians, the annual New Orleans Jazz and Heritage Festival, etc. It is easy enough to see how this archive cleaves upon such thematic lines. Smith's curiosity was boundless; the universe of his images can be organized into many constellations. But the ultimate character of the body of work is linear and continuous. In keeping a chronological record of his production, Smith showed not only the richness of the culture that fascinated him, but its cyclical

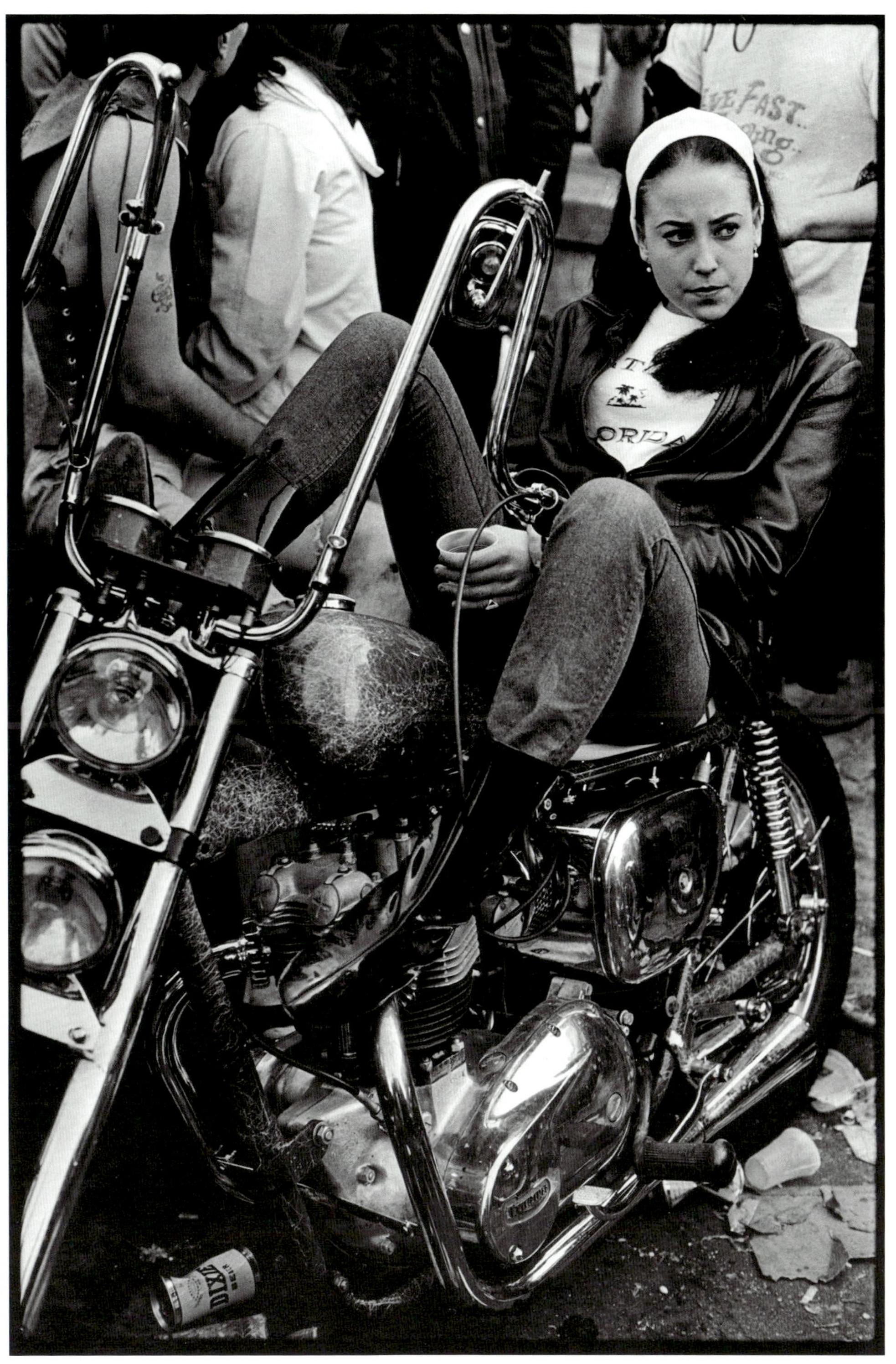


**MARDI GRAS DAY** | FRENCH QUARTER, NEW ORLEANS; 1968

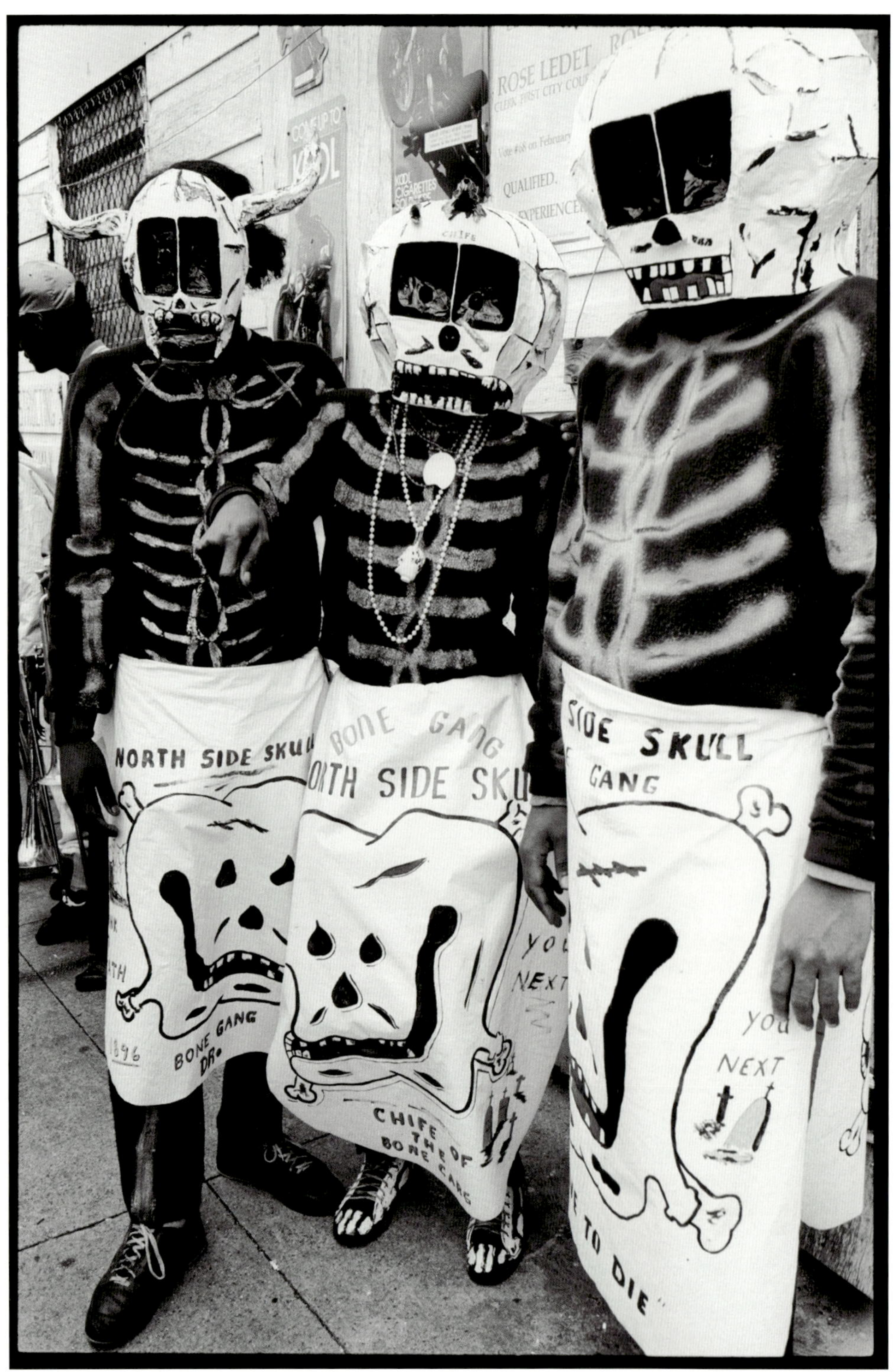


**NORTH SIDE SKULL & BONE GANG, MARDI GRAS DAY** | NEW ORLEANS; 1990

nature and the interrelatedness of its activities. The public manifestations of New Orleans music, referenced above, are sprinkled throughout the calendar, with many of the same musicians and community members participating in each. Against the backdrop of distinctive neighborhoods, architecture, and food ways, these musical traditions form a unique urban identity. Though Smith's work often focuses on the individual as culture-bearer (Antoine "Fats" Domino, Professor Longhair, and Mardi Gras Indian big chiefs Bo Dollis, Allison "Tootie" Montana, and Larry Bannock, for example), his underlying intent was to transcend the individual in order to better illustrate a given segment of society.

When viewed against the background of what can only be considered a white, middle-class upbringing, Smith's emergence as a denizen of the mostly African American world of social aid and pleasure clubs, brass bands, Mardi Gras Indian tribes, and spiritual churches seems both rebellious and quixotic. That he was able to discover, enter, respond to, and be largely accepted by these elements within New Orleans culture is testament to his perseverance, open-mindedness, and perspective on what was unique and important about the city. Some might feel that Smith's work spins gold from straw, but for him, he was hammering existing gold into forms accessible to wider audiences.

In this quest, he was preceded by others, notably the dedicated amateur still- and motion-picture photographer, New Orleanian Jules Cahn, and to a lesser degree, photographic artists Ralston Crawford and Lee Friedlander. Cahn's work is an important precedent to Smith's, not for any obvious influence of the older Cahn on the younger photographer, but for the sense of grounding that it provides Smith's pictures. Cahn's work predates Smith's by at least a decade (Smith's photographic outpouring began about 1968) and in many ways marks the beginning of a yet-to-be interrupted half-century of documentation of African American neighborhood cultures and the music of New Orleans. The work of Crawford and Friedlander, both "outsiders" albeit frequent visitors to New Orleans, tends to focus on a generation of musicians and a style of New Orleans music that was largely in transition when Smith arrived on the scene. A short list of others whose photographic contributions underscore the richness and vitality of the subject includes (in alphabetical order) Matt Anderson, Harold Baquet, Syndey Byrd, Keith Calhoun, Luke Fontana, Sylvester Francis, Chandra McCormick, Leo Touchet, Eric Waters, and Christopher Porché West. The effect of the whole underscores the notion that the culture and activities that Smith, his predecessors, and successors present to the viewer are not monolithic but highly nuanced.

As much as he would have liked to devote a career entirely to what he termed "following the music," Mike Smith was a working photographer with paying clients, jobs he didn't always like, and deadlines. He even photographed the occasional wedding. One folder of documents in the archive labeled "wedding job" illustrates his individual approach to what was often viewed as a formulaic task. Correspondence with an engaged couple from California reveals the photographer and his clients discussing the site of the ceremony (a New Orleans jazz club) and the selection of bands (Treme Brass Band was one possibility) to provide the music. Atypical of many such arrangements, Smith told the couple that he would turn over all of the processed film to them after the event, distancing himself from the standard (and lucrative) reprint phase of the wedding photography business. His rationale was simple: the photographs the couple found less important just after the wedding might, with the passage of time, become more important. As their lives changed, so too might their perception of which images best captured their relationship.

Beginning in 1974 Smith was an assignment photographer with the Black Star Publishing Company. Black Star's commissions were varied, coming from the diverse fields of editorial, industrial, and marine photography. Between 1974 and 2004 income derived from Black Star assignments funded much of Smith's self-directed work in New Orleans. In one sense, he was his own most difficult client. Driven by self-imposed discipline, Smith pushed himself to a degree that few others would demand and fewer still would undertake.

Though the city of his birth remained at the heart of his life's work, he sought analogues for New Orleans culture elsewhere in Louisiana and the world. Smith's photographs of Cuba (he made a number of trips to the island nation), in particular, reveal many of the same subjects, social activities, and themes he explored in his New Orleans work: activities ranging from rodeos to field labor, and from music to social patterns, all seemingly underscored by the importance of learned and inherited craft. The people and folkways of Cuba impressed him tremendously, eliciting his greatest talents as a photographer. Multiple visits, and the comfort Smith acquired in New Orleans with cultures other than his own, proved valuable when he visited Cuba. Though other images that Smith made abroad are filled with the characteristic energy of his photographs, those made in Cuba seem to incorporate the same spontaneity that is so much a part of his New Orleans pictures.

In the early years of the 21st century, a neurological disorder began to affect Michael P. Smith. By late spring 2005, some months before Hurricane Katrina visited its destruction on New Orleans and the Gulf Coast, he had ceased active photography. The loss of life and cultural property precipitated by Katrina, and the flooding and displacement that followed, serve as reminders of the fragility of any culture. A number of the locations and individuals shown in Smith's photographs were struck by the storm. The disruption of lives and destruction of buildings certainly altered New Orleans's musical landscape, but changes to this world had been happening throughout Smith's photographic career. Important figures passed away, and younger generations transformed existing traditions, sometimes seamlessly. The photographs and supplementary materials of the Michael P. Smith Archive at The Historic New Orleans Collection document specific episodes of life in New Orleans, but in the aggregate, they chronicle the nearly imperceptible changes that move cultural traditions forward while still maintaining their status as traditions. For these reasons and others, Smith's archive, though quite recent by temporal standards, represents a whole that cannot be effectively filtered through any one viewpoint. It is the chronicle of an era, embodying in some way the cause-and-effect study of history. It is fortunate that such a dedicated and talented visual artist took this task upon himself.

Today, perhaps more than ever before, we come to equate an image of something with a person, place, or object, using the flat surrogate for the fully dimensioned thing itself. Anyone who has seen musicians perform, trekked to the New Orleans Fair Grounds in April and May, or participated in the thick of a street parade, knows how false a comparison this is. Mike Smith's photographs are not substitutes for these people and things, but rather are paths to a different way of understanding and appreciating attributes of the city and its culture. And as objects, when cared for properly, they are durable and lasting. When the music no longer hangs in the air, when the applause at the end of a performance has faded, and when the casket has found its final repose, Michael Smith's work remains as a touchstone.

**JOHN H. LAWRENCE & JUDE SOLOMON** | EXHIBITION CURATORS
THE HISTORIC NEW ORLEANS COLLECTION

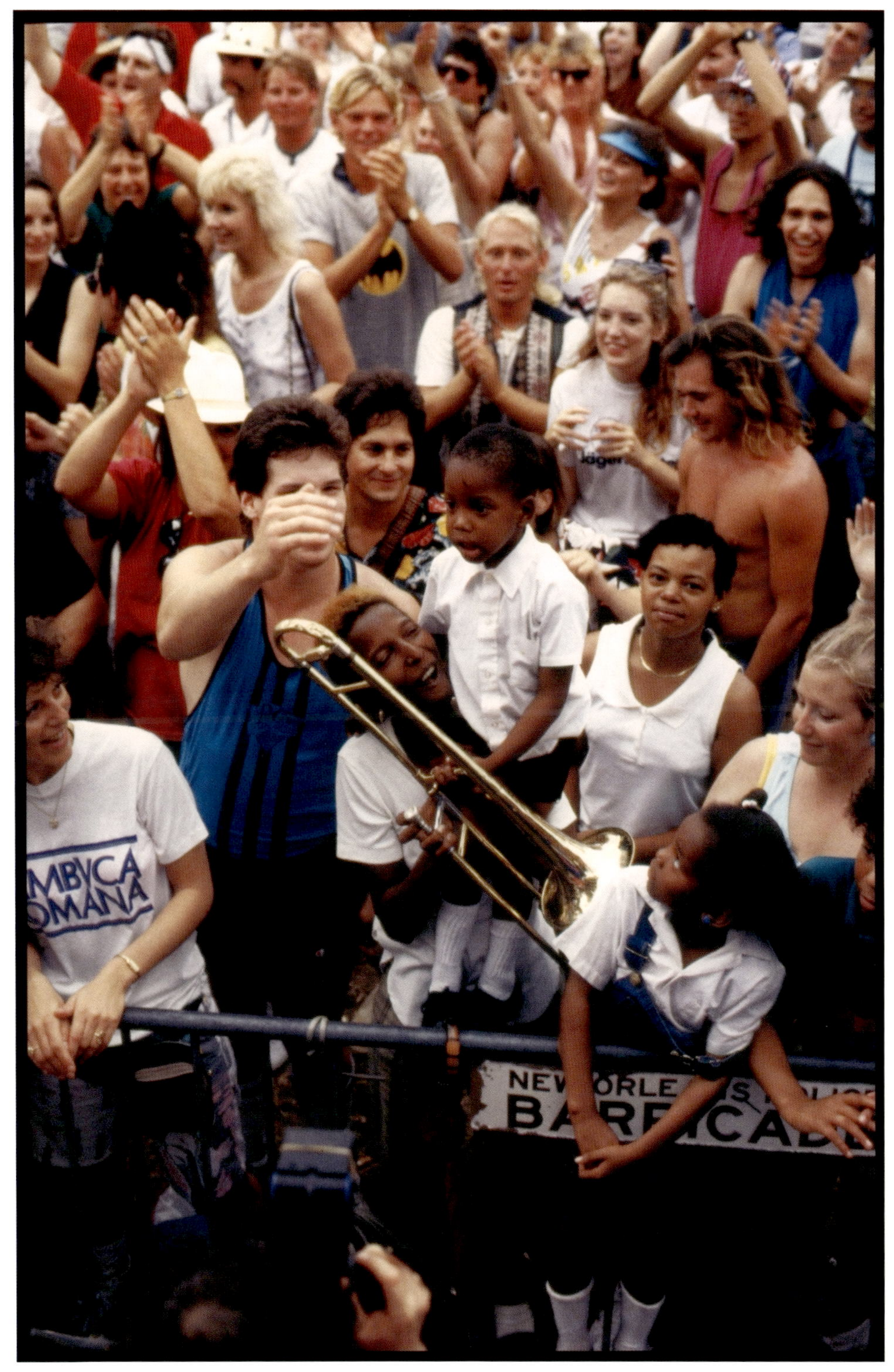

**TROMBONE SHORTY** | JAZZ FEST, NEW ORLEANS; 1990

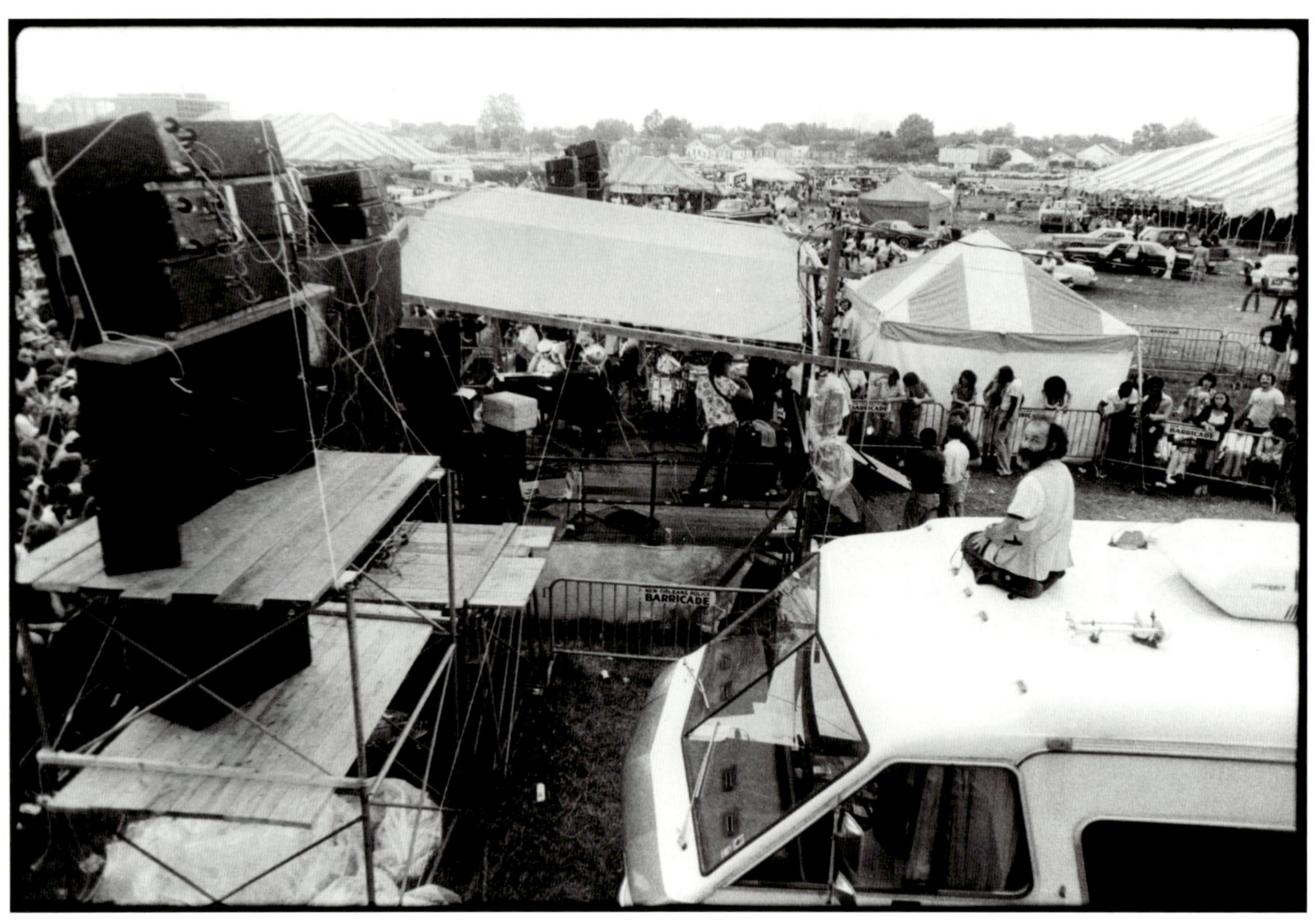


**MICHAEL P. SMITH ON VAN AT JAZZ FEST** | BY AN UNIDENTIFIED PHOTOGRAPHER; 1980s

## UP CLOSE AND SPIRITUAL

The best way—some might say the only way—to listen to music is to be totally conscious and present during the moment it's being created. On the most memorable occasions, the presence of the singer or instrumentalist in performance transmits a palpable energy that runs through every person listening and watching, so that one no longer has the experience of passively being on the receiving end, but of being a fully participating, necessary part of the action. That isn't to say that concert DVDs or live recordings aren't valuable at some level, but they only offer one part of the total immersion experience that requires the performance to be live and in person, with the artist delivering a real-time event, full of surprise and nuance. Although one can dance, sing, or even cheer to a prerecorded event, no substitute exists for having been there when it took place.

Because very few of us are immune to the experience of getting caught up in a great live musical performance, the fundamental reason for the remarkable four-decade success of the New Orleans Jazz and Heritage Festival—known to all as Jazz Fest—is that it has consistently brought together artists and listeners in a cathartic embrace that makes nearly everyone want to keep coming back for more. A dear friend who attended for the first time in 2008 quickly came to the conclusion that, despite the nonstop embellishments provided by the food, weather, crafts, and spirited antics of attendees, Jazz Fest's essence lies in the unfolding love affair between musician and fan. Taking that as a starting point, the key to any great Jazz Fest performance seems to lie in the degree and intensity with which the artist is transformed during the course of his or her performance, which usually means that everyone who has gathered together to share that moment is also caught up in the transformation.

More than any photographer of his generation, Michael P. Smith's artistic contribution as the "official" photographer of Jazz Fest for more than thirty years lay in ceaselessly attempting to capture that precise moment in a musical performance when the transfer of energy from musician to listener transmits an electrical charge.

Whether it is the classic mid-1970s funk style of Irma Thomas (1975) viewed from backstage framed by the crowd, or the sheer magnetism of Al Green's smile (1995) as he plays peek-a-boo between his fingers, what comes across today is that these performers are giving their all, and Michael Smith was the foremost witness to it. Describing Smith's role as witnessing should come as no surprise to anybody who knows the breadth of his work, particularly his dedication to photographing African American folk and vernacular traditions in southern Louisiana. From spiritual churches to jazz funerals and second lines, Smith was perpetually on the lookout for the same kind of ecstatic channeling of the spirit that he eventually conveyed through his Jazz Fest photographs. In fact, the symbiosis between the two bodies of work offers ample opportunities for future scholars to explore the links between them.

Not surprisingly, my first real awareness of Smith's work occurred in the Gospel Tent, sometime in the early 1990s, as it dawned on me that the images hung around the inside of the tent hadn't changed since the last time I'd been there, or the time before that. Not only were they consistent in quality and intensity, they were nearly all signed by the same person. From Mahalia Jackson at the inaugural festival, to an Aaron Neville photograph of more recent vintage, Smith's work was reinforcing a narrative in which the Gospel Tent is a site where, year after year, gospel artists take their place in a long line of predecessors whose ringing voices are layered on top of each other, like an echoing chorus that lingers in the air well after the tents have been folded up and put away until next year. Each gospel chorus or small ensemble knows the history of what happened on that stage in years past, and while it seems to require a distinct act of faith each time it happens, what keeps belief alive, as in all great rituals, is the continual reminder of the great heights achieved by our forerunners. Within the larger act of faith as it is shared by others, Smith's photographs serve as visual documents that pull the narrative together.

This last point is clearest when one stops to consider the range of artists Smith documented at Jazz Fest between 1970, the year of its inception, and 2004, the last year he took photographs at the event. Because Smith was already very comfortable documenting Mardi Gras Indians, jazz parades, funk parties, and gospel services, it was a natural fit for him to be documenting the Mighty Chariots of Fire, the Meters, and the Wild Tchoupitoulas on their respective stages, or following Danny Barker as grand marshal of a fairgrounds parade featuring the Onward Brass Band. But he also prided himself on doing justice to Jazz Fest's more eclectic side, so that distinguished zydeco artists, from the late Beau Jocque and Boozoo Chavis to the current generation of Rosie Ledet and Terrance Simien, are well represented throughout his work, as are such Cajun music counterparts as D. L. Menard and Christine Balfa. Blues is also thoroughly covered in his photographs, with revered figures like B. B. King and Snooks Eaglin lovingly documented year after year. More than any other genre, Smith was drawn to that particular brand of New Orleans funk / R & B embodied by the musicians he photographed the most: Professor Longhair, Dr. John, Allen Toussaint, the Neville Brothers. But he was also present for Zap Mama, Jimmy Cliff, and the Temptations, as well as countless artists whose connection to New Orleans music entails at least one degree of separation. Like all die-hard Jazz Fest fans, Smith kept up a frenetic pace during both fest weekends, chasing his favorite musical artists from stage to stage. Unlike the rest of us, however, he came home with an archive of images that continue to provide tangible shape to the collective memories of thousands.

Another of Michael P. Smith's great talents was as an editor of his own work, and his two published volumes of Jazz Fest photographs are more than adequate testimony to his skill at selecting the one frame out of dozens that leaves an indelible impression on the viewer's imagination. In fact, the degree to which Smith's published work has defined how Jazz

Fest was, and continues to be, visualized by prospective visitors hundreds and even thousands of miles away will probably never be fully known, but it is increasingly clear that he is the one visual artist whose impact on the festival's public image is immeasurable. The present sample of Smith's photographs is a relatively subjective interpretation based on a range of curatorial factors, chosen from the full selection of black-and-white prints and color transparencies made available by The Historic New Orleans Collection from the Michael P. Smith Archive. Thanks to the attention drawn to its existence by Jude Solomon, curator of the archive, it was possible to work with a pre-selection of photos that Smith had made for the years 1997 and 1998, which is at least one reason why there is a disproportionately large number of photographs included from those two years.

In general, despite the understandably greater attention given to the work that Smith produced while Jazz Fest was still expanding its audience base, the photos from the 1990s are probably his best work. As Smith's involvement with Jazz Fest moved into its third full decade, his innate compositional sense, combined with his increased knowledge of each performer's style, enabled him to frame his subjects more naturally. Younger artists like John Mooney (1991), Jason Marsalis (1997), and Anders Osborne (1995) project their fully matured selves outward to the world, while veterans such as Pharoah Sanders, Ruth Brown, and Taj Mahal command the stage with the weight of true icons. What all the 1990s images share is a heightened degree of intimacy with their subjects, a sense of kinship built up over years of close-up encounters with the individuals who inspired Smith to document their artistry.

For anybody who's tried, the biggest challenge in explaining Jazz Fest to somebody who has never attended is that there is simply no adequate way to communicate the specific feelings that the event generates, short of physically dragging someone to the New Orleans Fair Grounds for a firsthand encounter. Most non-initiates struggle to visualize how Jazz Fest could be all that different from any other big concert event or cultural festival, and these are the people for whom a collection of Michael P. Smith's Jazz Fest photos might be the best possible form of seduction. Except for the music itself, to thousands of Jazz Fest fans, regardless of whether or not they recognize his name, what Smith did was communicate through black-and-white and color static images an experience that is virtually impossible to reproduce in any medium. In essence, he managed the incredible feat of capturing the heart and soul of live music without making a sound.

**DAN CAMERON** | CURATOR
THE CONTEMPORARY ARTS CENTER

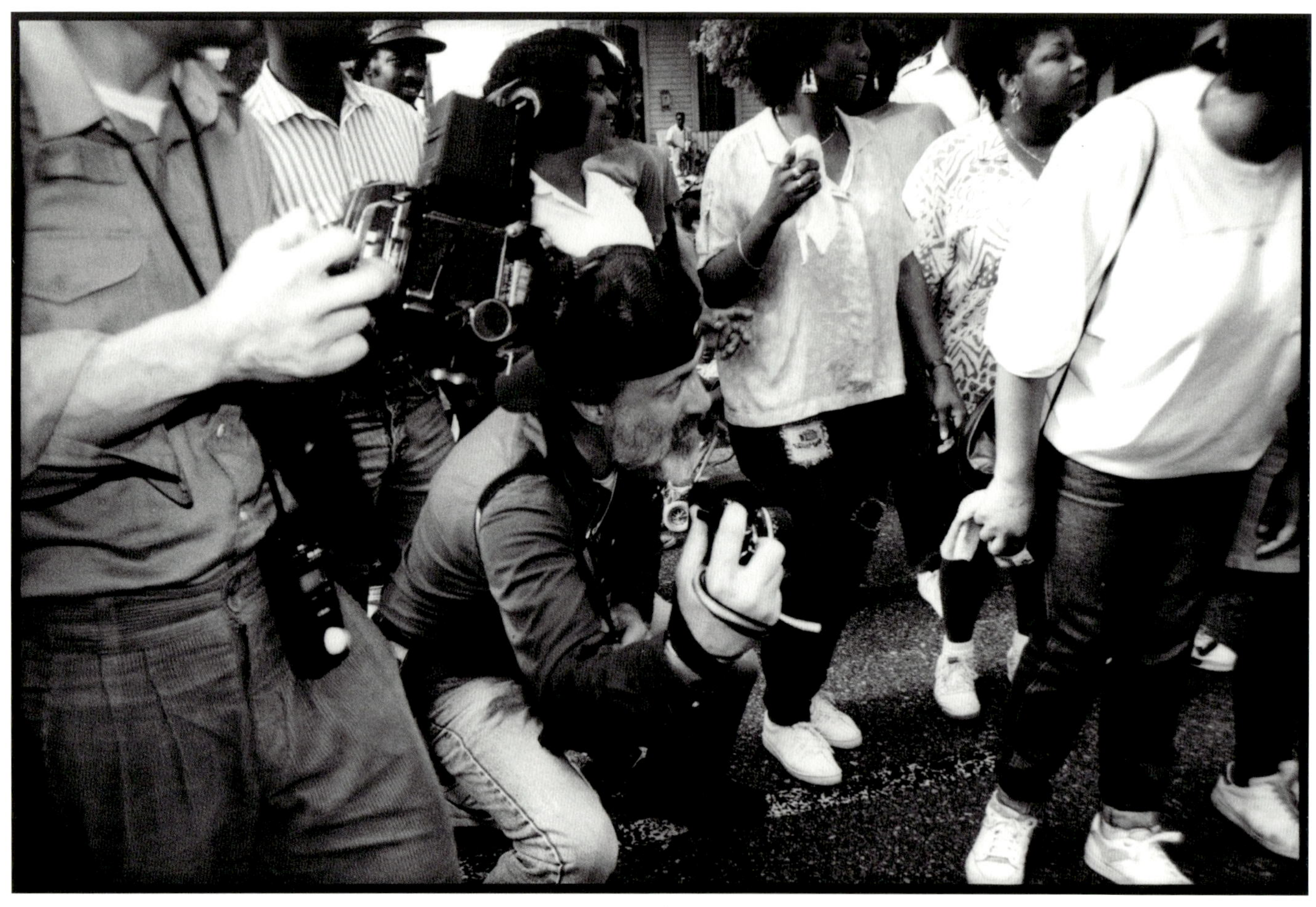

MICHAEL P. SMITH PHOTOGRAPHING BO DOLLIS ON SUPER SUNDAY | BY CAROLYN LONG; MARCH 19, 1989

## REMEMBERING MIKE SMITH

We met in 1973 at a salon hosted by Clarence John Laughlin in his vast apartment on top of the Upper Pontalba Building. Clarence, the esteemed Surrealist photographer then in his late sixties, had belatedly gained international notice; he still took a bus across town to use a darkroom on Edgar Stern's Bamboo Road estate. Clarence's flat, with thousands of books and many pictures, was hot. His guests ran from serious collectors to shaggy-haired artists. After Clarence lectured about his photographs, people mingled among the beautiful books, sipping bad wine. That's when Mike Smith told me Richard Nixon was a war criminal. I hated the Vietnam War too. Smith, who was older than me by a dozen years, had a laser-like intensity. That's probably why he meant so much to Clarence.

"Laughlin would often call [Smith] in the middle of the night either to talk for hours or to ask a favor," writes Laughlin biographer A. J. Meek. Mike was getting immersed in jazz funerals and folk culture, so different from his mentor's stylized Romanticism. Smith helped him prepare traveling exhibitions. In the biography, Meek recounts one trip the pair made to Chicago:

> In Chicago, having searched for a cheaper hotel, they stayed in a bordello. "The girls were working out of their rooms," [Smith] said. Laughlin and Smith often walked for hours searching for a cheaper meal and then were diverted by a bookstore where Laughlin would spend further hours and much of his money.

Imagine that! Clarence and Mike, *radicals,* patrolling Chicago for used books while the beds were banging back at the lodge. Unlike Clarence, a supreme eccentric, Mike had ample irony in his blood supply. "Some of my work follows in his footsteps though I don't think you'd find Clarence in Dorothy's Medallion photographing Big Linda," he mused, years later, of the quirky little club on Orleans Avenue where Walter "Wolfman" Washington played guitar as Big Linda danced in a cage, wrapped in a boa constrictor.

Our friendship grew slowly toward a reciprocal view of the mythical essence in the music, second lines, and folkways of the city—a spiritual topography made from neighborhood life.

When Tipitina's opened in 1977 he confided that he was one of the founders—put up $1,000. He knew that would impress me. I was pulling all-nighters, cranking out long articles, reading like an addict, scheming for real payback. He rationalized his commercial shoots on oil rigs as making Mammon pay for his art. The mainstream media had scant interest in Mardi Gras Indians and storefront churches. Today an image-makers' army converges for parades and festivals. Thirty years ago, as his visual odyssey took shape, the value of that culture was far less widely shared.

In 1979 I produced a documentary about musical families. He gave me the brother-in-law rate to use some of his spiritual church photographs. He gave me a photograph of a female bishop, holding a tambourine at an altar. It rests framed a few feet from where I type. Ah, Mike.

In 1984, I sat in the shotgun house he and filmmaker Karen Snyder shared on Short Street, listening to him recount a dispute with Mardi Gras Indians. "They think I'm ripping off the culture!" I had never seen him angry. The house was packed with books, photographs, and posters. Stacks of music placards, handbills, and memorabilia showed his eye for a hidden culture. All so neatly arranged. "I give them photographs!" he continued, frustration rising. *They'll come around,* I said. *Just keep shooting.* "But this is serious!"

He was so innocent, so offended that the Indians could think of him as exploiting them, impervious to his investment of time and money. I saw it as one of those inevitable collisions when treaties of race and class must be negotiated. He showed me his letter to Yellow Pocahontas Big Chief Tootie Montana, explaining his stance. *Don't send it,* I said. *Give it time.* I worried that a long letter might provoke more conflict. He sent the letter, and mended his fences.

Upholding egalitarian principles was elemental to his world view. Justice, fairness, righteousness in the best sense, meant more to Michael P. Smith than to most people I have known. Artists and writers are not known for practicing virtue as he did. In time, we quit talking politics because we agreed. When idealism fades and you see brute power's ignorant force, the mind searches for humankind's best impulses. What I loved about his work was not just the spontaneous street choreographies, frozen in time, and religious folk in trance-like exaltation, but how he melded with a vision of spirit tides transcending an unjust city.

In 2001, at the onset his neurological illness, the photographer David Richmond asked me to do an interview profile for *Gambit:* "Get his life down right." Mike was weaker, his memory flagging, but still verbal. Richmond videotaped him through that afternoon.

"I always tried to catch an attitude in the way people were expressing themselves, or their other selves, their nominally wilder selves," Mike reflected. "I think of myself as a historian and documentarian. So my photography is a form of memory to share an event with a larger audience."

Richmond had his own problems after Katrina. I hope he held onto the tapes. I don't know how much other video exists of Mike in self-reflection. He was actually a rather modest man.

His neurological illness was well advanced before Katrina. After the storm, Karen made sure he got around, seeing friends as so many of us tried to remake a semblance of the world we had. The "cultural wetlands" he championed had taken an enormous beating, the people in communities he documented treated as expendable items. So many of the spiritual churches Mike captured were destroyed in the flood. Mike was mute, literally unable to speak. At one gathering I sat by him, telling him how glad I was for the work he had done, the history he had captured. What did he think behind those large eyes? Mayor Nagin worked hard to keep the working poor—the second line culture Mike chronicled—from coming back. How much did the political blight haunt Mike Smith's silent years? I visited him at home, bedside, two days before he died. A glimmer of light touched his eyes. How much more I wish we had said.

JASON BERRY

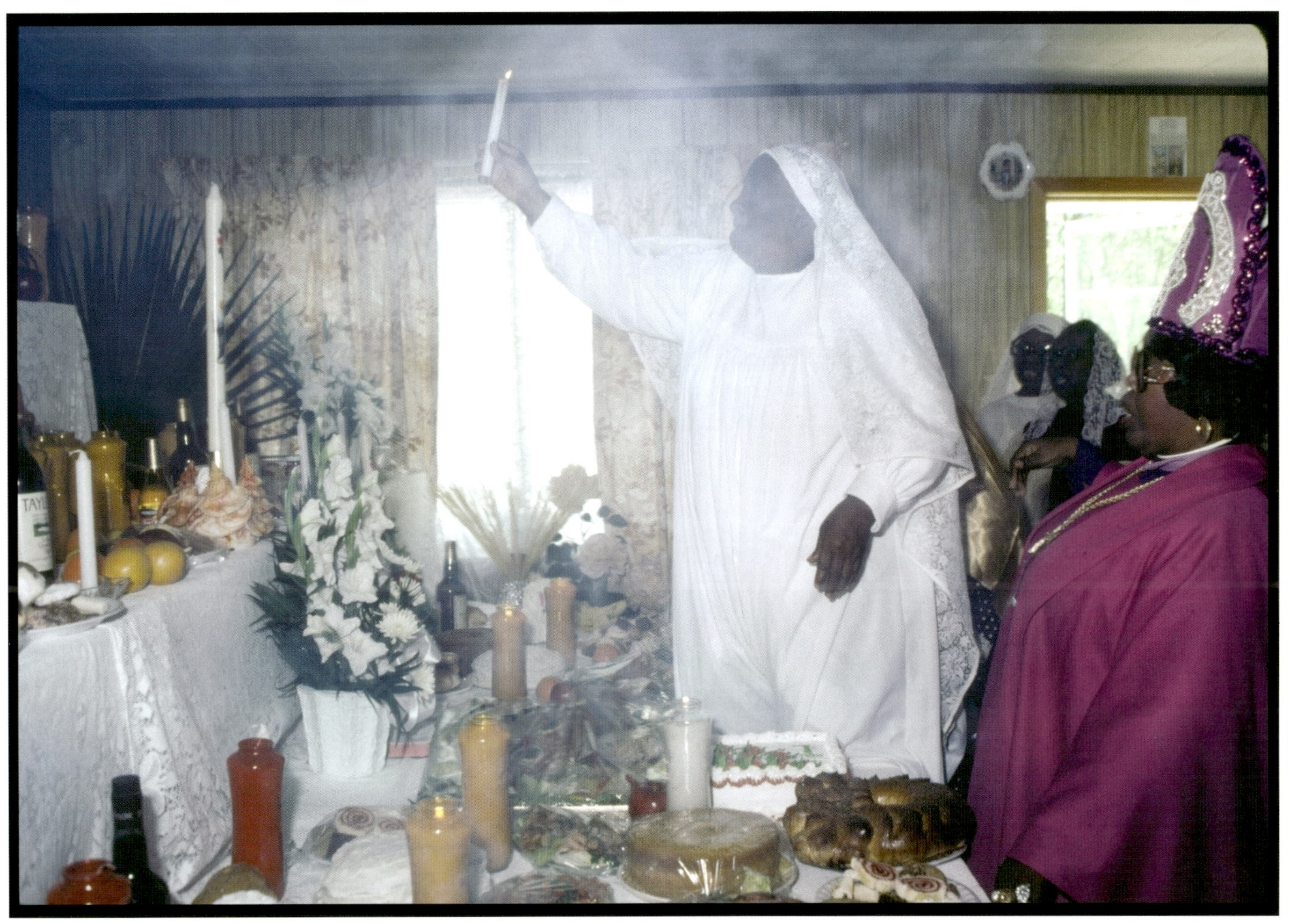

**ALTAR, INFANT JESUS OF PRAGUE SPIRITUAL CHURCH** | SEVENTH WARD, NEW ORLEANS; 1983

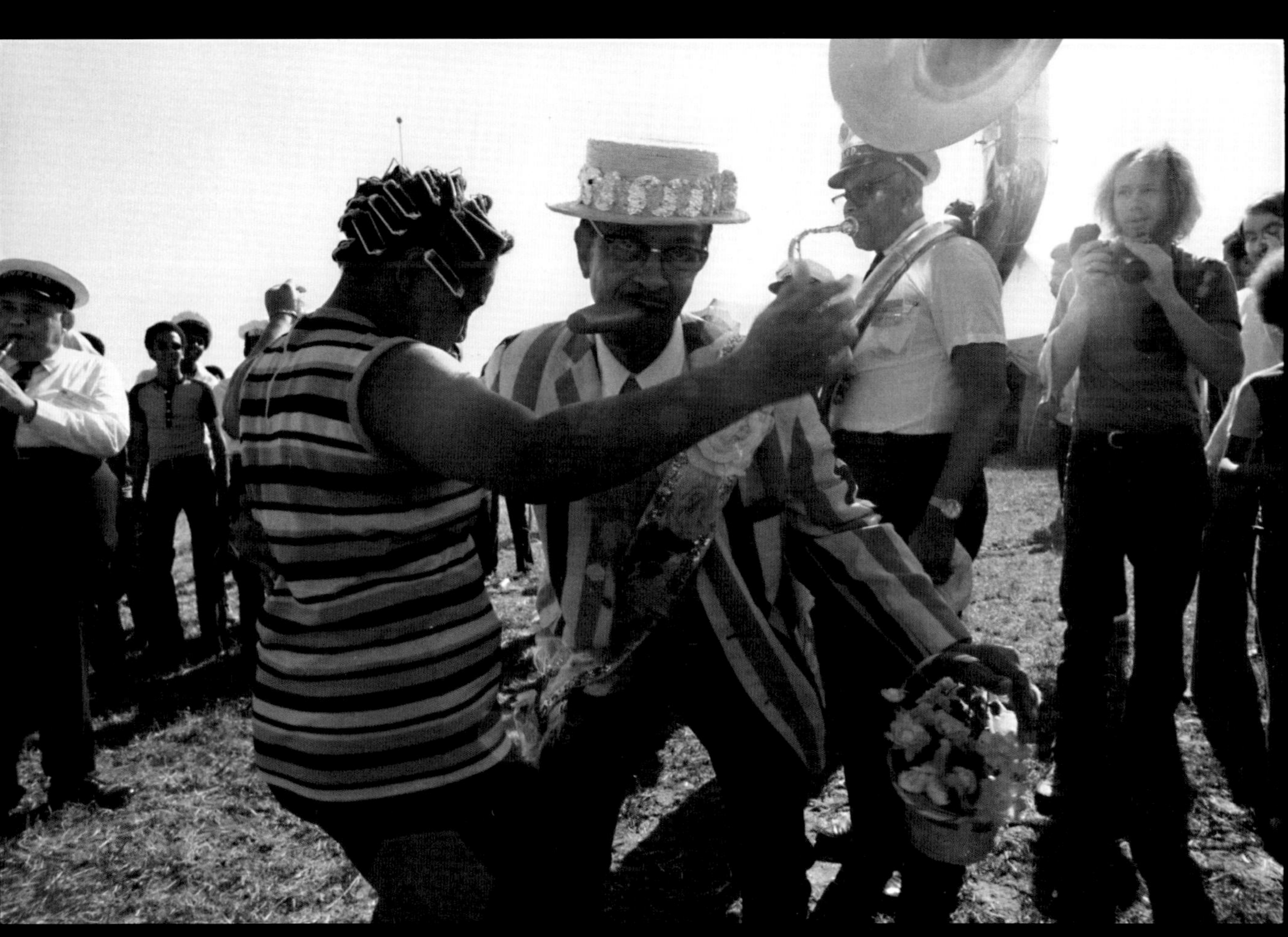

DANNY BARKER DURING TRADITIONAL JAZZ PARADE | NEW ORLEANS, JAZZ FEST; 1973

## NEW ORLEANS

The city of New Orleans is the setting for most of Smith's photographs. In addition to large bodies of work with consistent themes, the archive is sprinkled with images of sheer visual exuberance that characterize the Crescent City's neighborhoods and citizens.

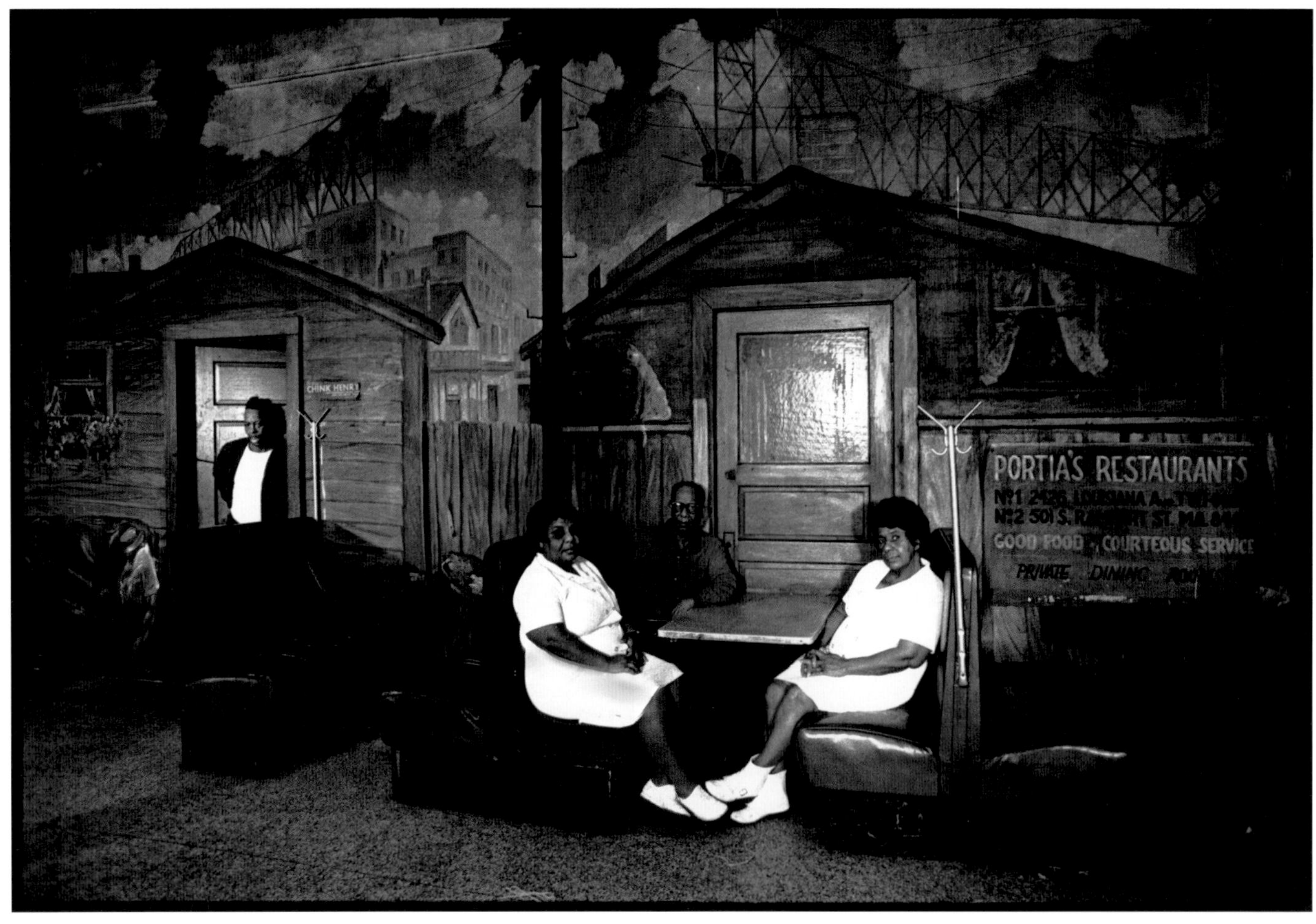


PORTIA'S RESTAURANT ON SOUTH RAMPART STREET | NEW ORLEANS; 1972

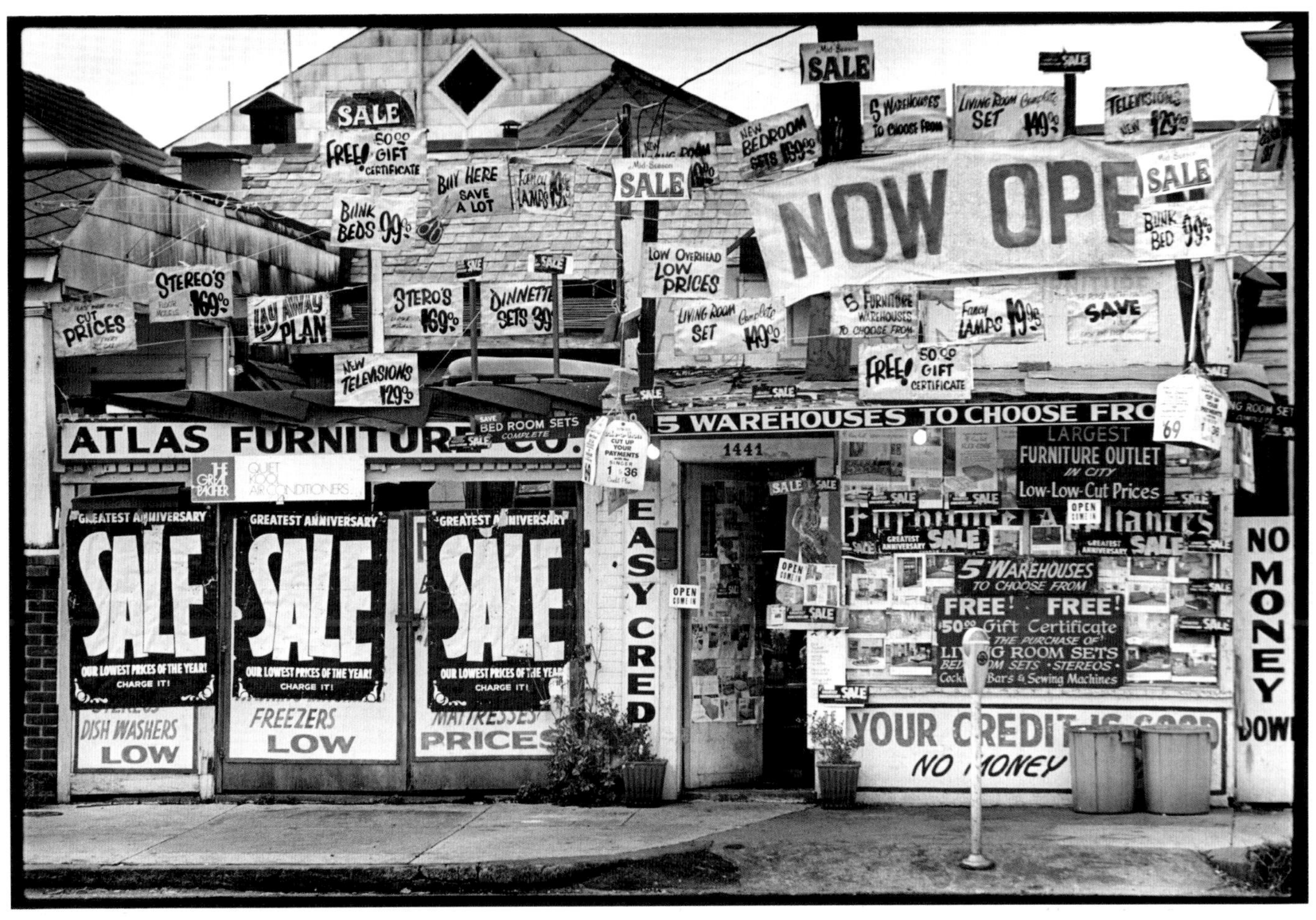


SALE, NORTH RAMPART STREET | FAUBOURG MARIGNY, NEW ORLEANS; 1972

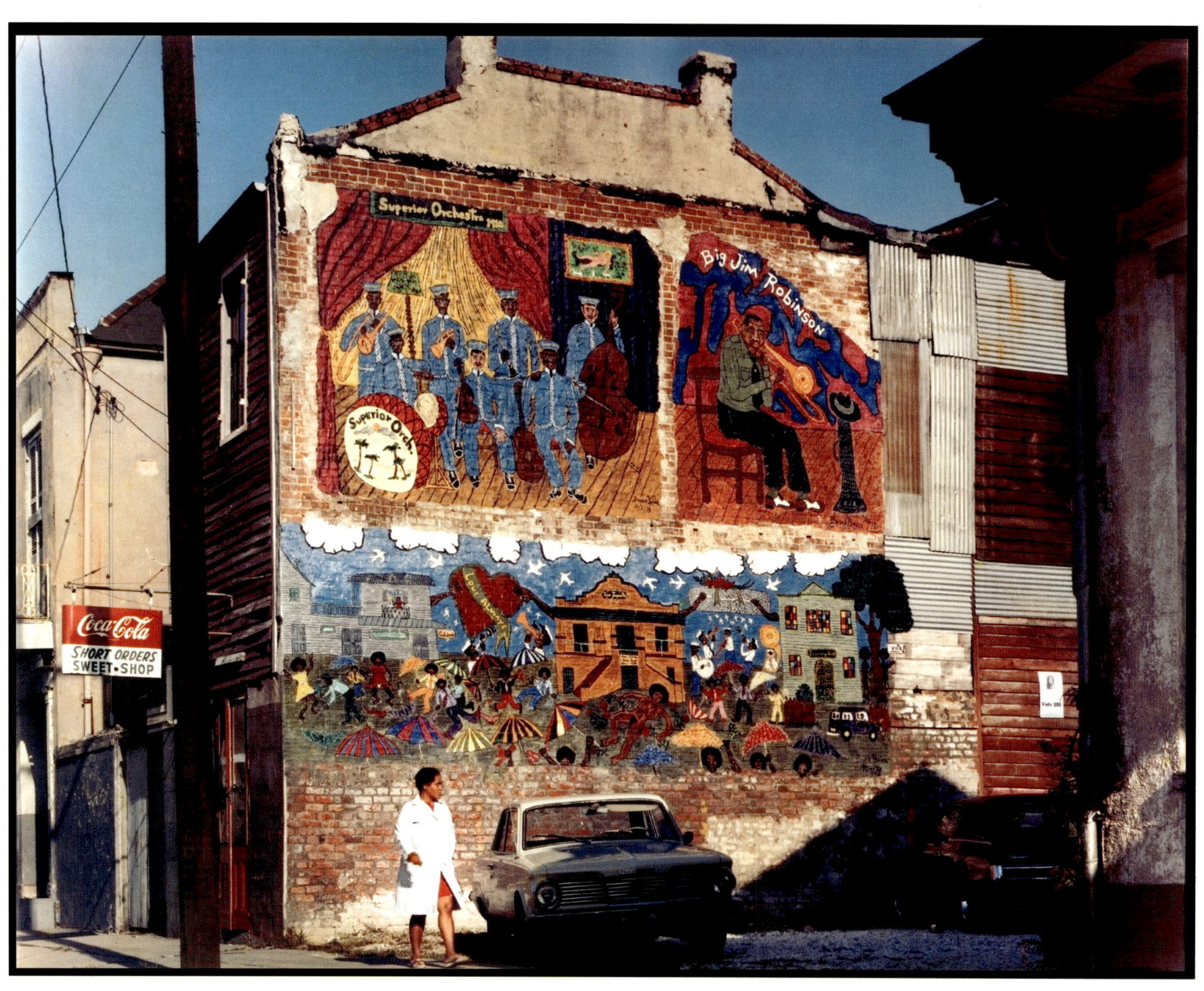


**BRUCE BRICE MURAL** | TREME, NEW ORLEANS; 1973

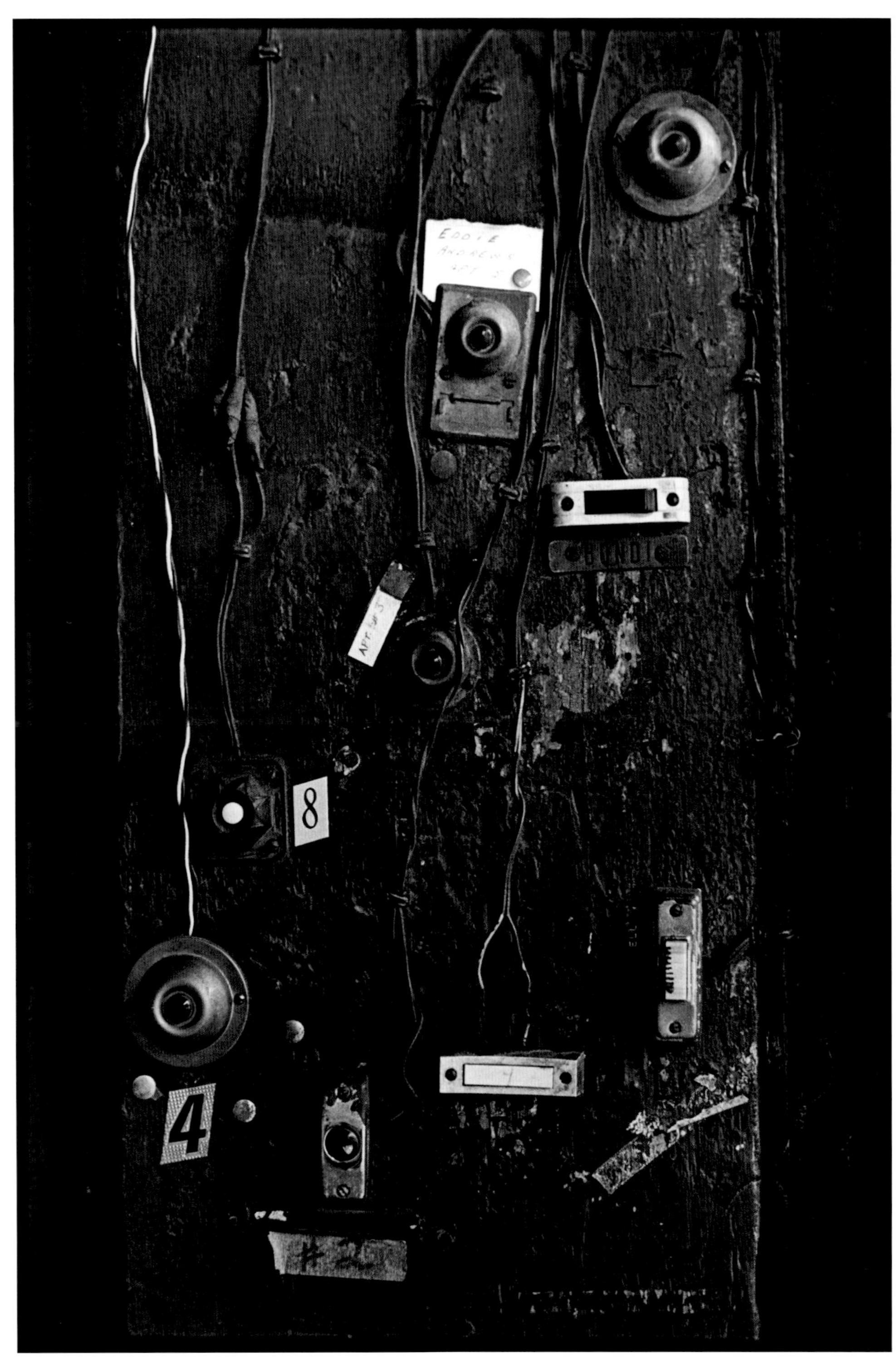


DOORBELLS | NEW ORLEANS; 1972

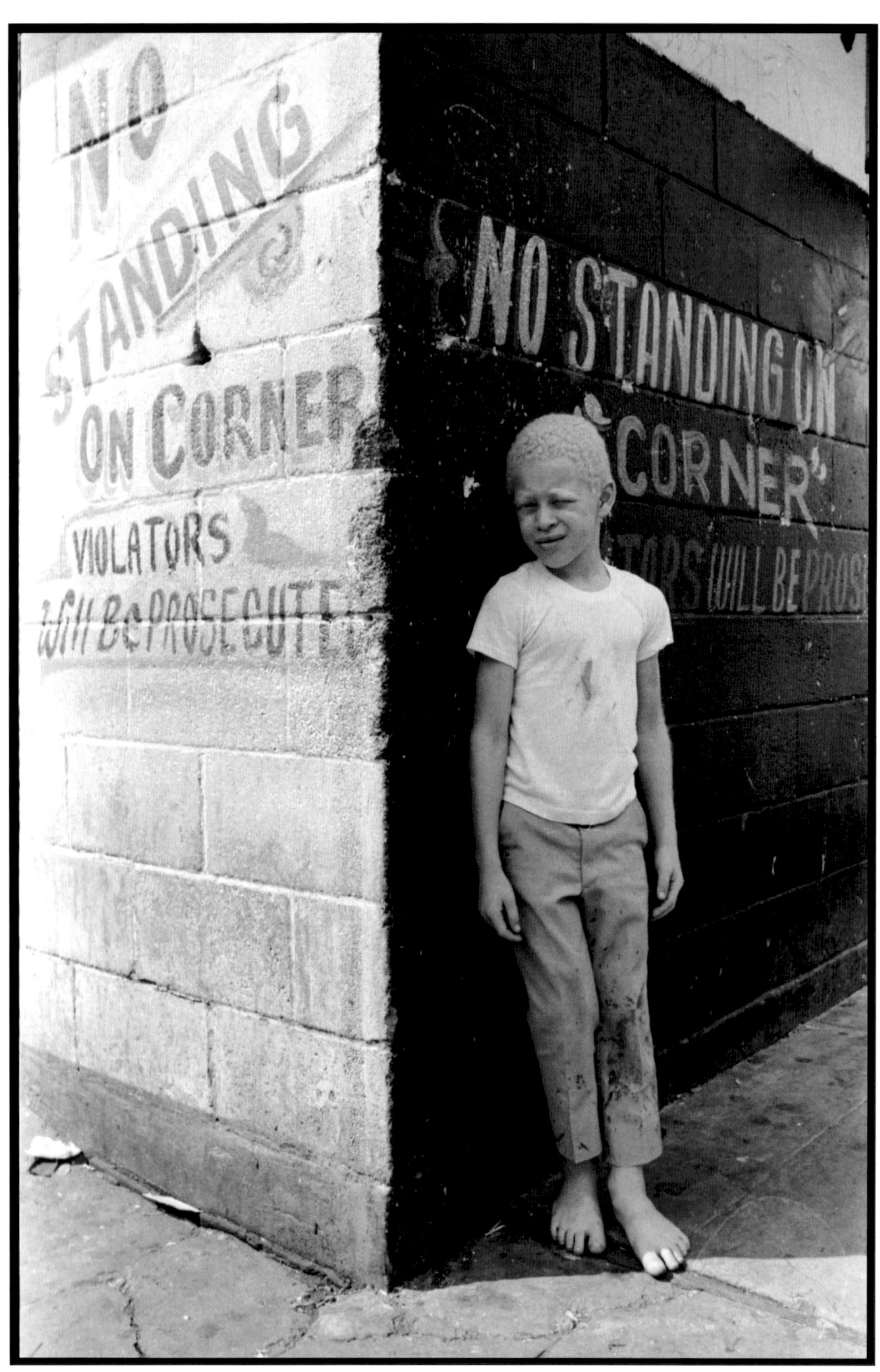


**NO STANDING ON CORNER** | NEW ORLEANS; 1973

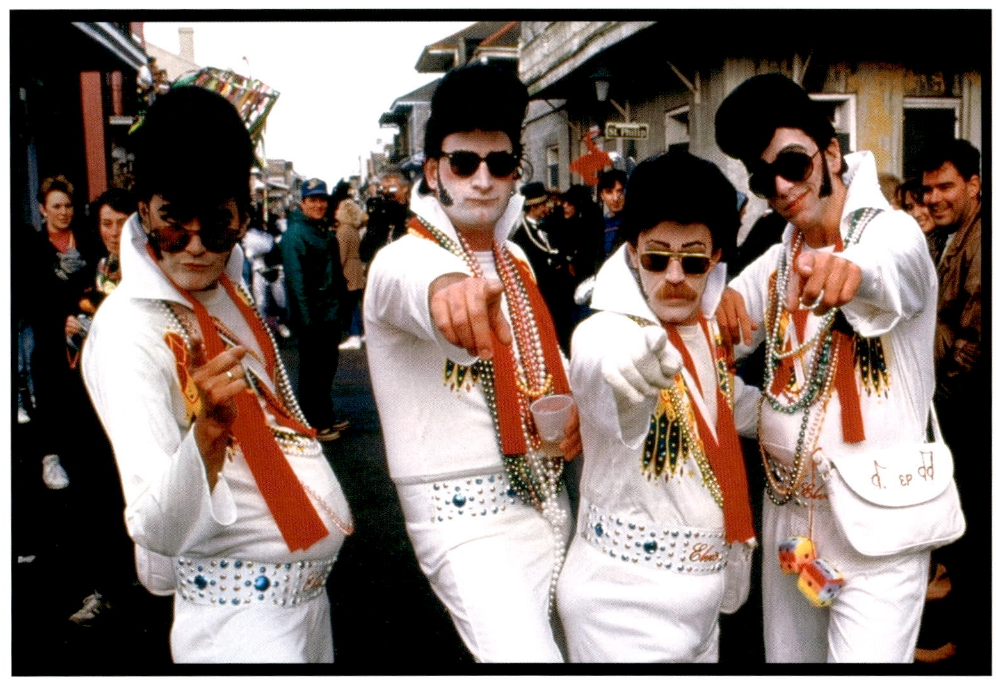

THE ELVISES, MARDI GRAS | FRENCH QUARTER, NEW ORLEANS; 1990

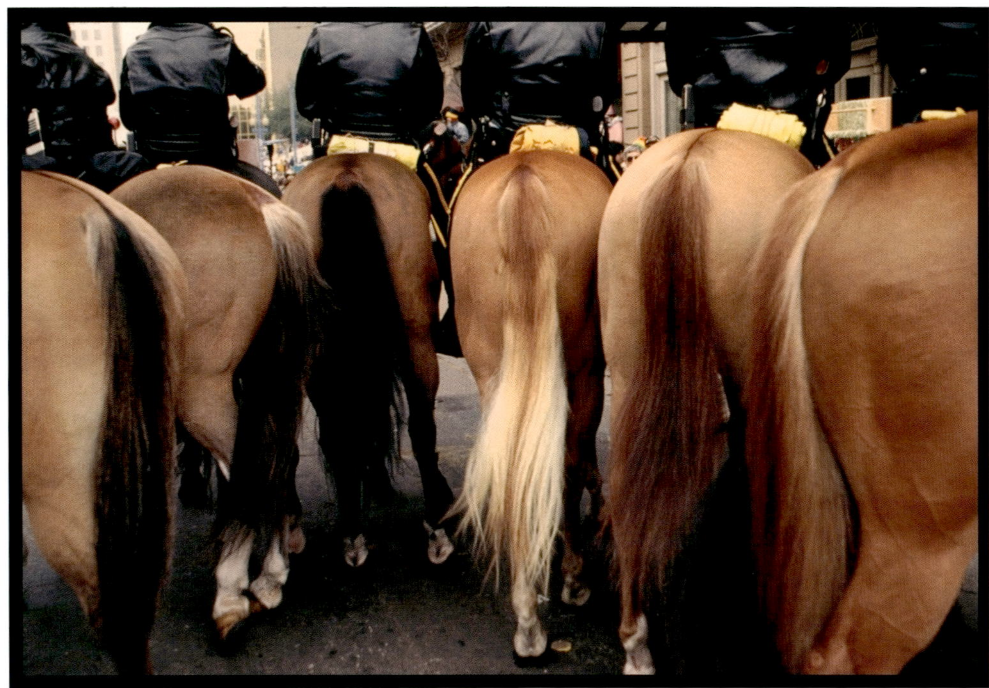

END OF THE PARADE | NEW ORLEANS; 1989

## SPIRIT WORLD

Smith's images of spiritual church ceremonies are landmarks in documenting an aspect of New Orleans's culture that is hidden from nearly all save those participating in it.

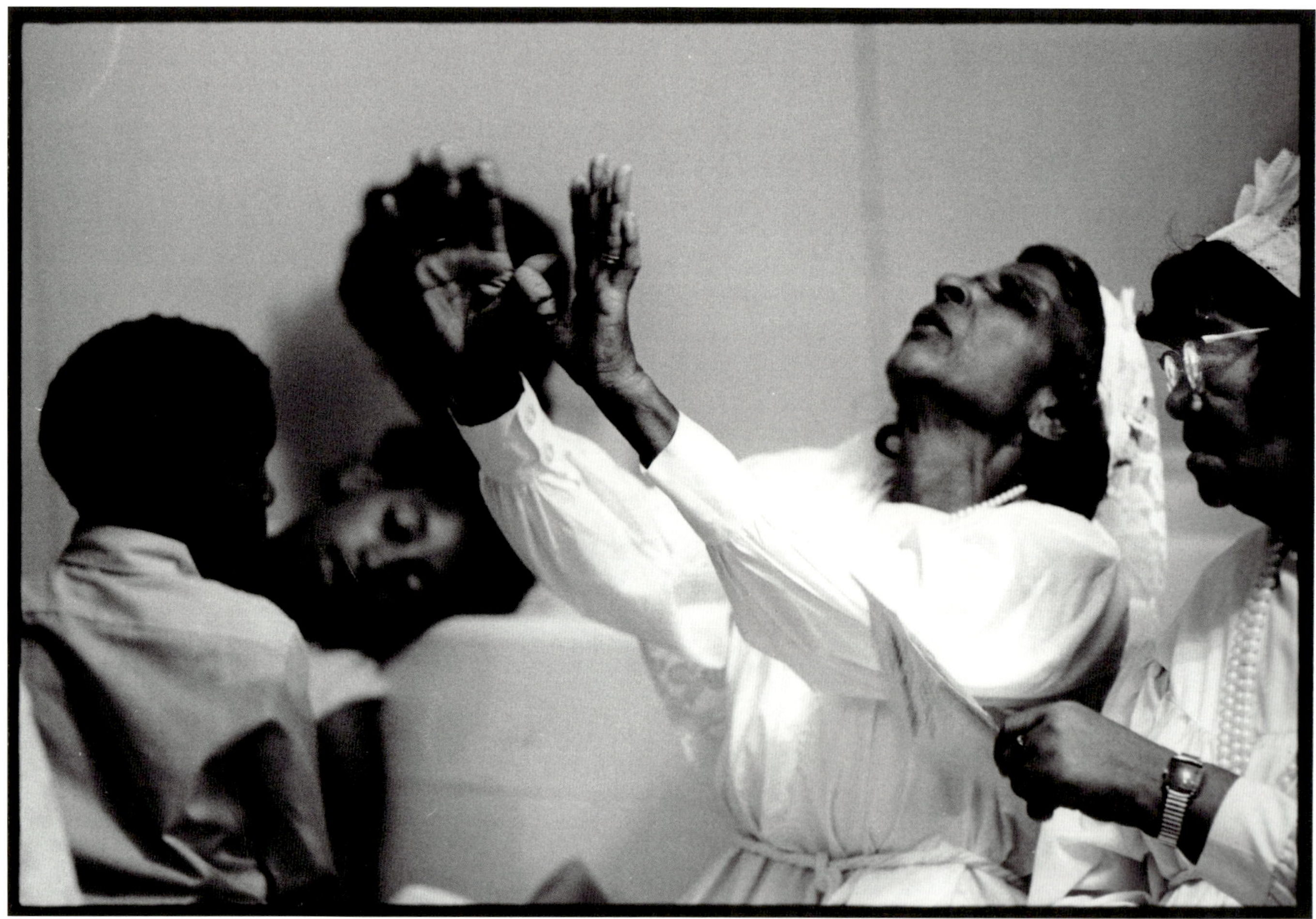

**HOLY FAMILY SPIRITUAL CHURCH** | LOWER NINTH WARD, NEW ORLEANS; 1973

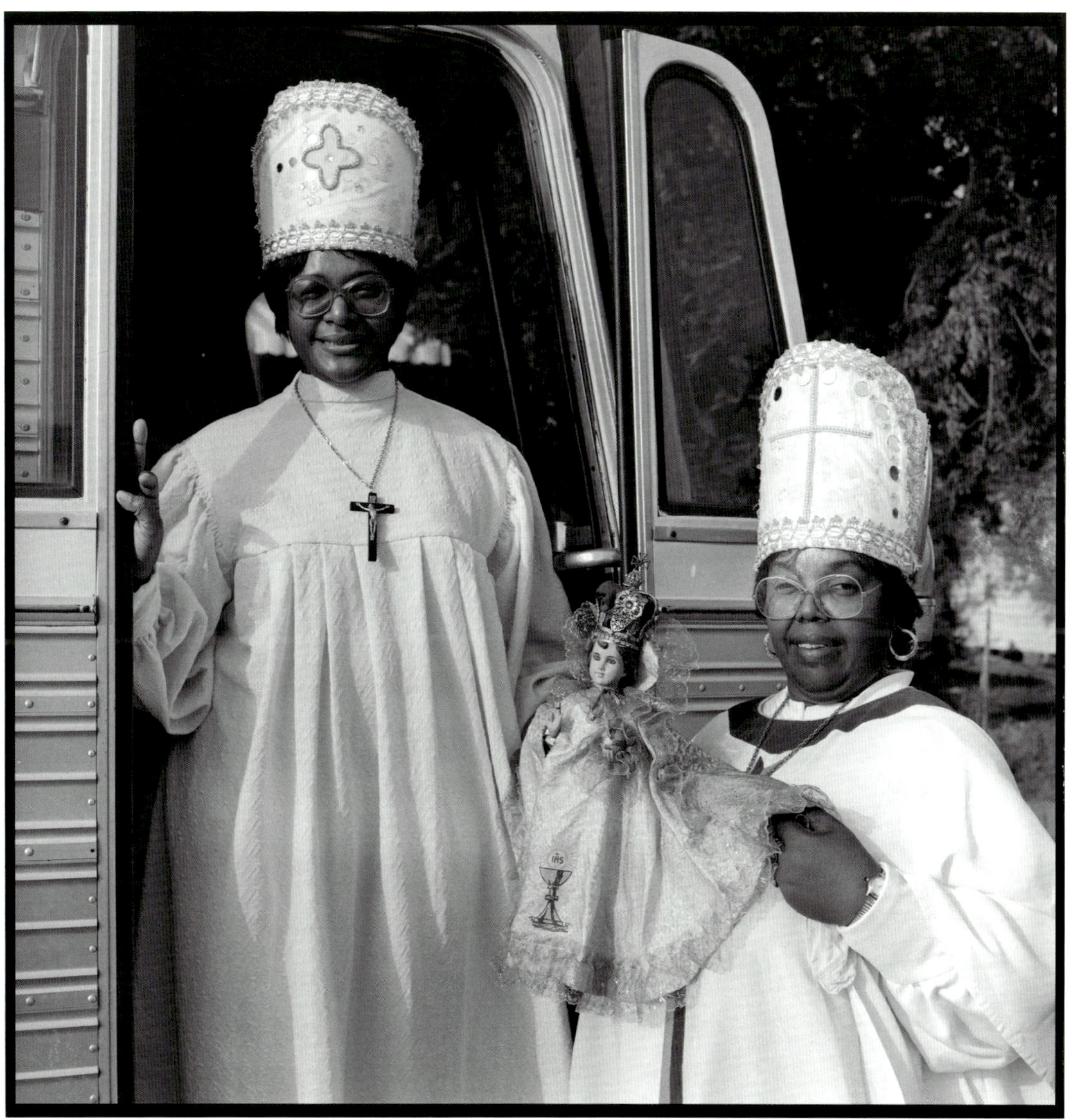

BISHOP LYDIA GILFORD (RIGHT) & UNIDENTIFIED CLERGY,
INFANT JESUS OF PRAGUE SPIRITUAL CHURCH | SEVENTH WARD, NEW ORLEANS; 1977

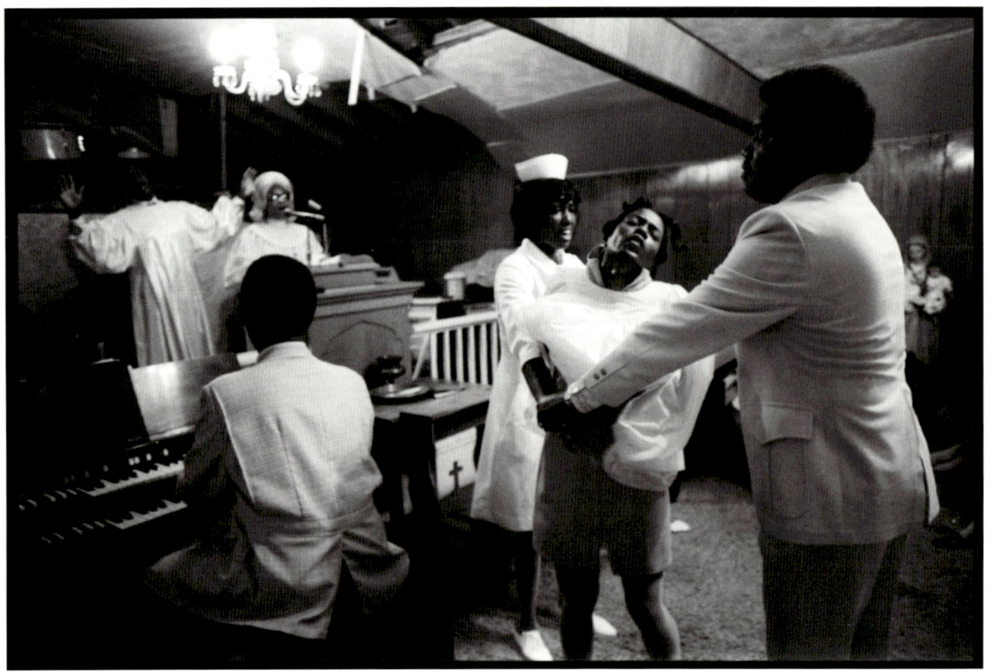

**"IN THE SPIRIT," HOLY FAMILY SPIRITUAL CHURCH** | LOWER NINTH WARD, NEW ORLEANS; 1973

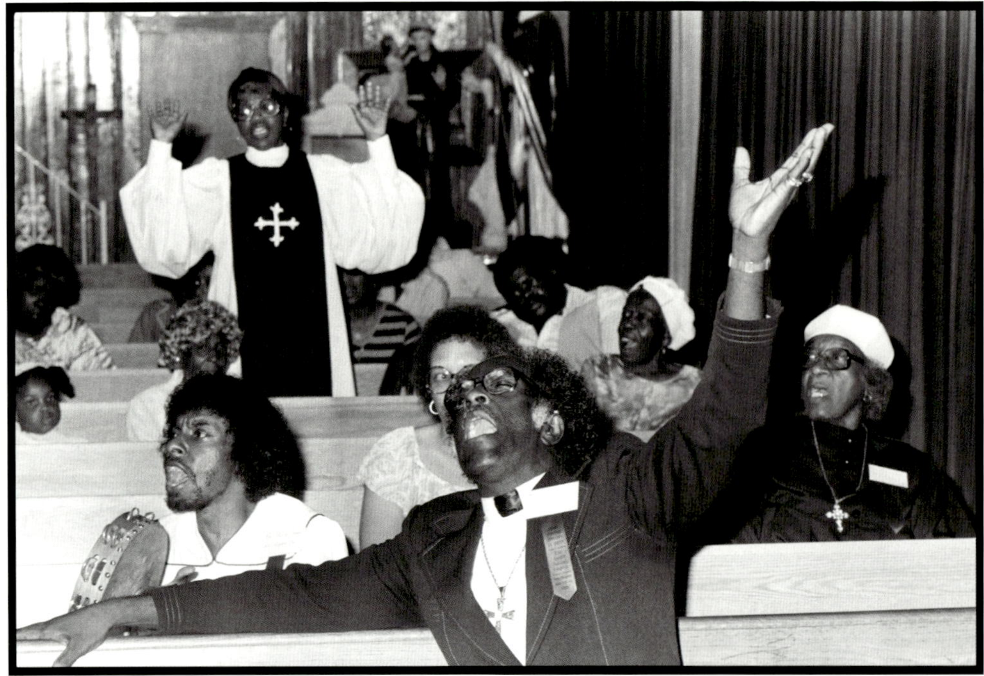

**ISRAELITE DIVINE SPIRITUAL CHURCH** | ST. ROCH, NEW ORLEANS; 1983

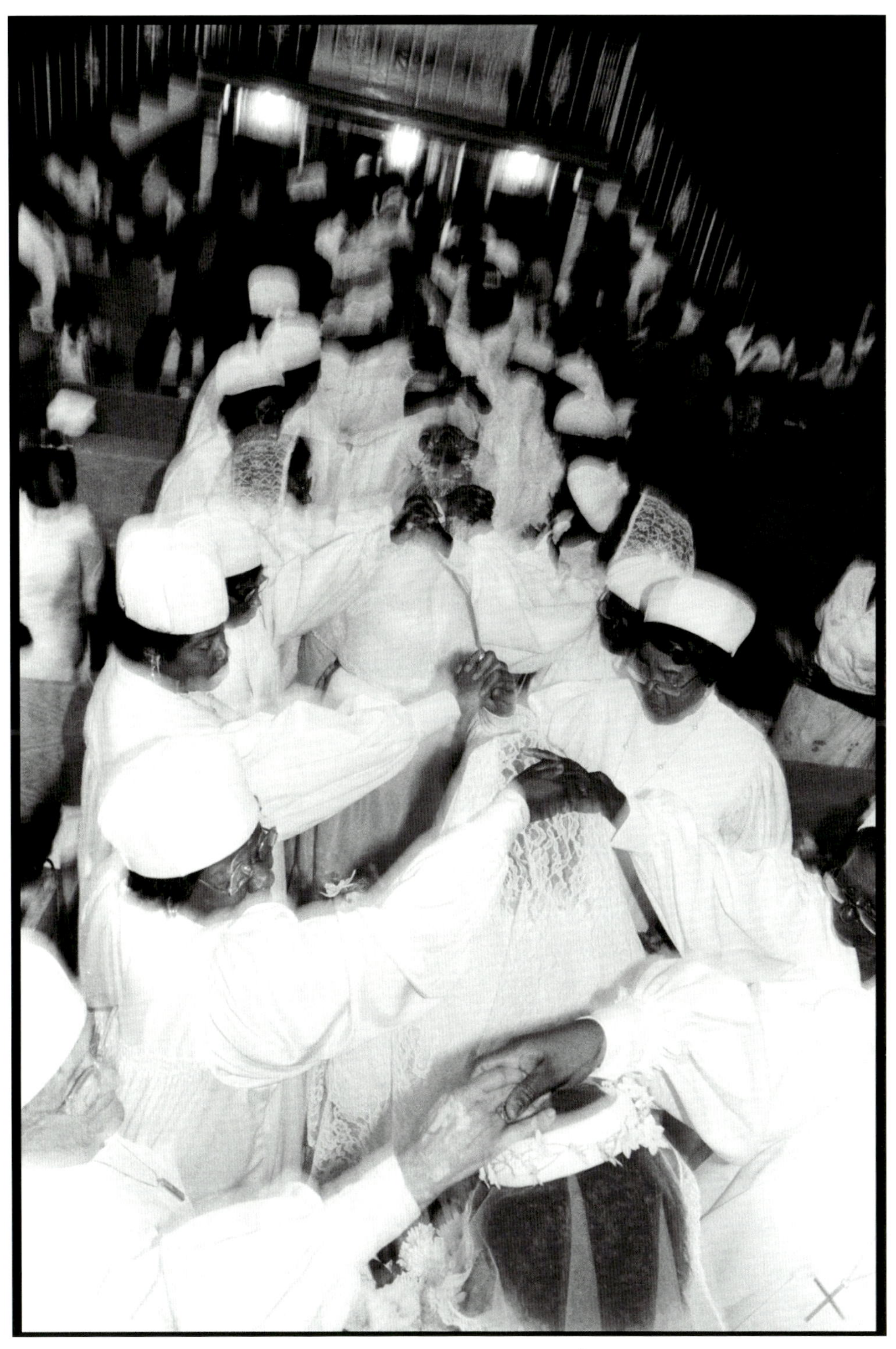

ORDINATION SERVICE, ISRAELITE DIVINE SPIRITUAL CHURCH | ST. ROCH, NEW ORLEANS; 1983

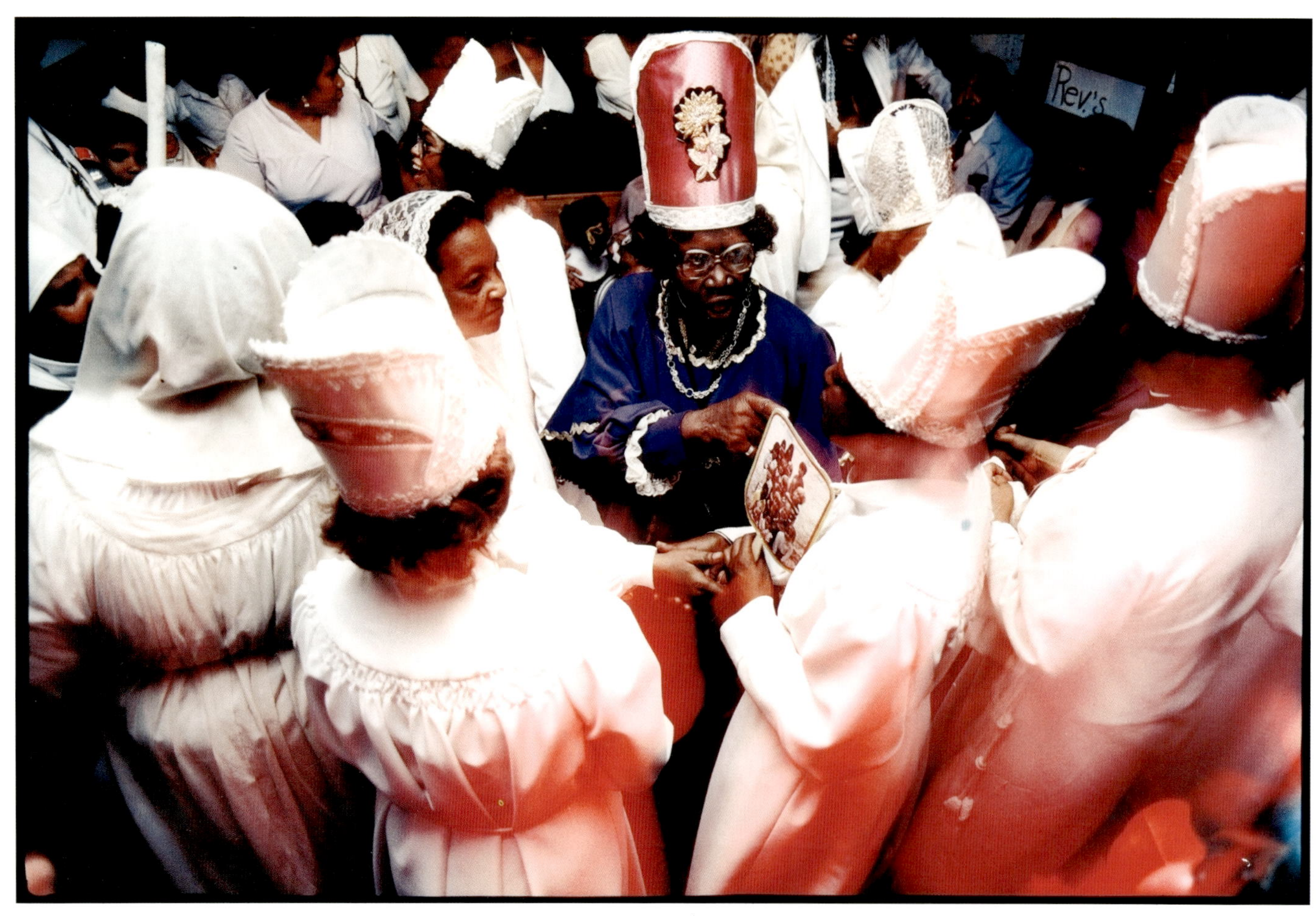


**ORDINATION SERVICE, INFANT JESUS OF PRAGUE SPIRITUAL CHURCH** | SEVENTH WARD, NEW ORLEANS; 1984

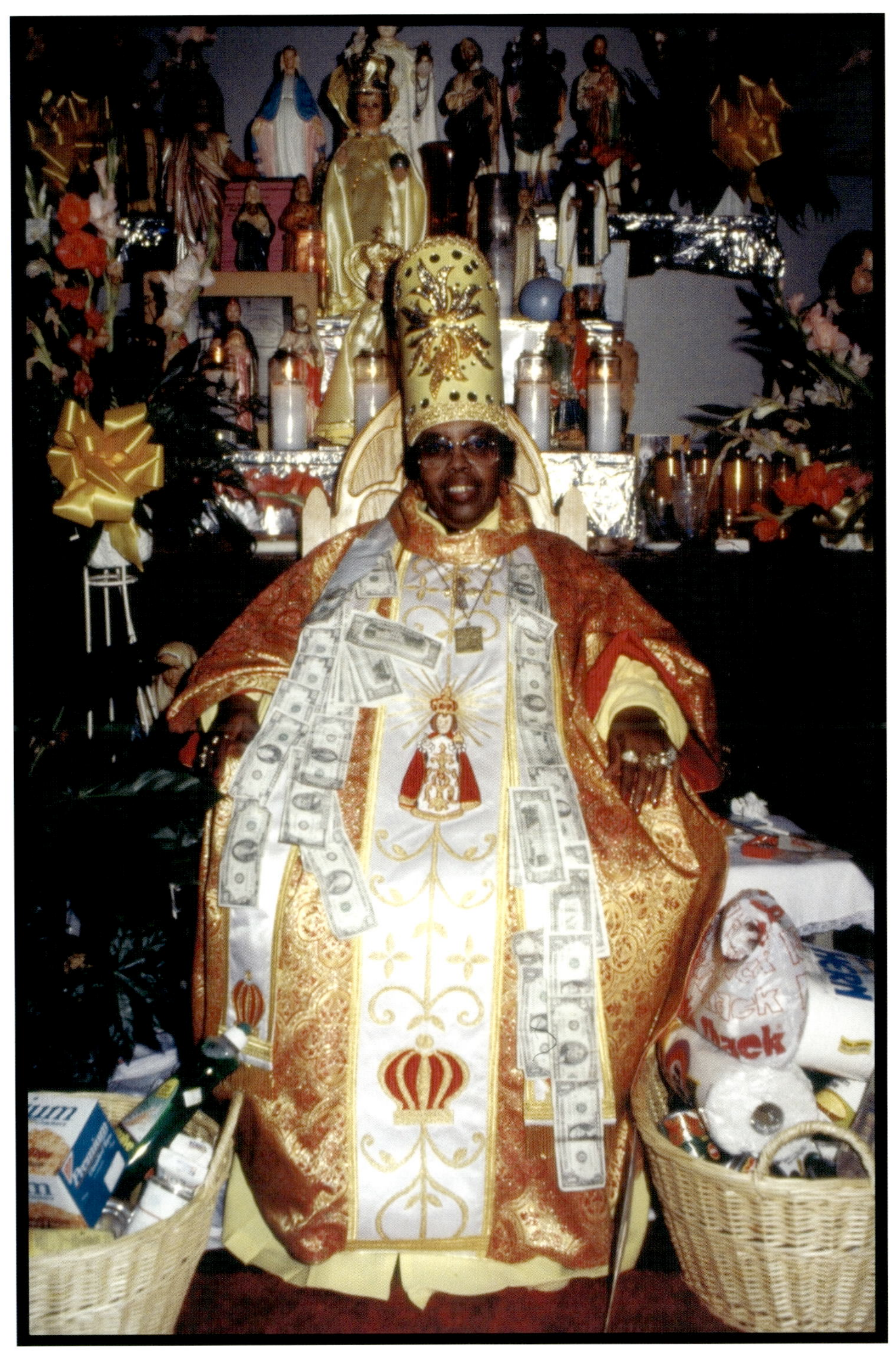

ARCHBISHOP LYDIA GILFORD SEATED IN FRONT OF ALTAR,
INFANT JESUS OF PRAGUE SPIRITUAL CHURCH | SEVENTH WARD, NEW ORLEANS; 1985

## RHYTHMS OF THE STREET

Though social aid and pleasure clubs are private organizations, some aspects of their activities are presented for public enjoyment. Chief among these are outings where members march accompanied by a brass band. Those not members of the club, the second line, follow with their own impromptu parade.

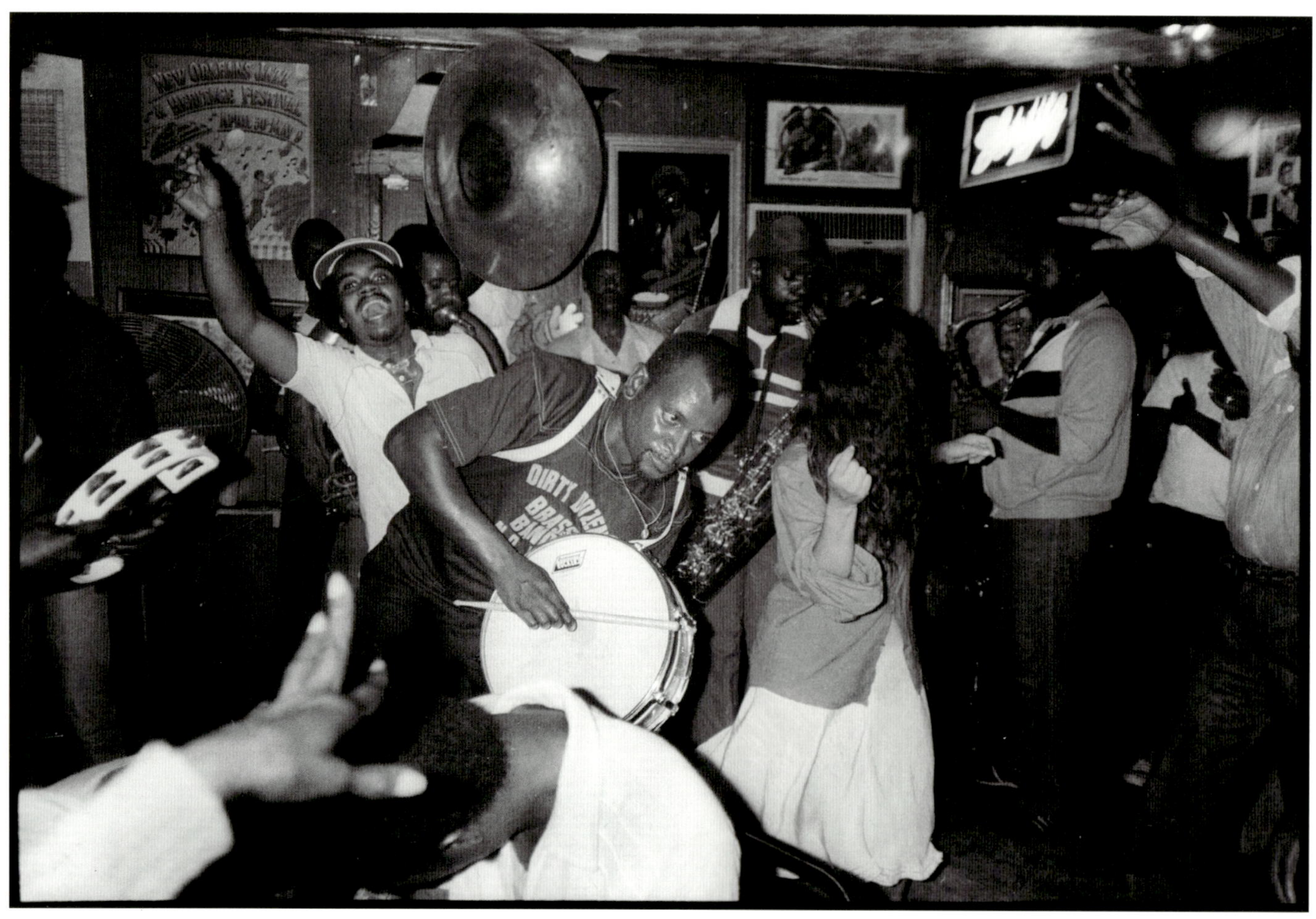

**DIRTY DOZEN BRASS BAND AT THE GLASS HOUSE** | CENTRAL CITY, NEW ORLEANS; 1982

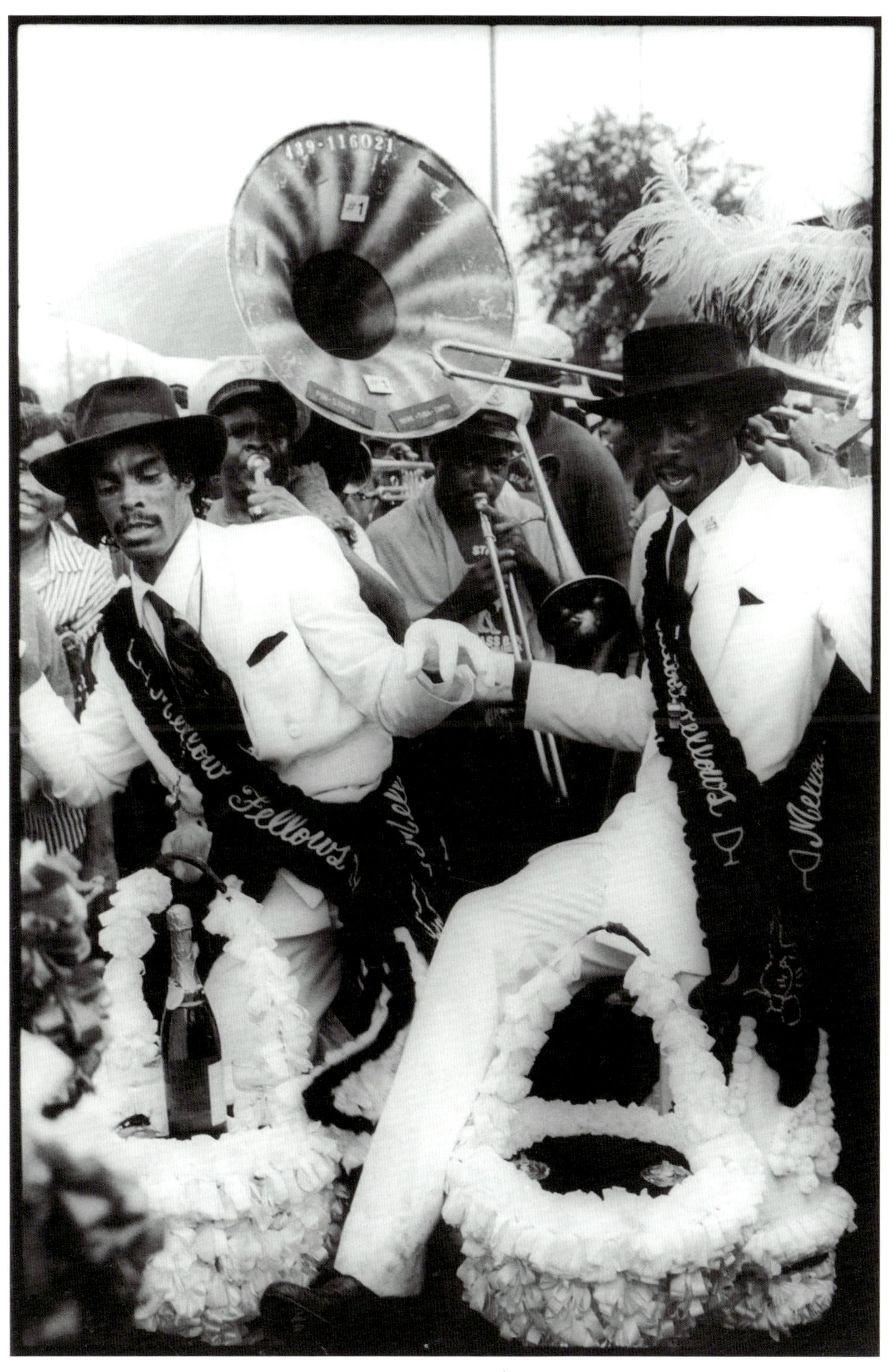


**MELLOW FELLOWS & YOUNG MEN OLYMPIAN PARADE** | CENTRAL CITY, NEW ORLEANS; 1985

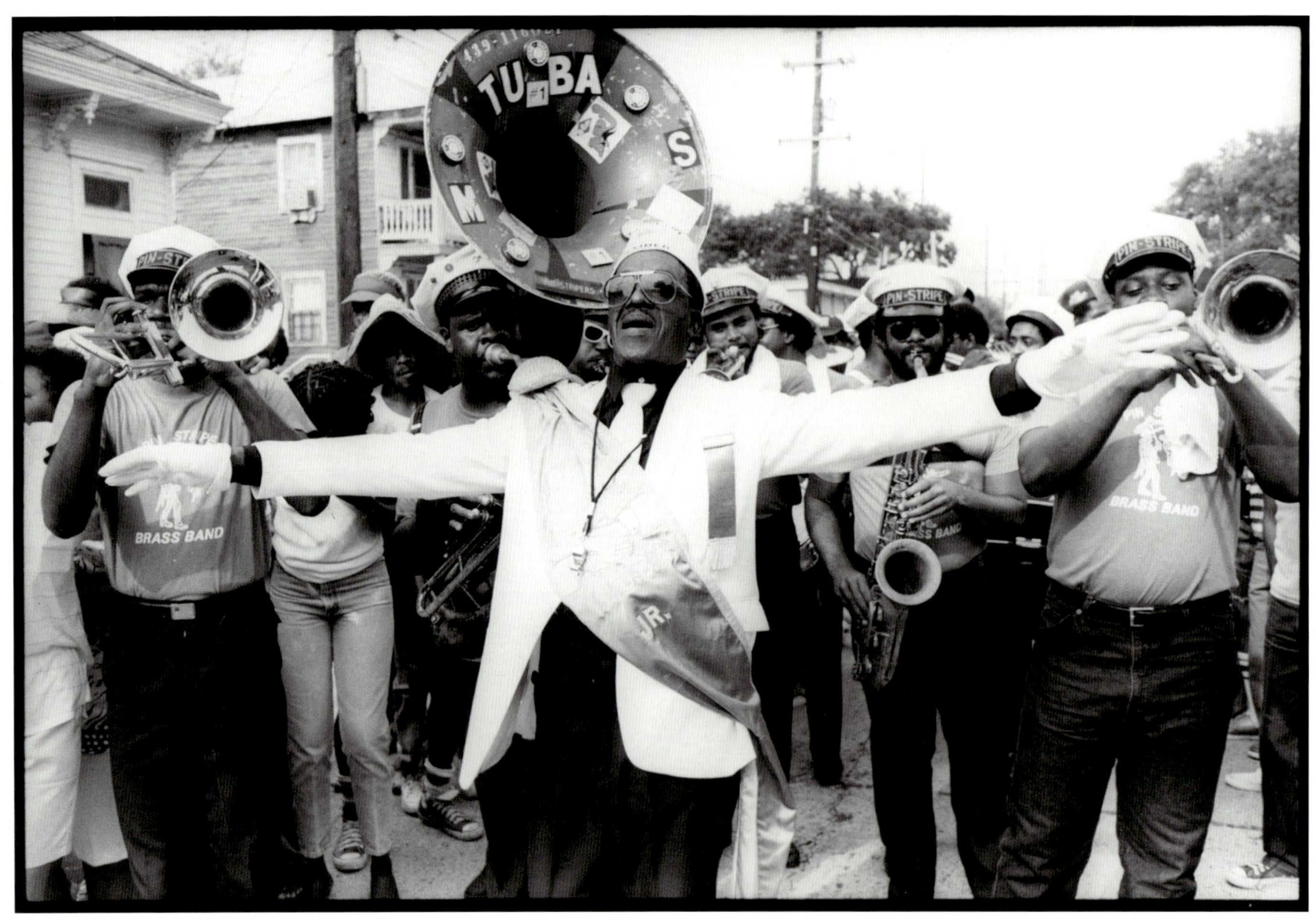


YOUNG MEN OLYMPIAN JUNIOR BENEVOLENT ASSOCIATION WITH THE PIN-STRIPE BRASS BAND | TREME, NEW ORLEANS; 1987

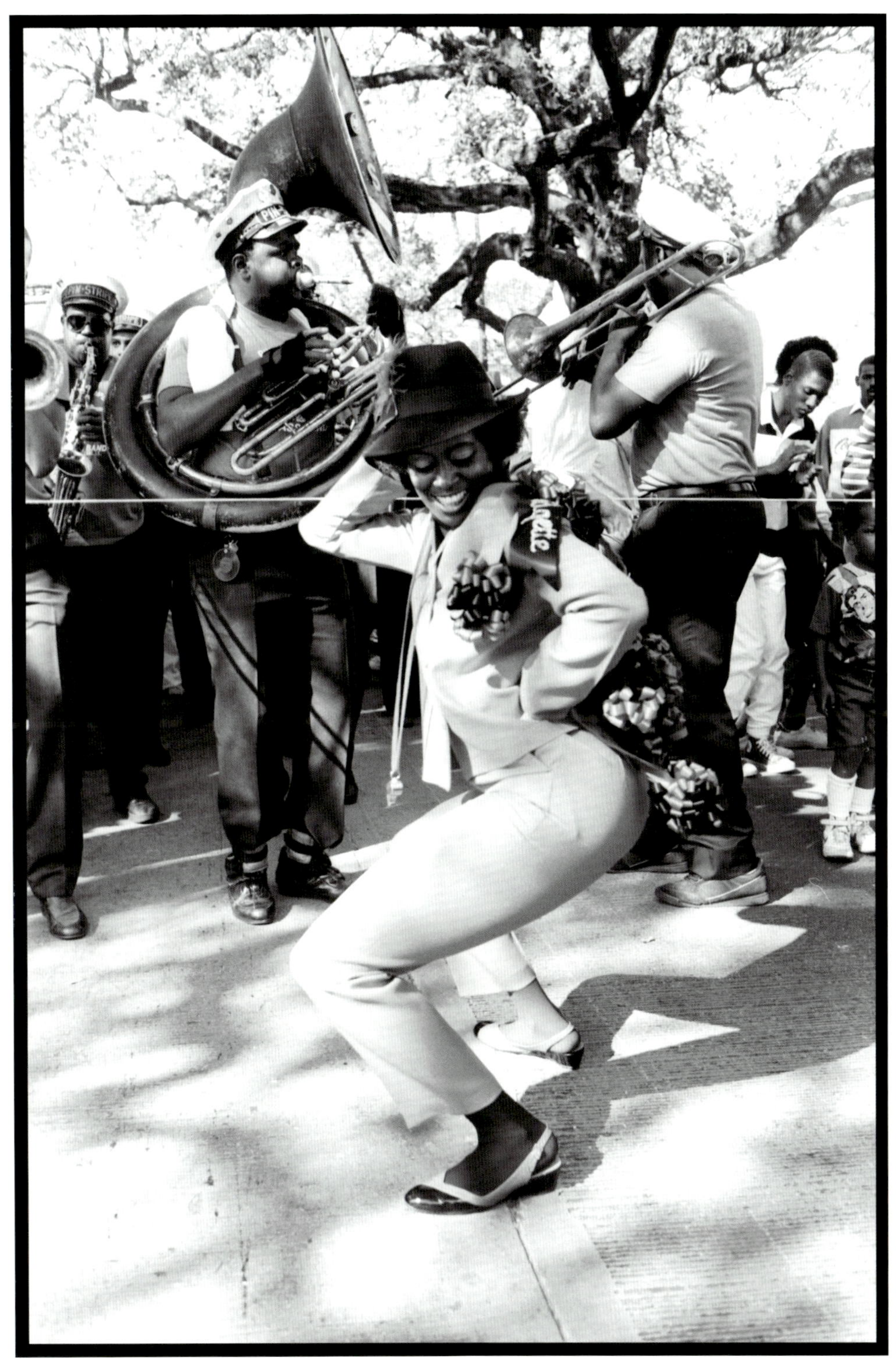

SECOND LINE JAMMERS SOCIAL & PLEASURE CLUB | NEW ORLEANS; 1987

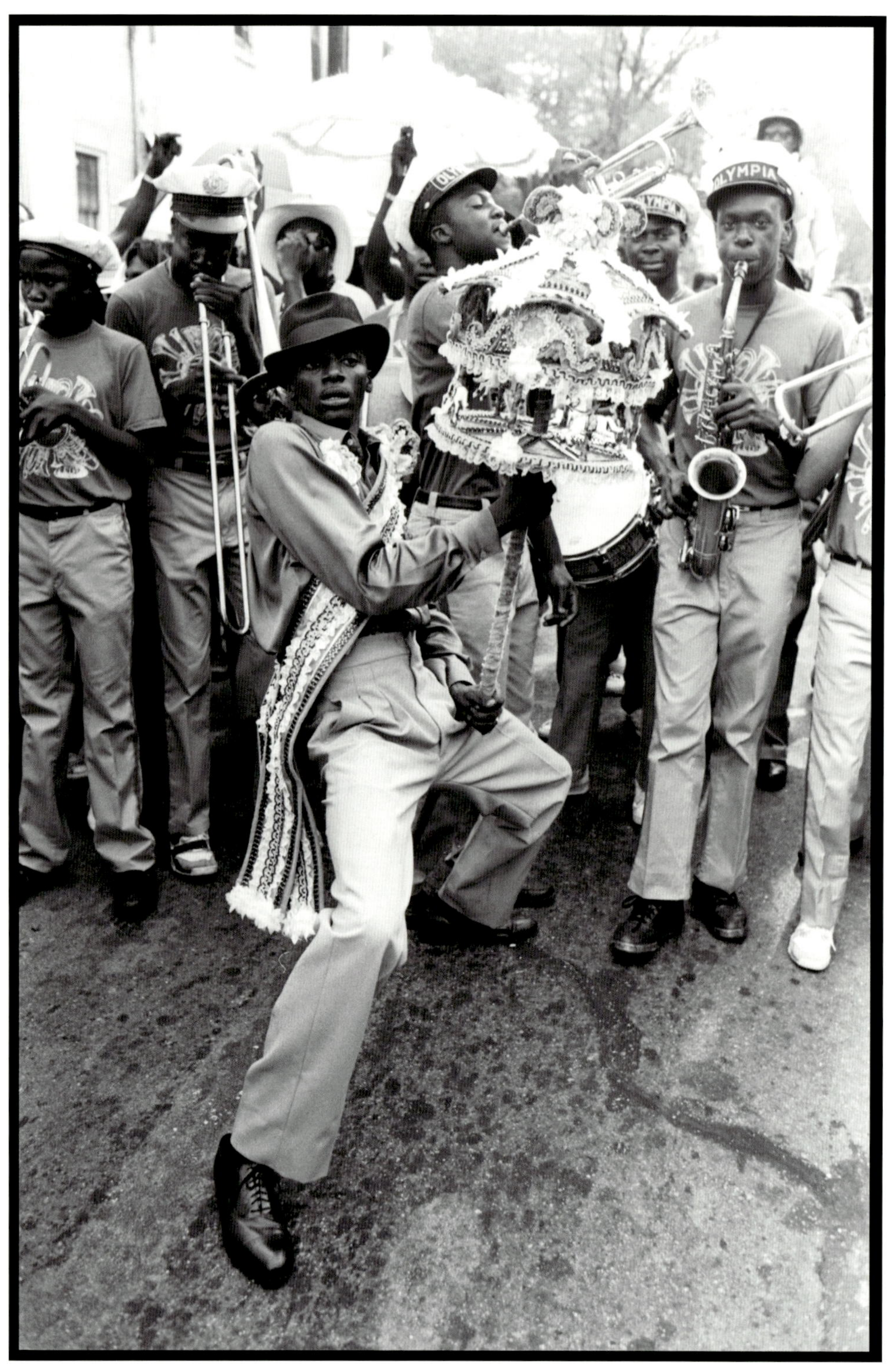


**SUDAN SOCIAL & PLEASURE CLUB, 3RD ANNUAL PARADE** | SEVENTH WARD, NEW ORLEANS; 1987

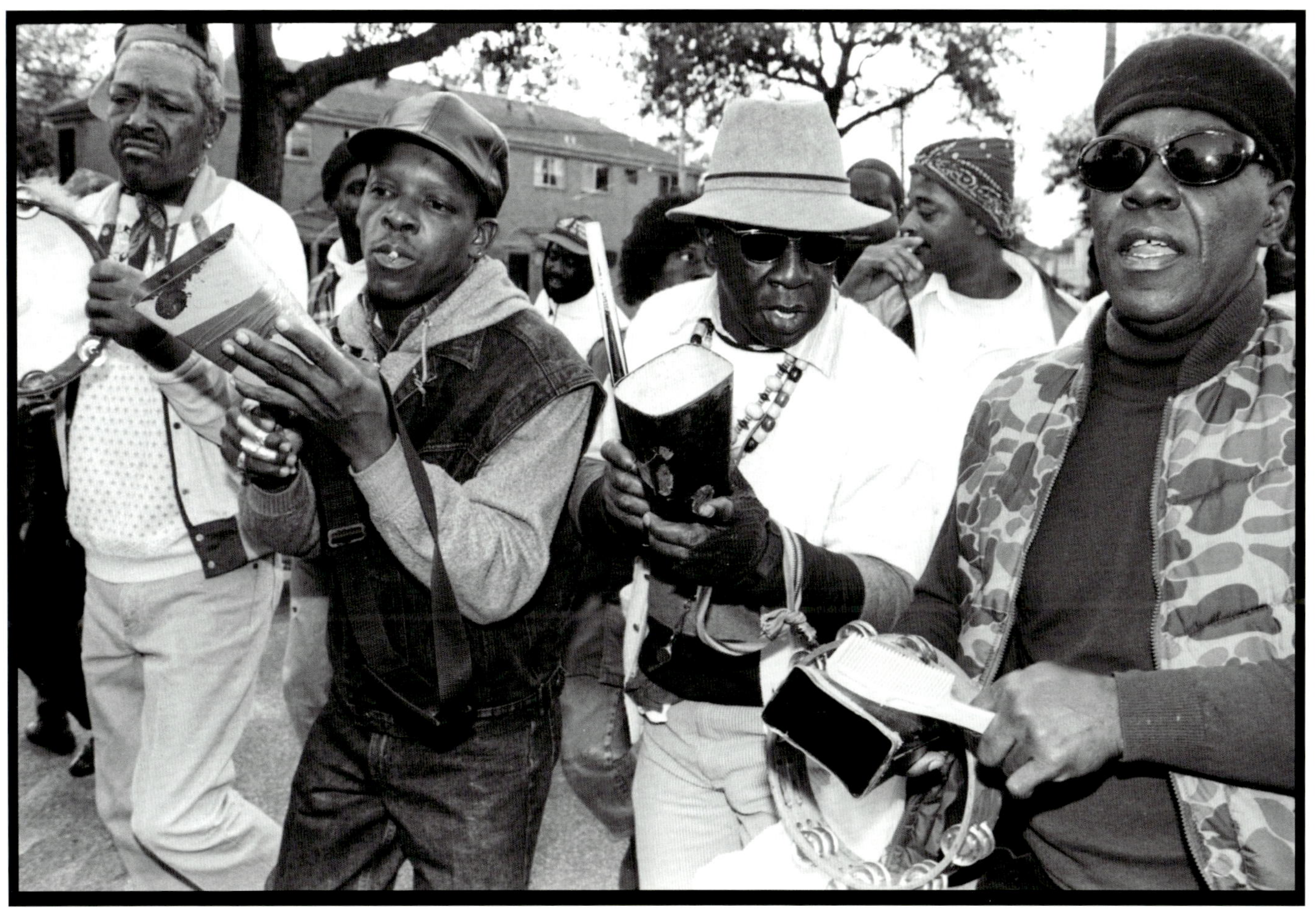

**SECOND LINERS WITH THE CALLIOPE HIGH STEPPERS** | CENTRAL CITY, NEW ORLEANS; 1994

## JAZZ FUNERALS

For decades, a burial and what the late jazz historian Dr. Curtis D. Jerde referred to as a "funeral with a band of music" were often specified benefits of membership dues paid to social and benevolent organizations. Because prominent jazz musicians were often involved, and some of the traditional songs played at the funerals were jazz standards, the umbrella term "jazz funeral" was coined.

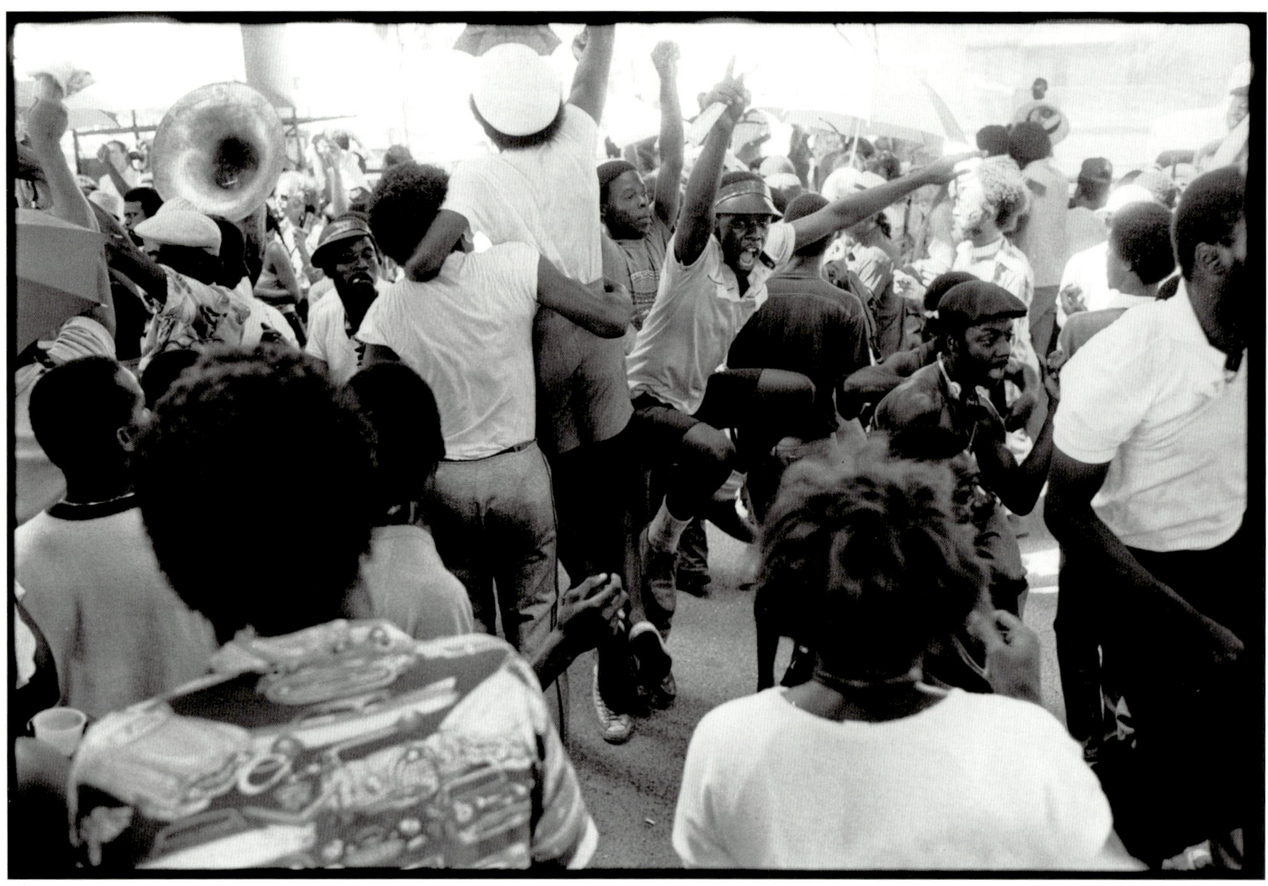

**FUNERAL OF DAVE "FATMAN" WILLIAMS** | SEVENTH WARD, NEW ORLEANS; 1982

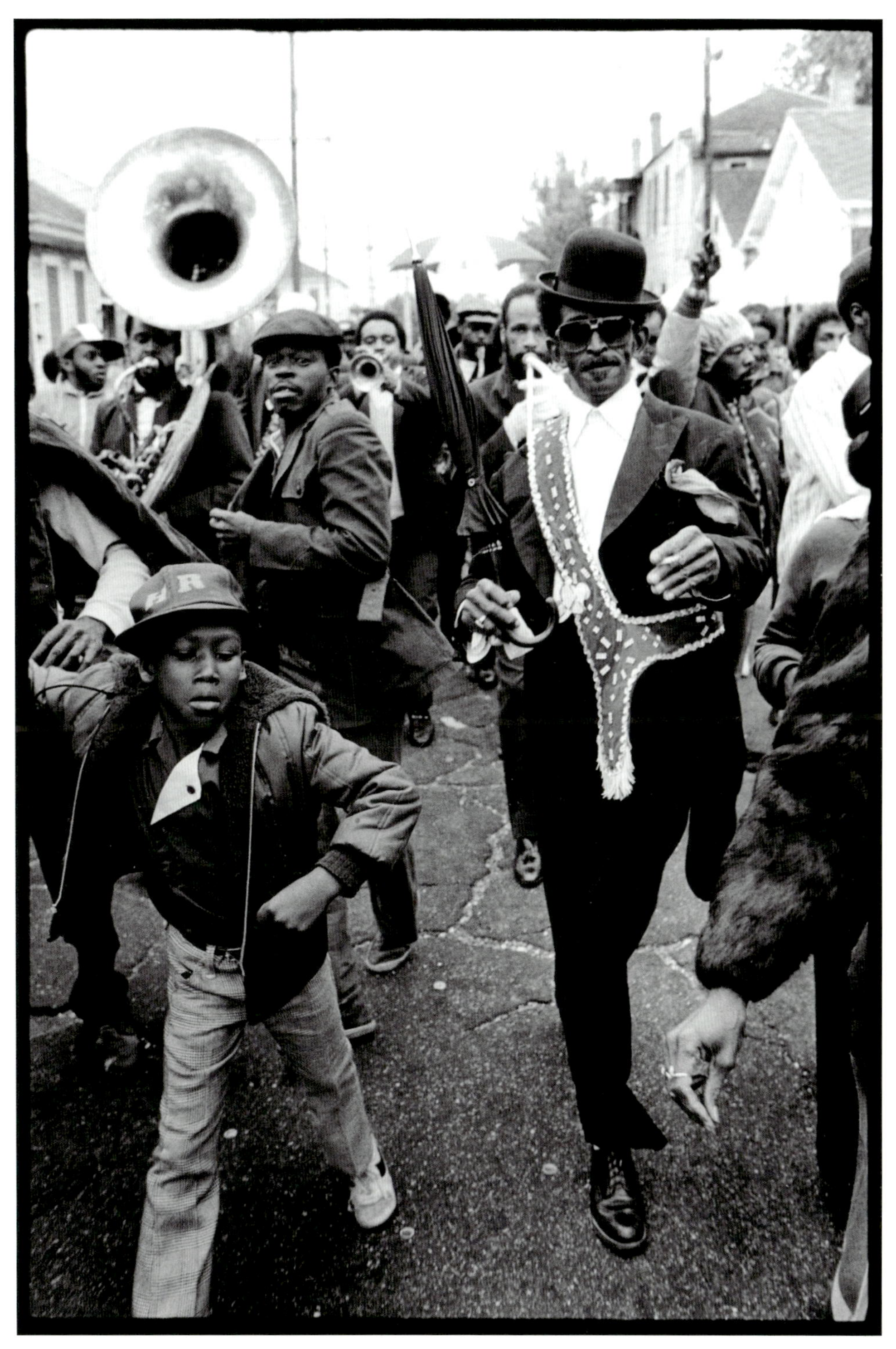

"UNCLE" LIONEL BATISTE LEADING FUNERAL PARADE FOR JIMMY "THE HAWK" RICHARDSON | TREME, NEW ORLEANS; 1983

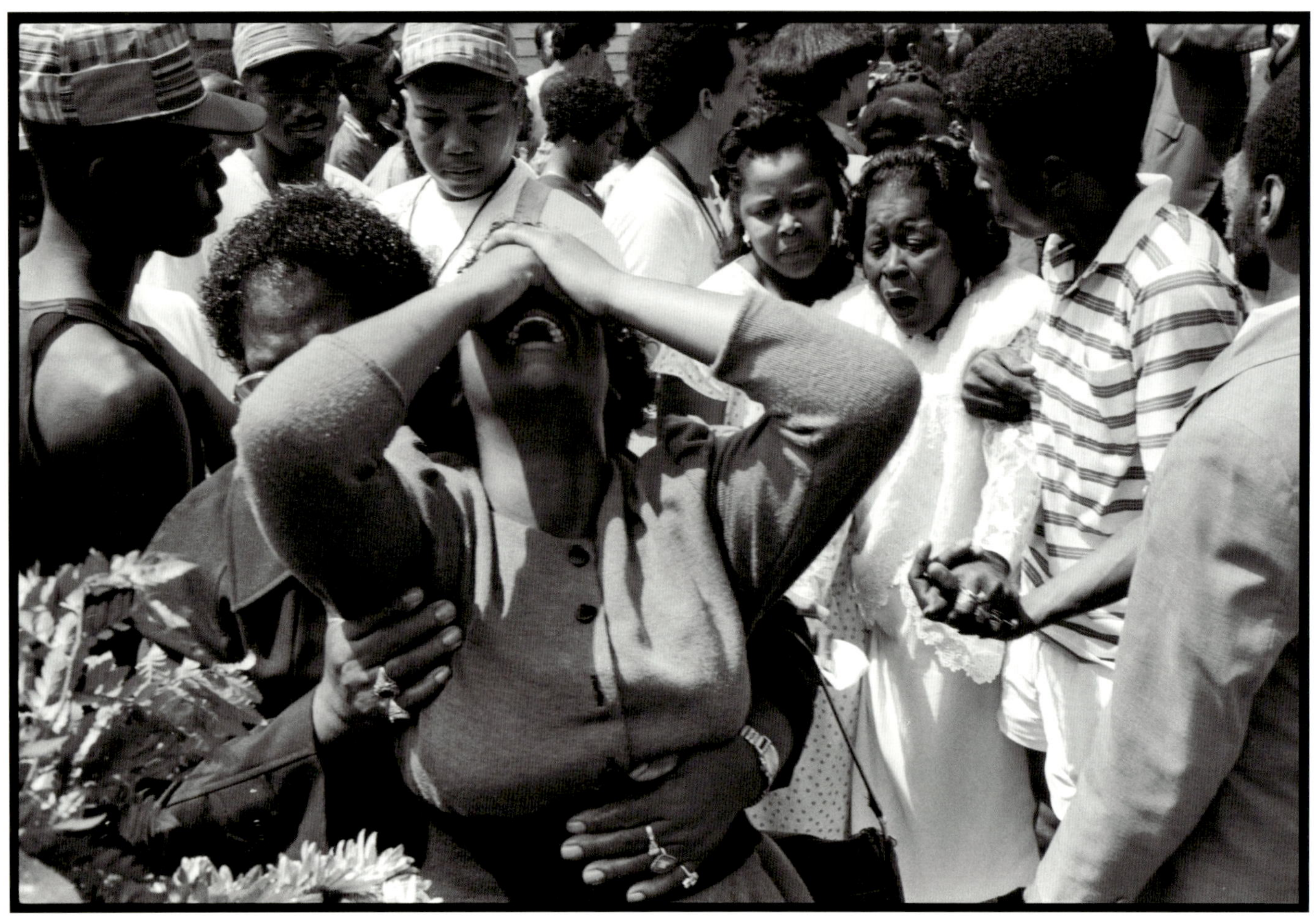

FUNERAL OF PHILLIP JOSEPH SHEZBIE JR. | SEVENTH WARD, NEW ORLEANS; 1990

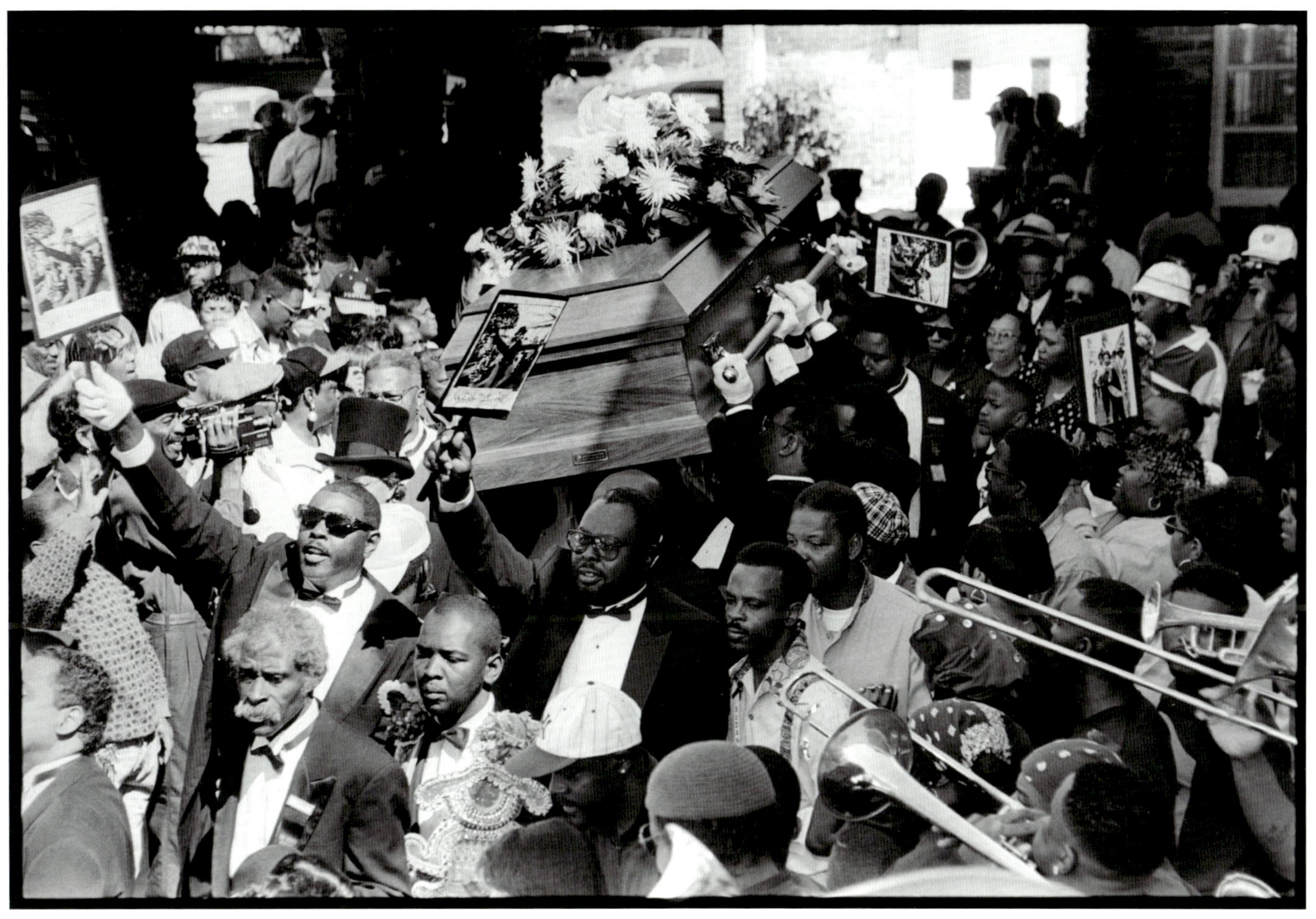

FUNERAL OF ALFRED "DUTE" LAZARD | TREME, NEW ORLEANS; 1995

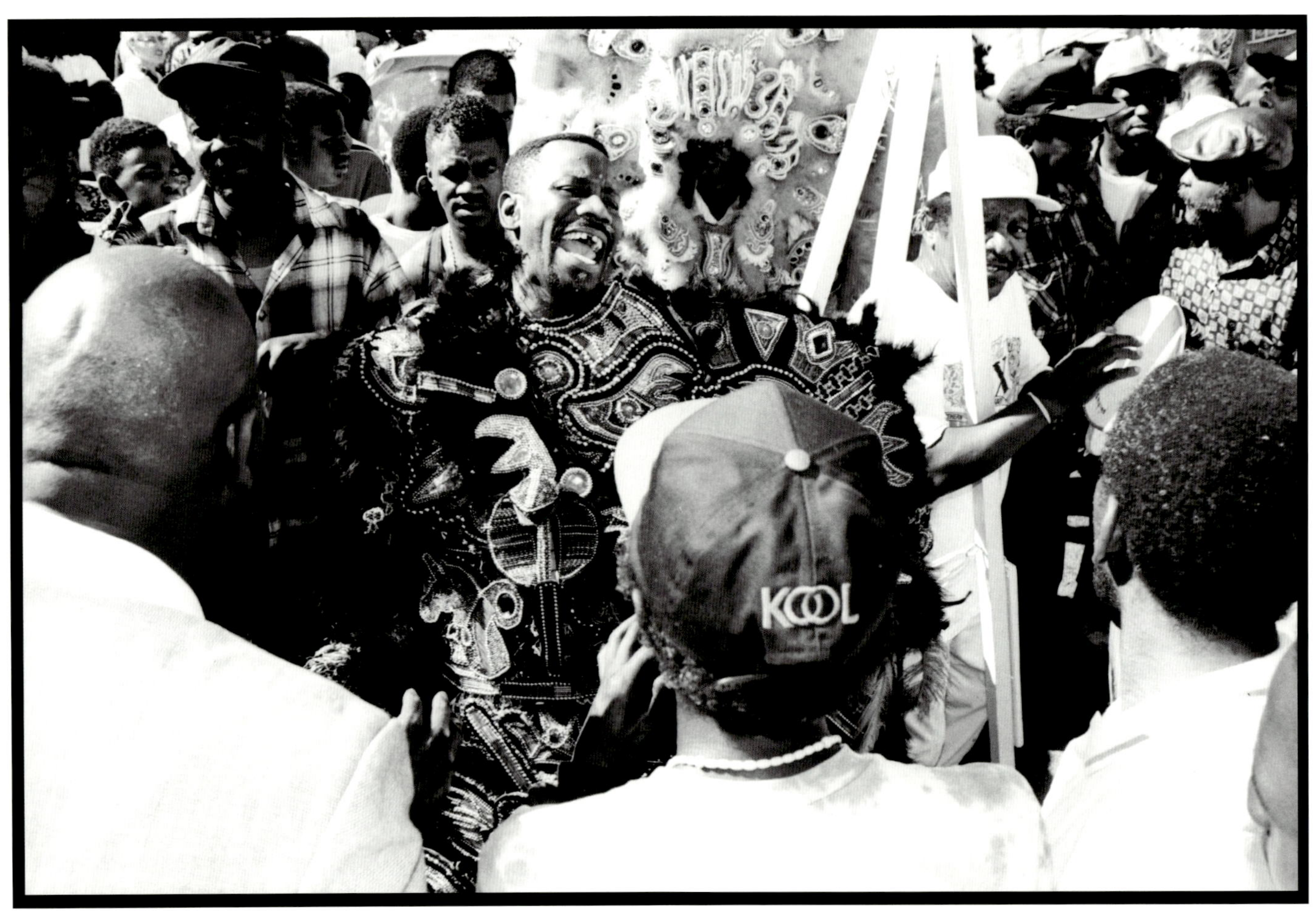


FUNERAL OF TAJU MALIK SMITH | TREME, NEW ORLEANS; 1995

## MARDI GRAS INDIANS

Dressed in elaborate hand-sewn and beaded suits that reference aspects of Native American and African cultures, African American marching groups—led by a "big chief"—parade in New Orleans neighborhoods on Mardi Gras, St. Joseph's Night, and Super Sunday. Uptown and Downtown groups have different traditions and neighborhood routes.

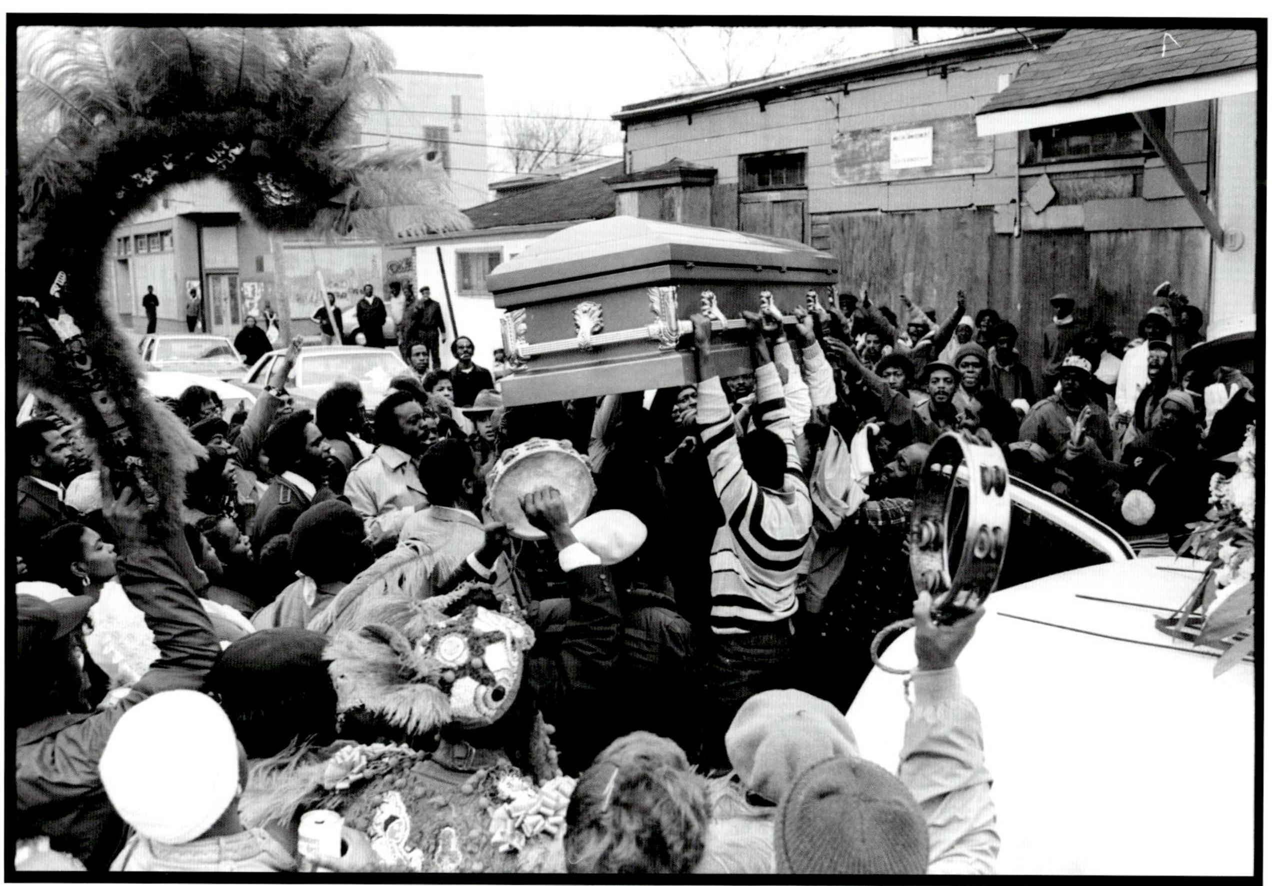

**FUNERAL OF JOHNNY "TOBA" TOBIAS, BLACK EAGLES, MARDI GRAS INDIAN TRIBE** | CENTRAL CITY, NEW ORLEANS; 1988

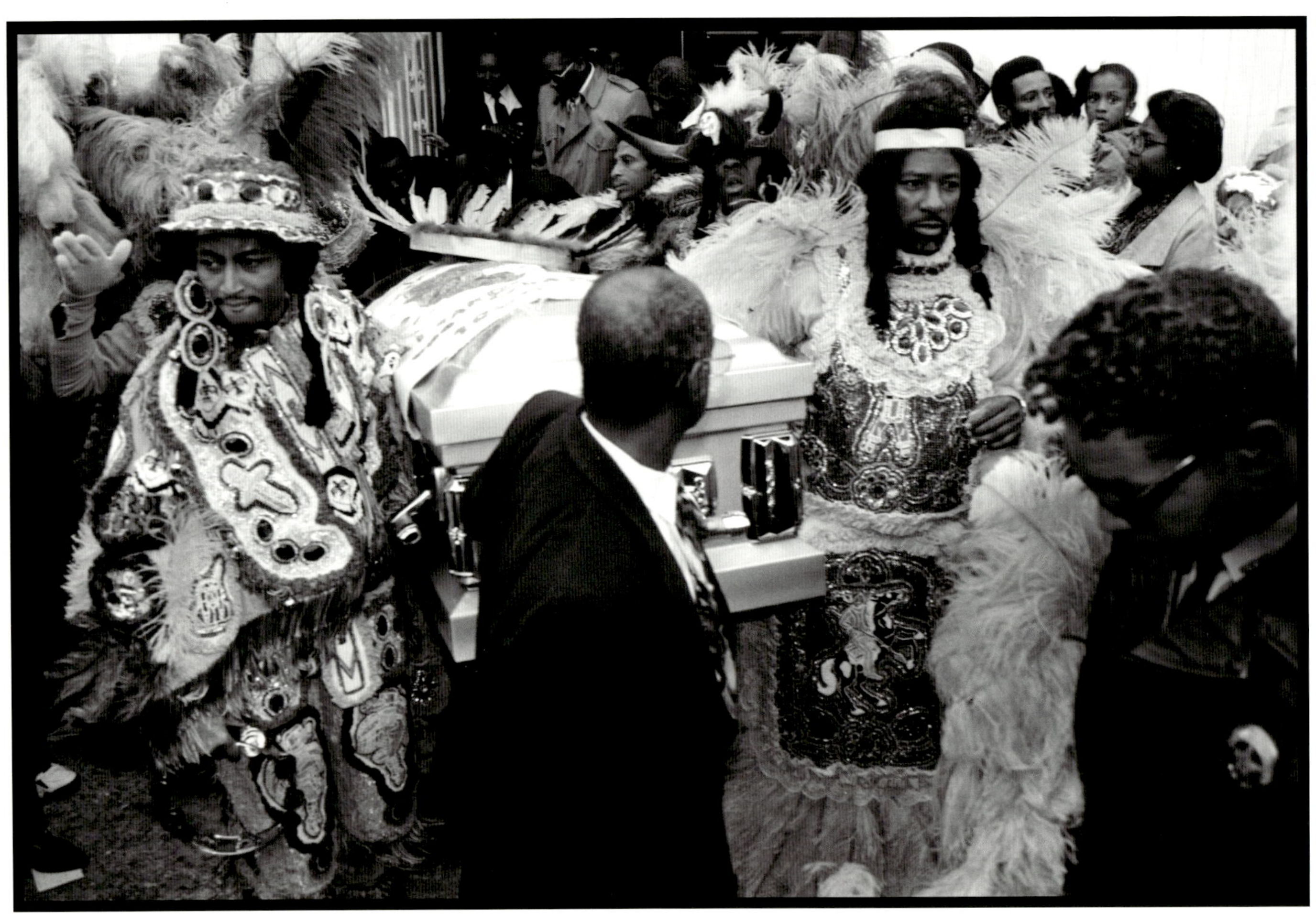

**FUNERAL OF ALEX BAILEY, SPYBOY FOR THE CREOLE WILD WEST MARDI GRAS INDIAN TRIBE** | BROADMOOR, NEW ORLEANS; 1996

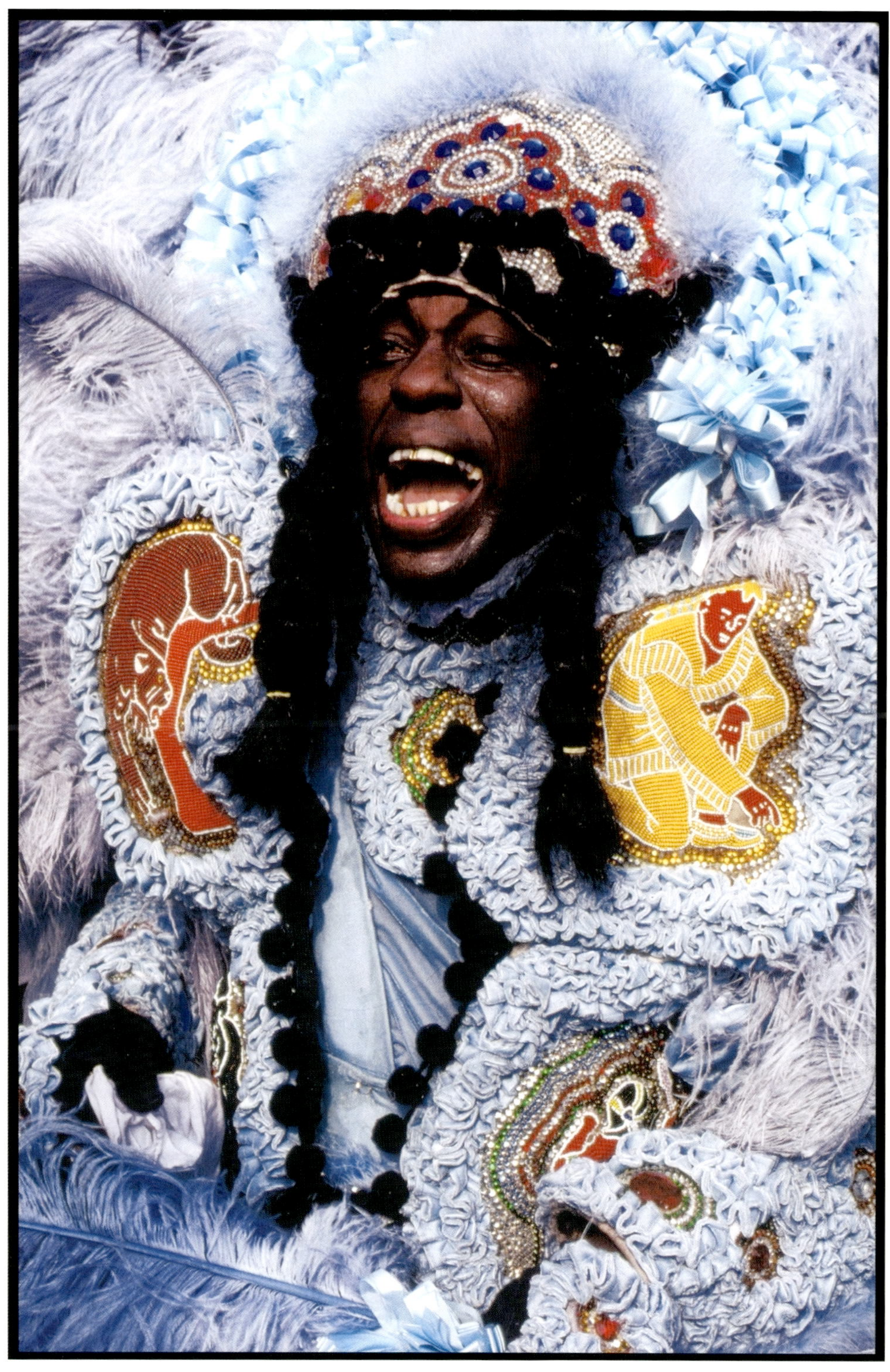

**BO DOLLIS, BIG CHIEF OF THE WILD MAGNOLIAS, MARDI GRAS DAY** | NEW ORLEANS; 1989

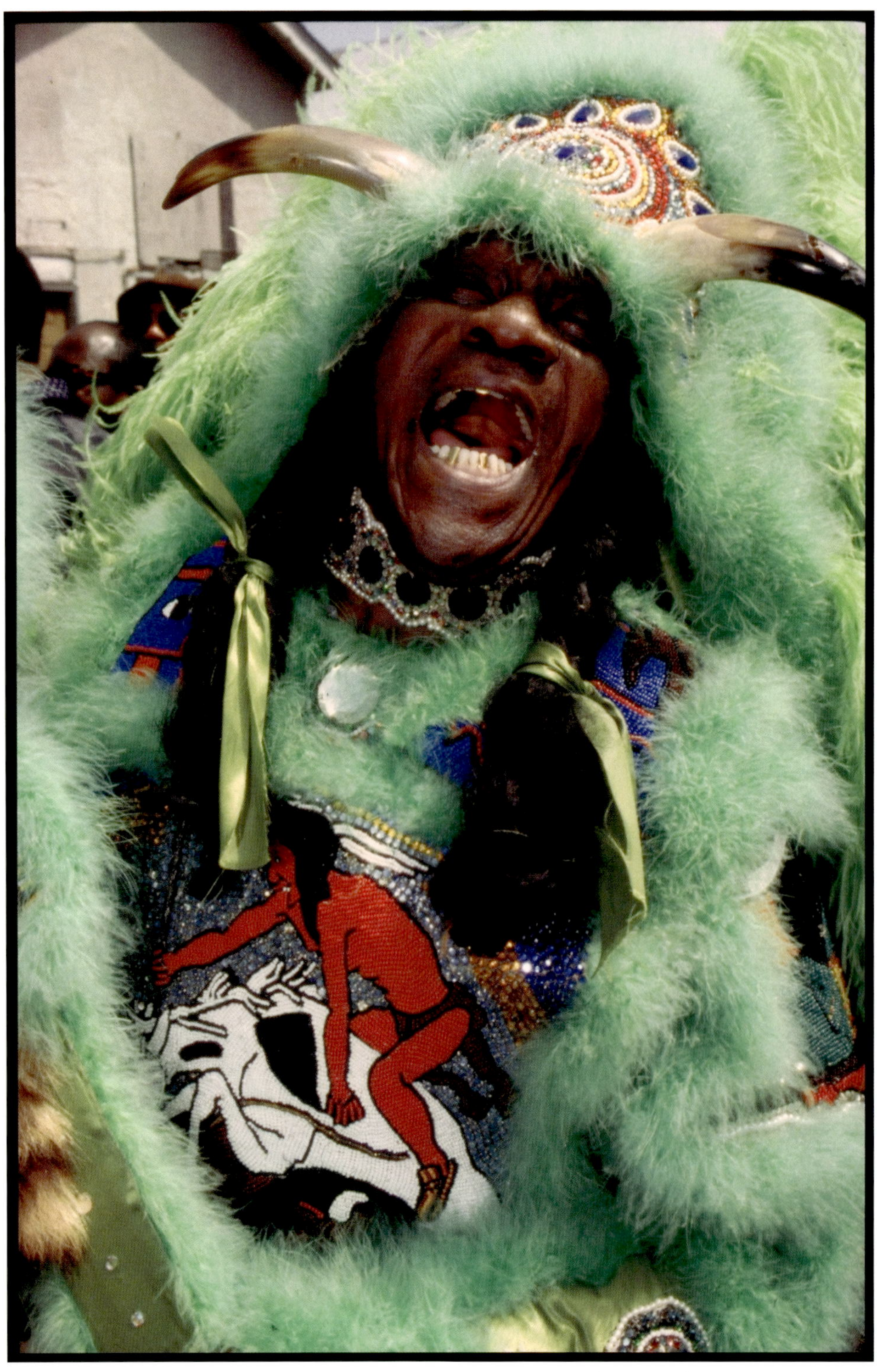

**LIONEL "DR. BIRD" OUBICHON, MEDICINE MAN, WHITE EAGLES** | NEW ORLEANS; 1993

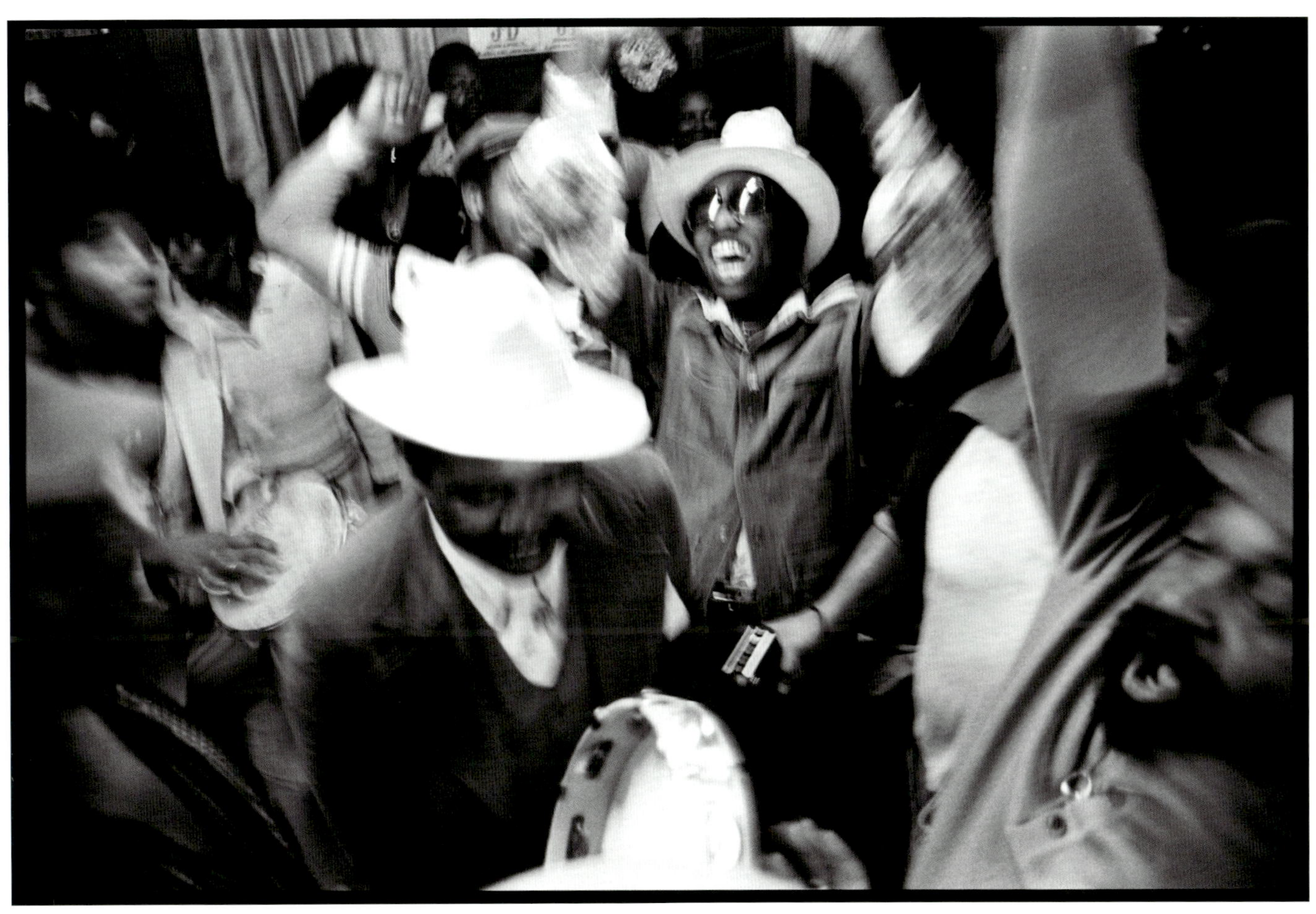

**INDIAN PRACTICE AT THE H & R BAR** | CENTRAL CITY, NEW ORLEANS; 1978

## TIPITINA'S AND MUSICIANS

Smith documented many performances at Tipitina's, a club that he helped launch. Located at the corner of Napoleon Avenue and Tchoupitoulas Street, Tipitina's showcases traditional New Orleans music and musicians. Smith did not limit his photographs of musicians to their appearances at Tipitina's or Jazz Fest. Instead, he captured them both on and off stage.

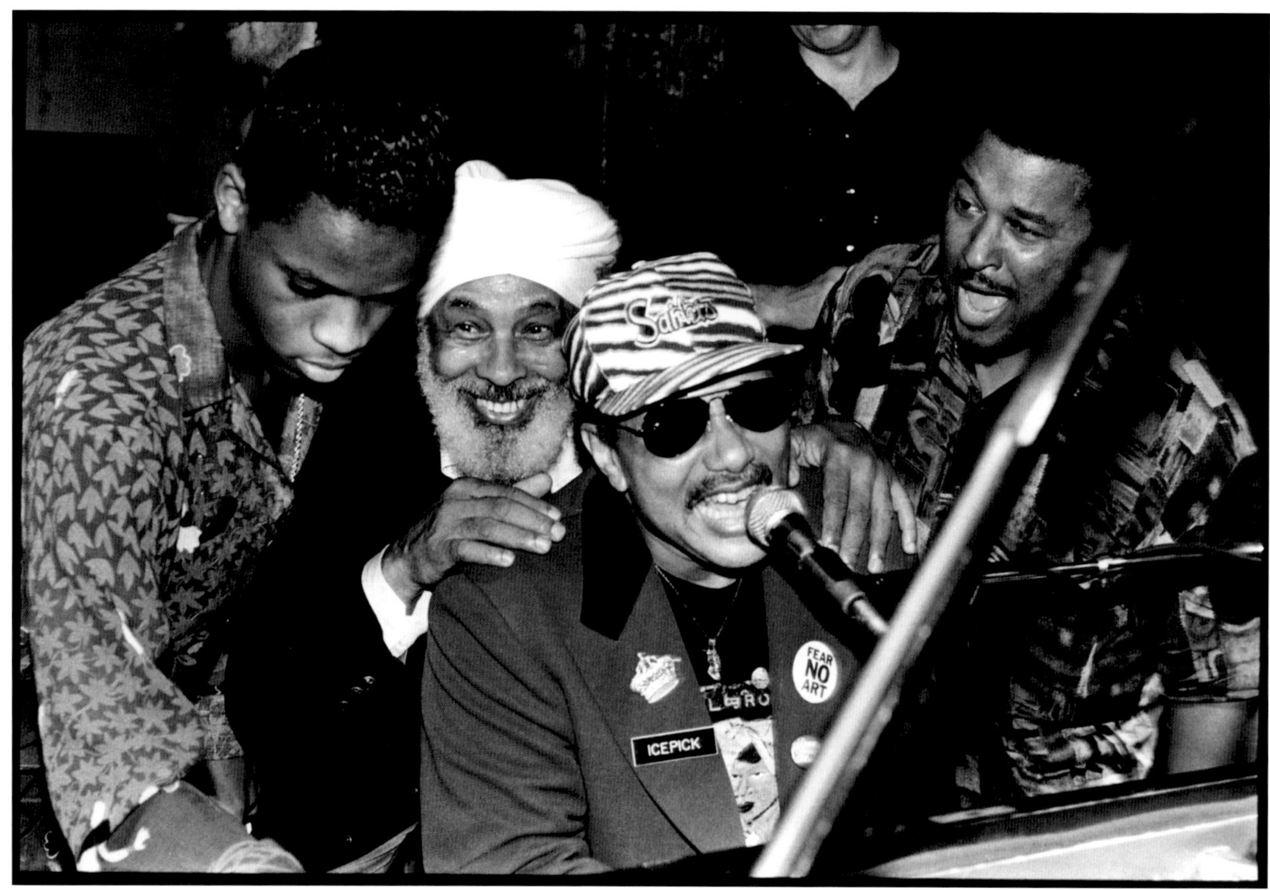


**PIANO NIGHT AT TIPITINA'S** (FROM LEFT TO RIGHT: DAVELL CRAWFORD, EDDIE BO, ART NEVILLE, AND WILLIE TEE) | NEW ORLEANS; 1991

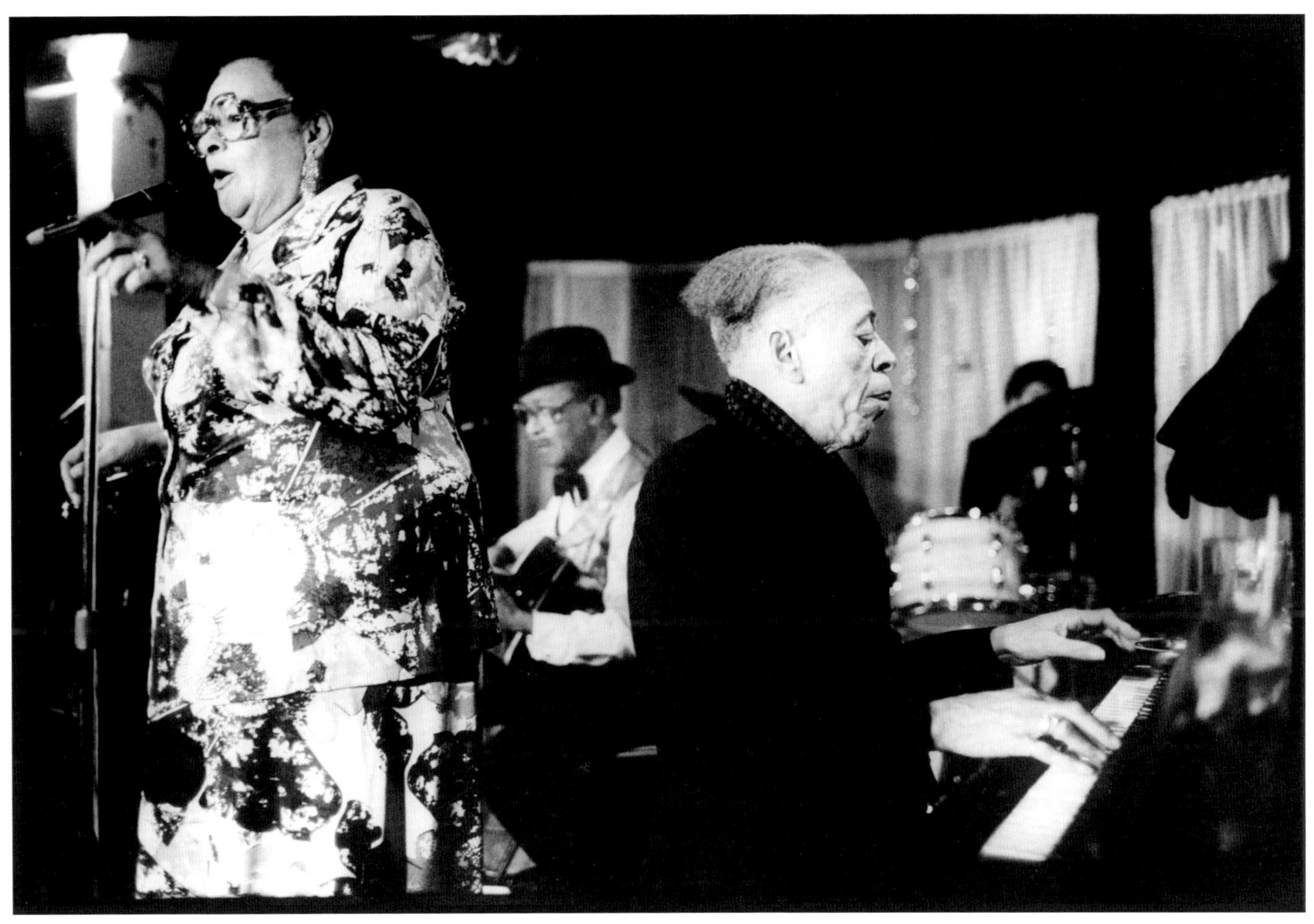

BLUE LU & DANNY BARKER WITH TUTS WASHINGTON AT TIPITINA'S | NEW ORLEANS; 1978

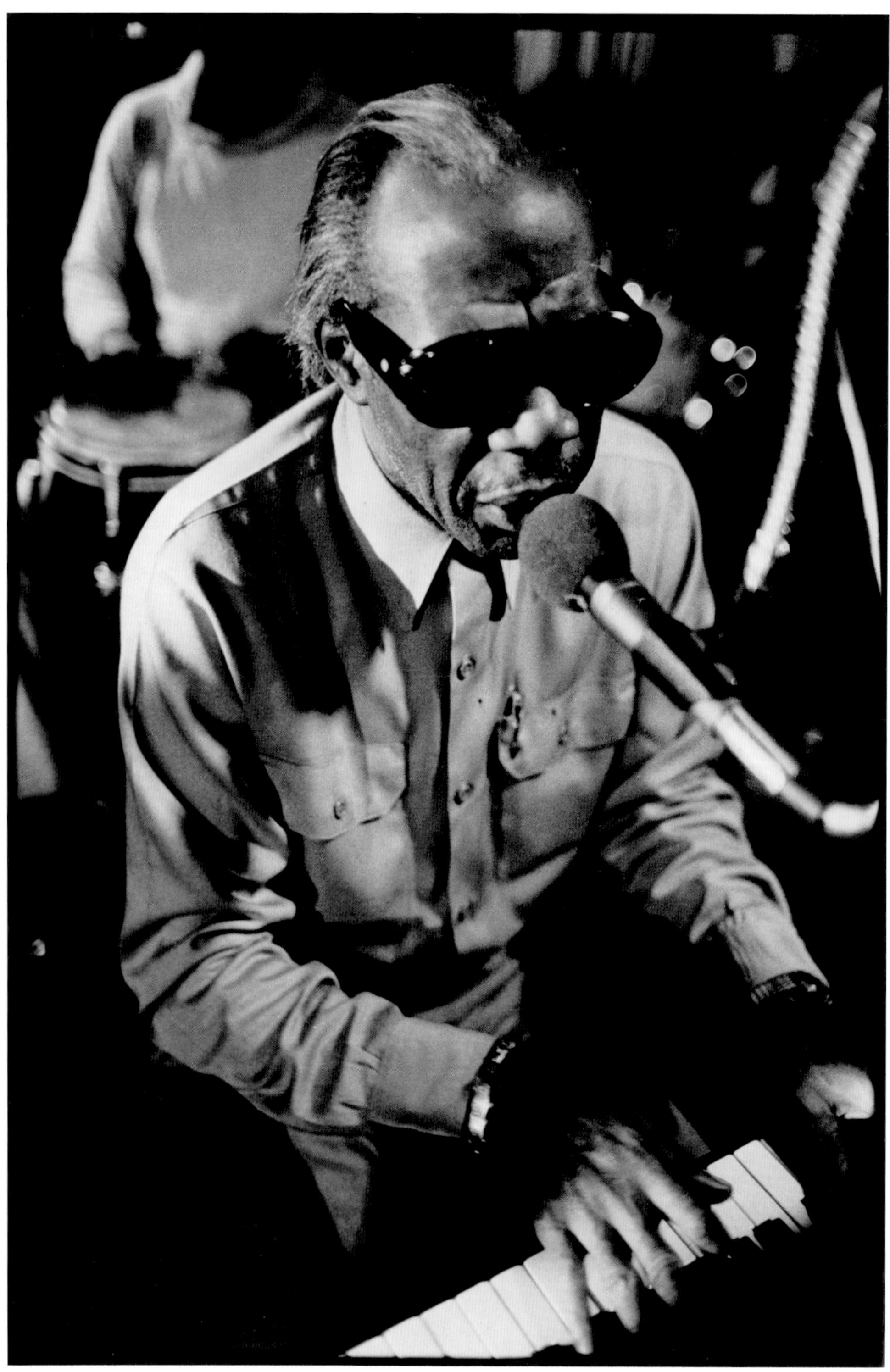

**PROFESSOR LONGHAIR AT TIPITINA'S** | NEW ORLEANS; 1978

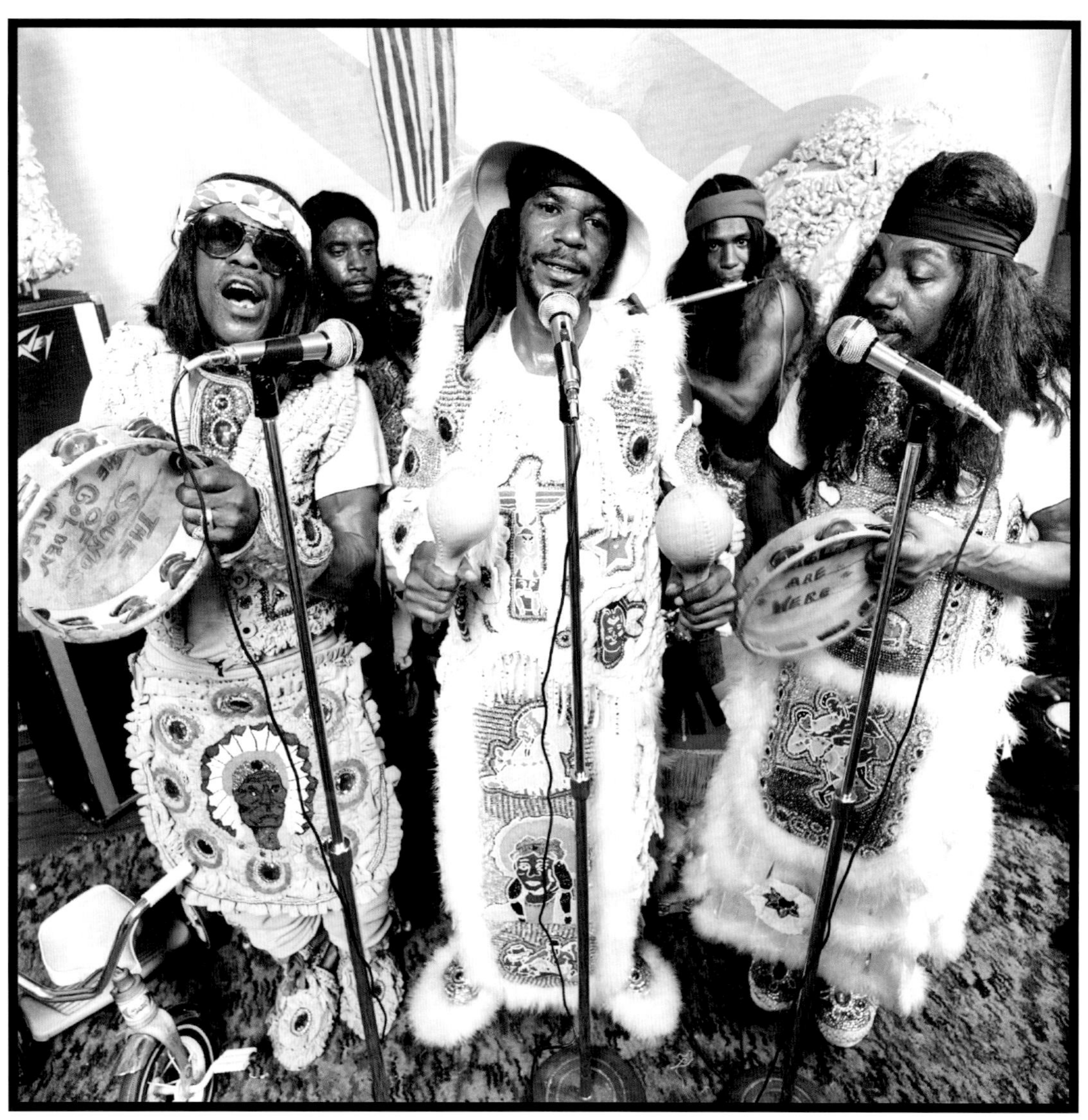

THE GOLDEN EAGLES MARDI GRAS INDIAN TRIBE (LEFT TO RIGHT: QUARTER MOON TOBIAS, BIG CHIEF MONK BOUDREAUX, AND ALLIGATOR JUNE JOHNSON) | NEW ORLEANS; 1978

## TRAVEL

Occasionally, Smith traveled away from his home base of New Orleans. When he made photographs outside of the Crescent City, his subjects often paralleled those found in his Louisiana work.

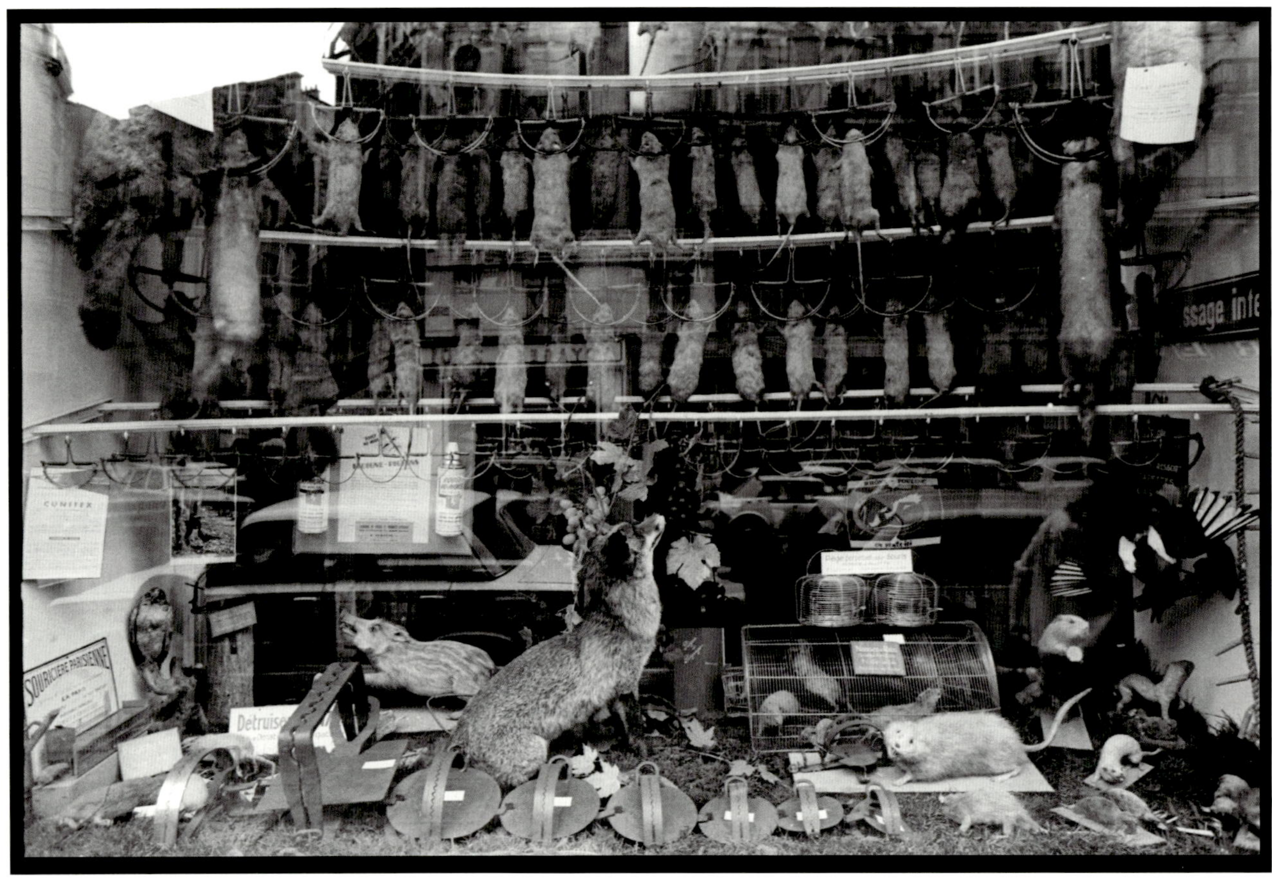

**EXTERMINATOR'S SHOP** | PARIS, FRANCE; 1971

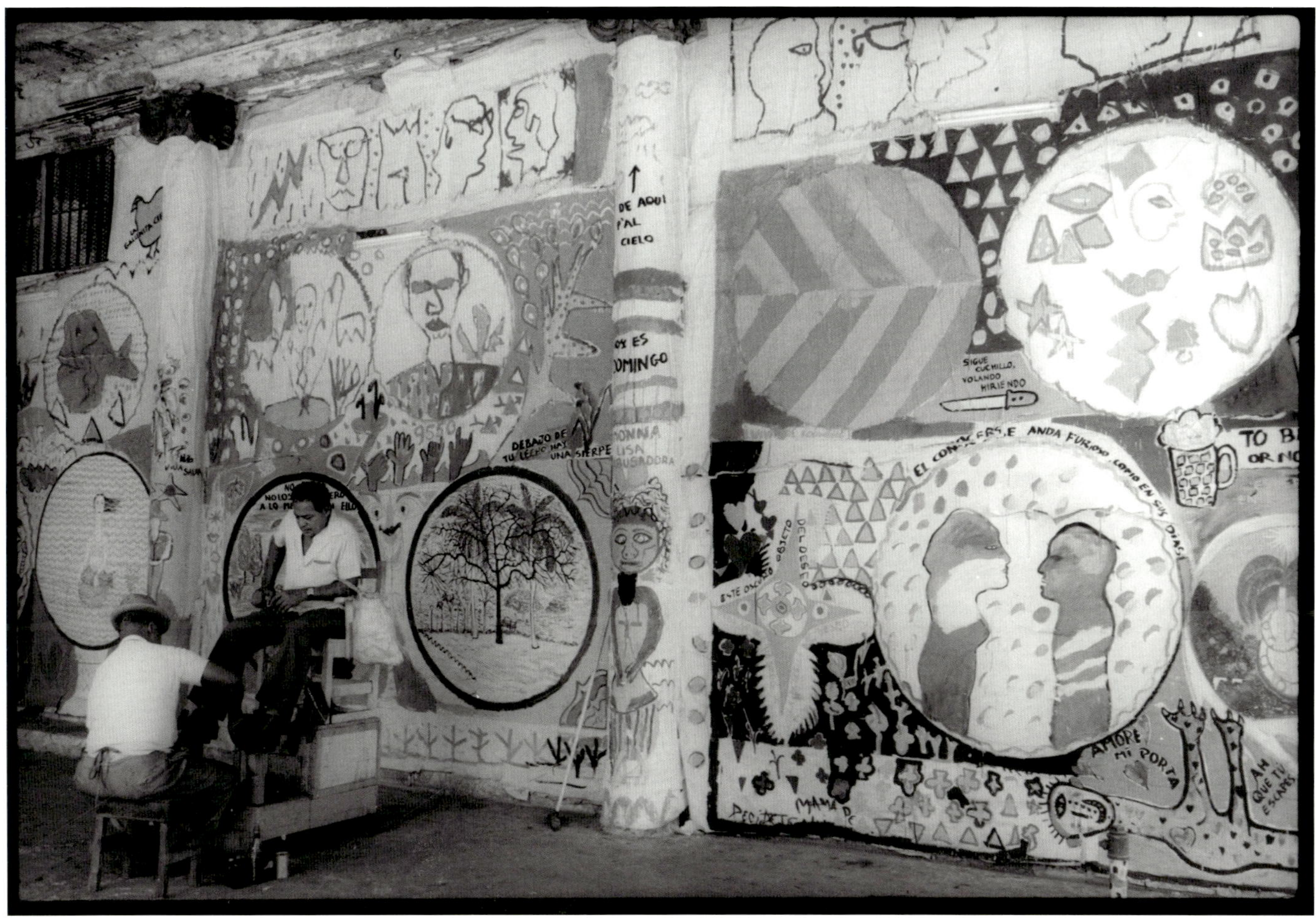


**GRAFFITI** | HAVANA, CUBA; 1984

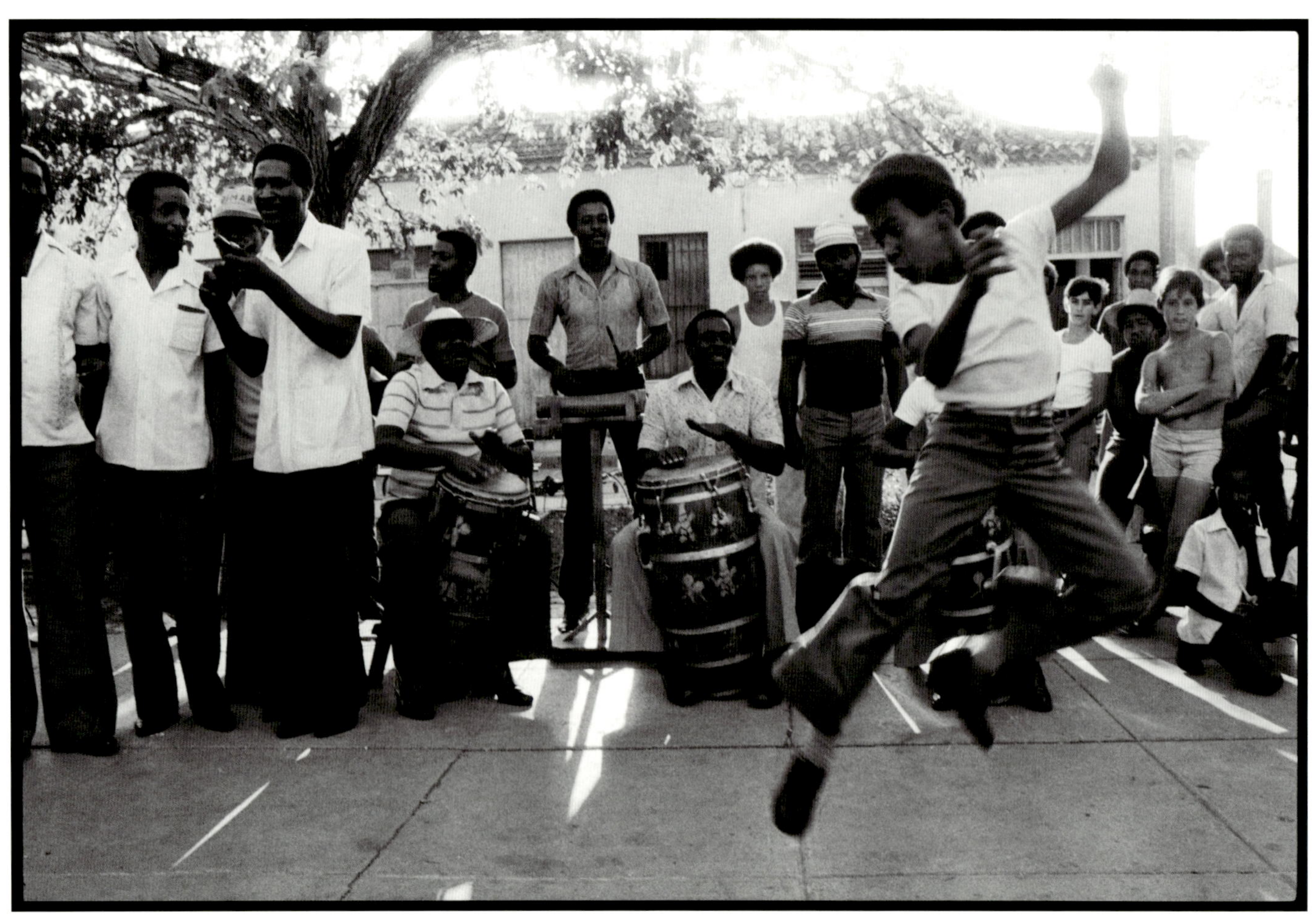

**DANCING WITH LOS MUÑEQUITOS** | MATANZAS, CUBA; 1984

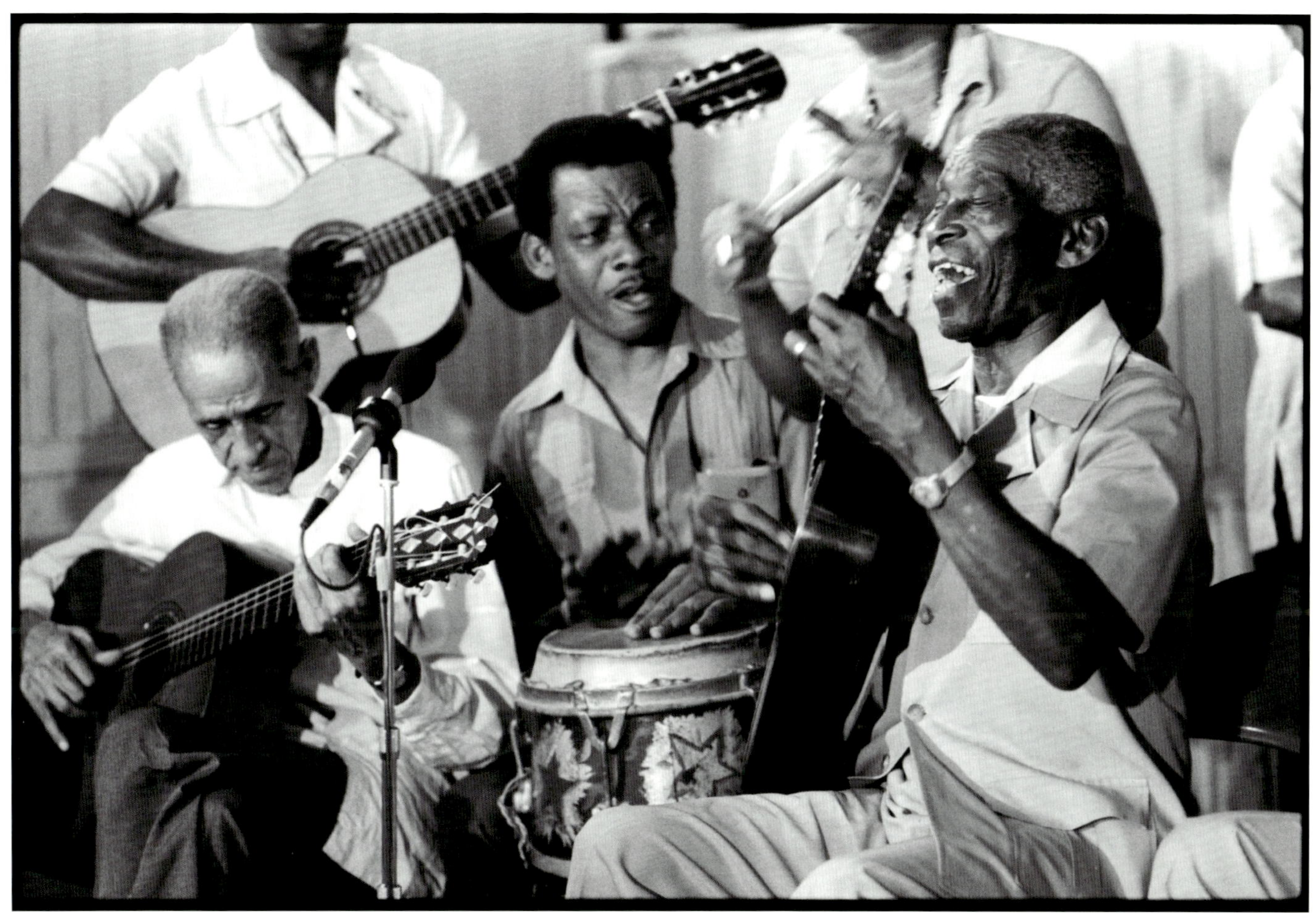

**ISAAC OVIEDO** (RIGHT) **& GROUP AT PEÑA DE BENITO** | NEAR HAVANA, CUBA; 1984

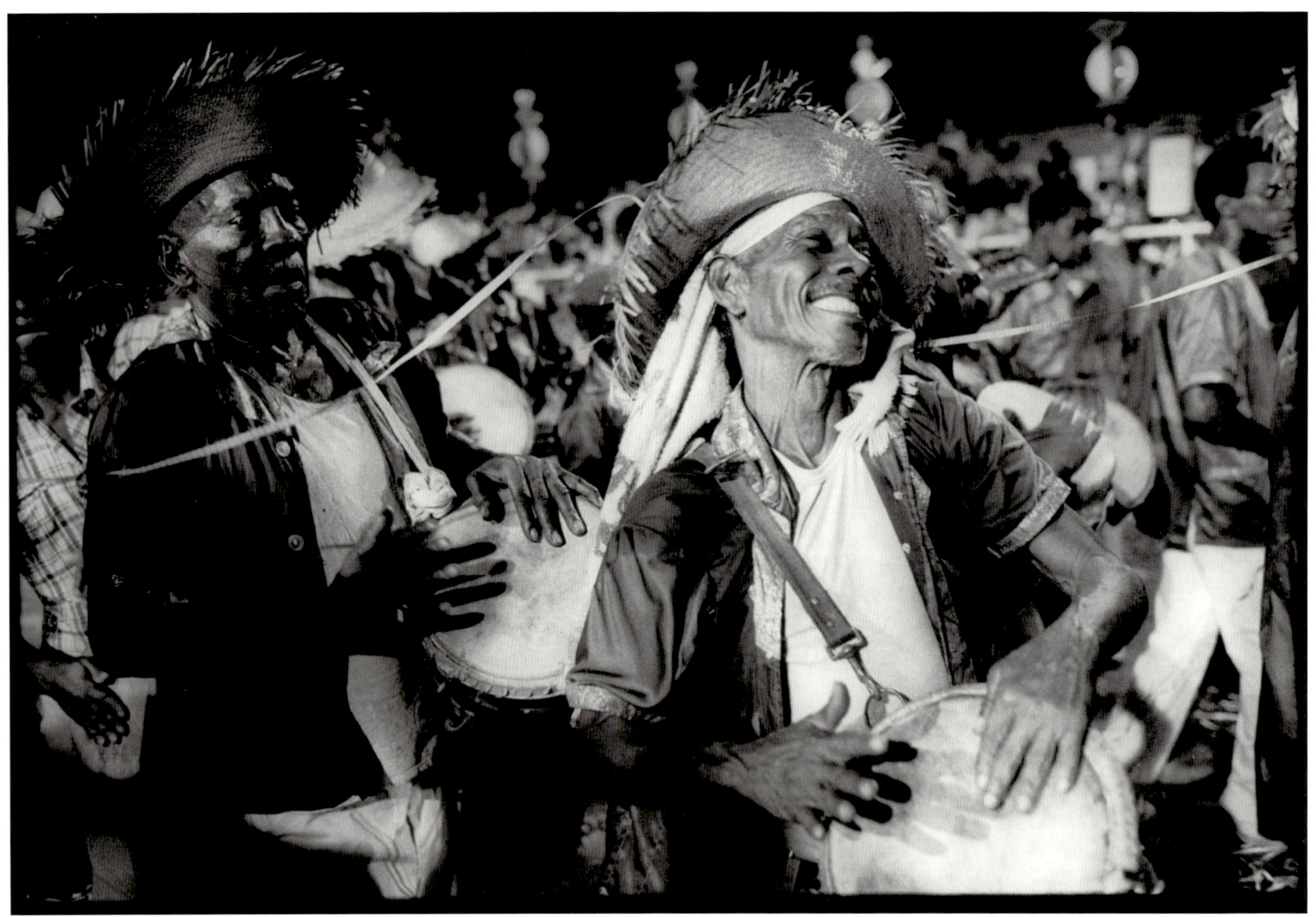

**CARNIVAL** | HAVANA, CUBA; 1984

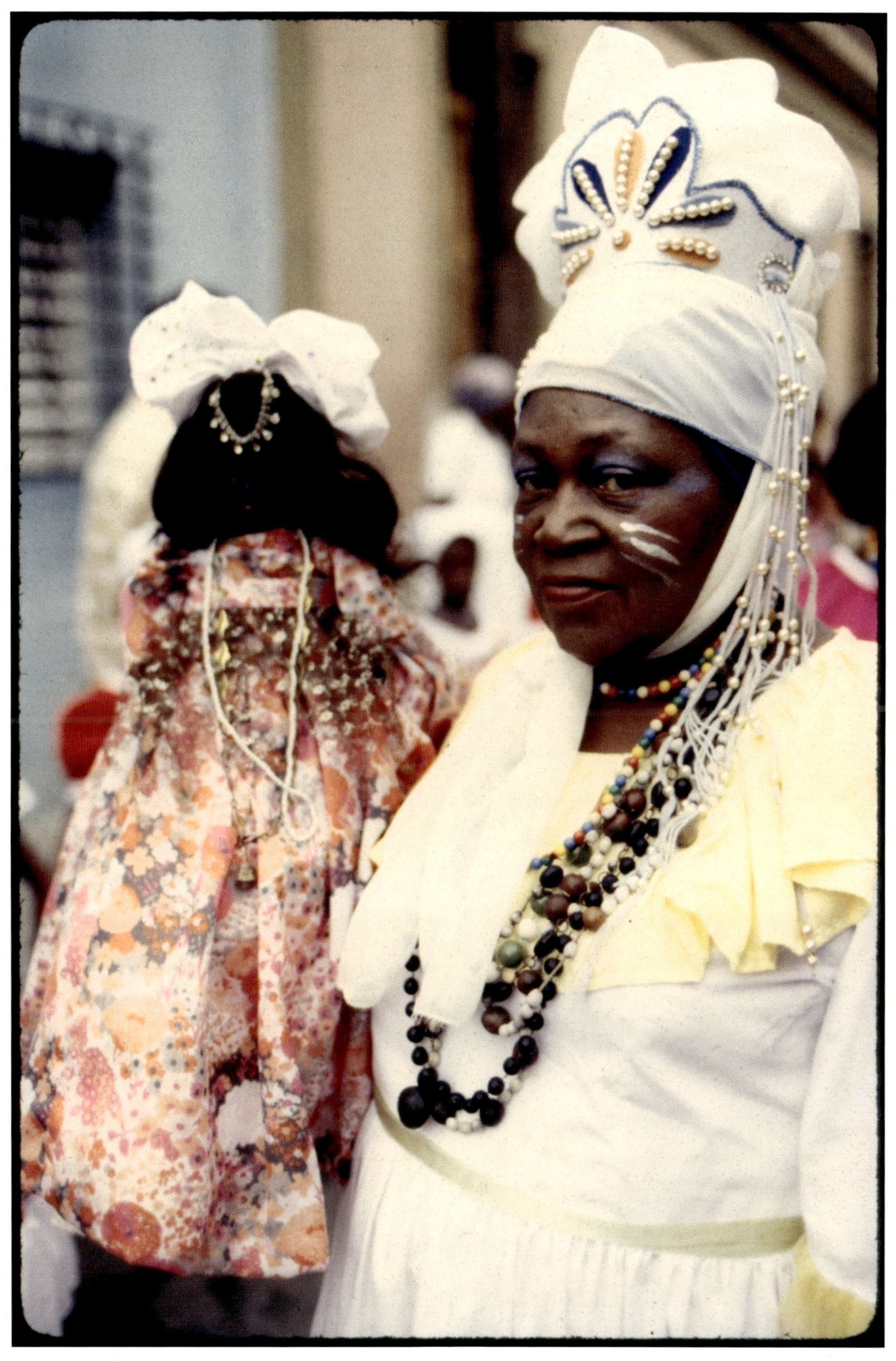

**CARNIVAL** | SANTIAGO DE CUBA, CUBA; 1984

## LOUISIANA FOLKWAYS

Louisiana traditional crafts, cooking, and other folkways are lived day to day but often publicly demonstrated at fairs and festivals. Smith's photographs of such activities show heritage practices in both environments.

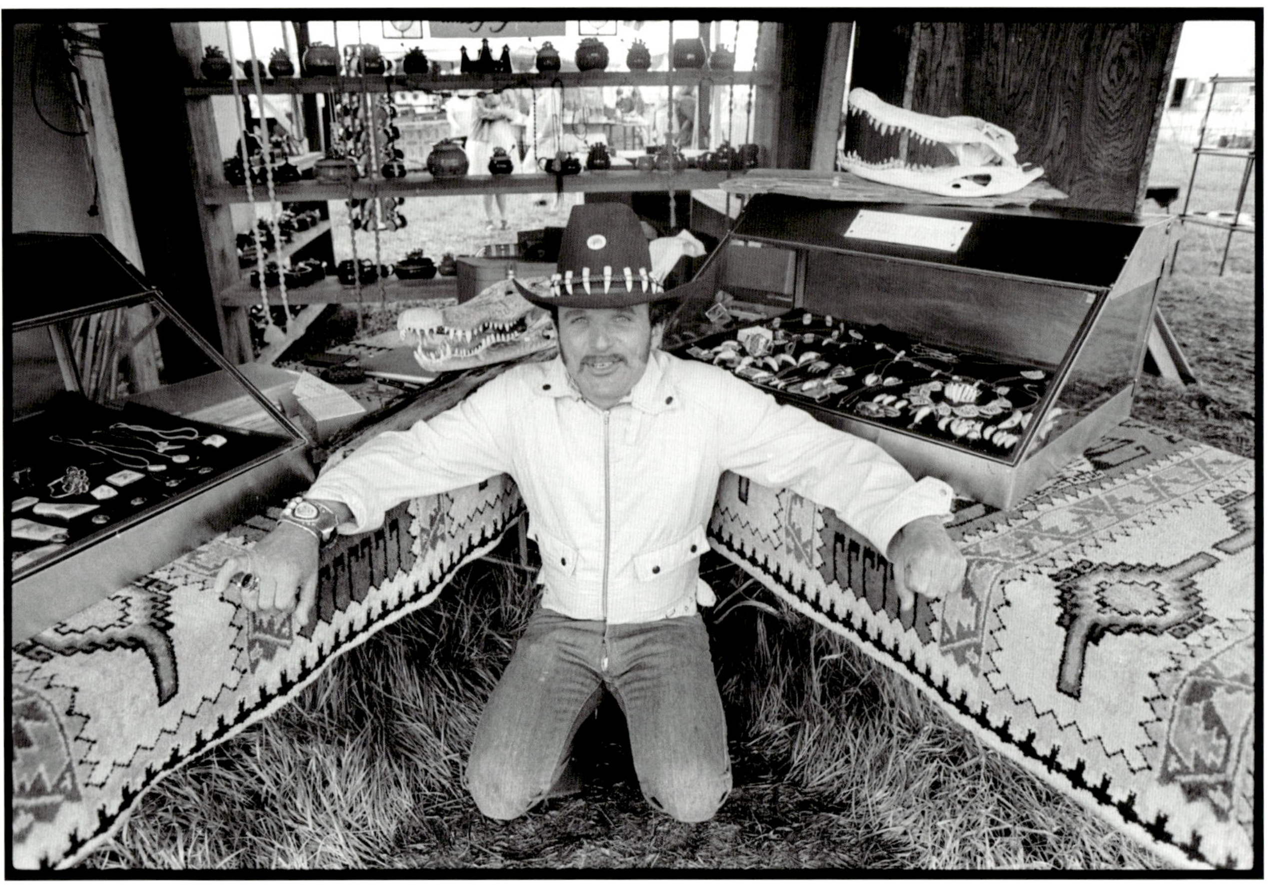

**JAKE JEGELWICZ, CRAFT BOOTH** | JAZZ FEST, NEW ORLEANS; 1980

Russell's Crab Hse U.S. 11, N. Shore, Slidell, La.
Knoledge of crabs handed down 4 generations already.

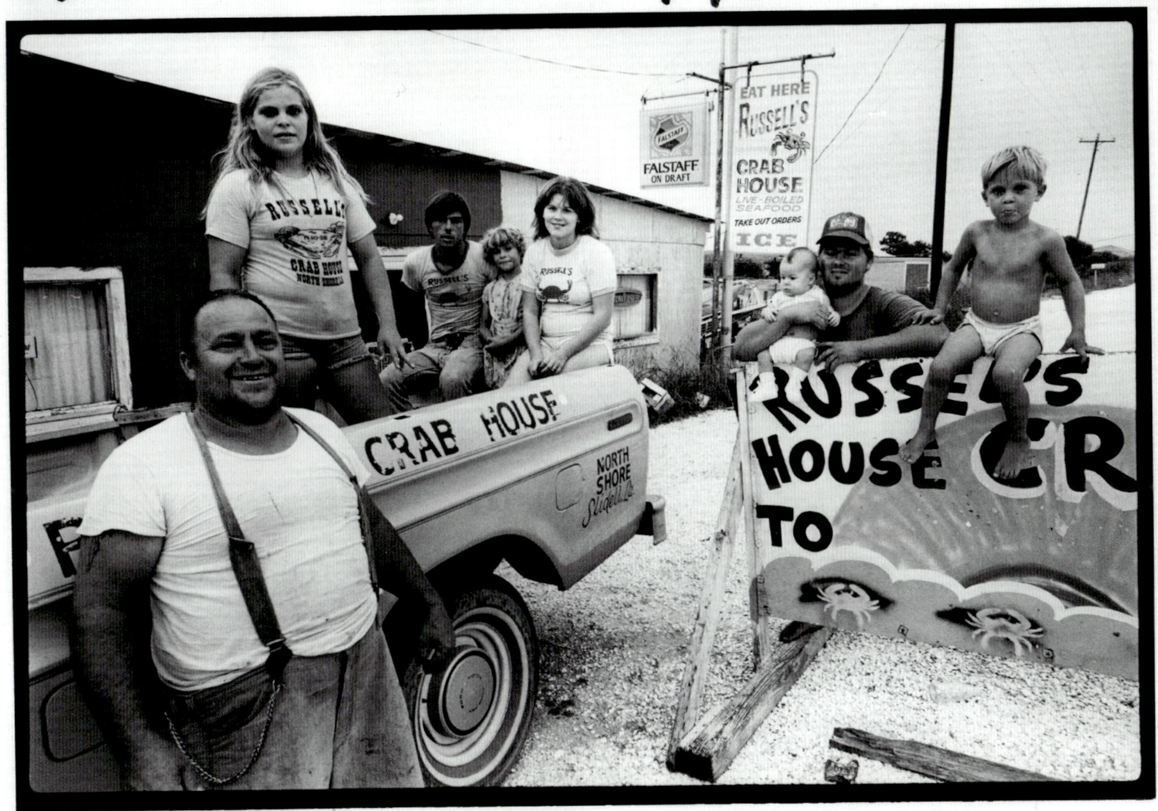


Russell Estain on Left is a 3rd generation crab man. Grandson will be 5th generation crabber

**CRABBERS PRESENT AND FUTURE** | SLIDELL, LOUISIANA; 1978

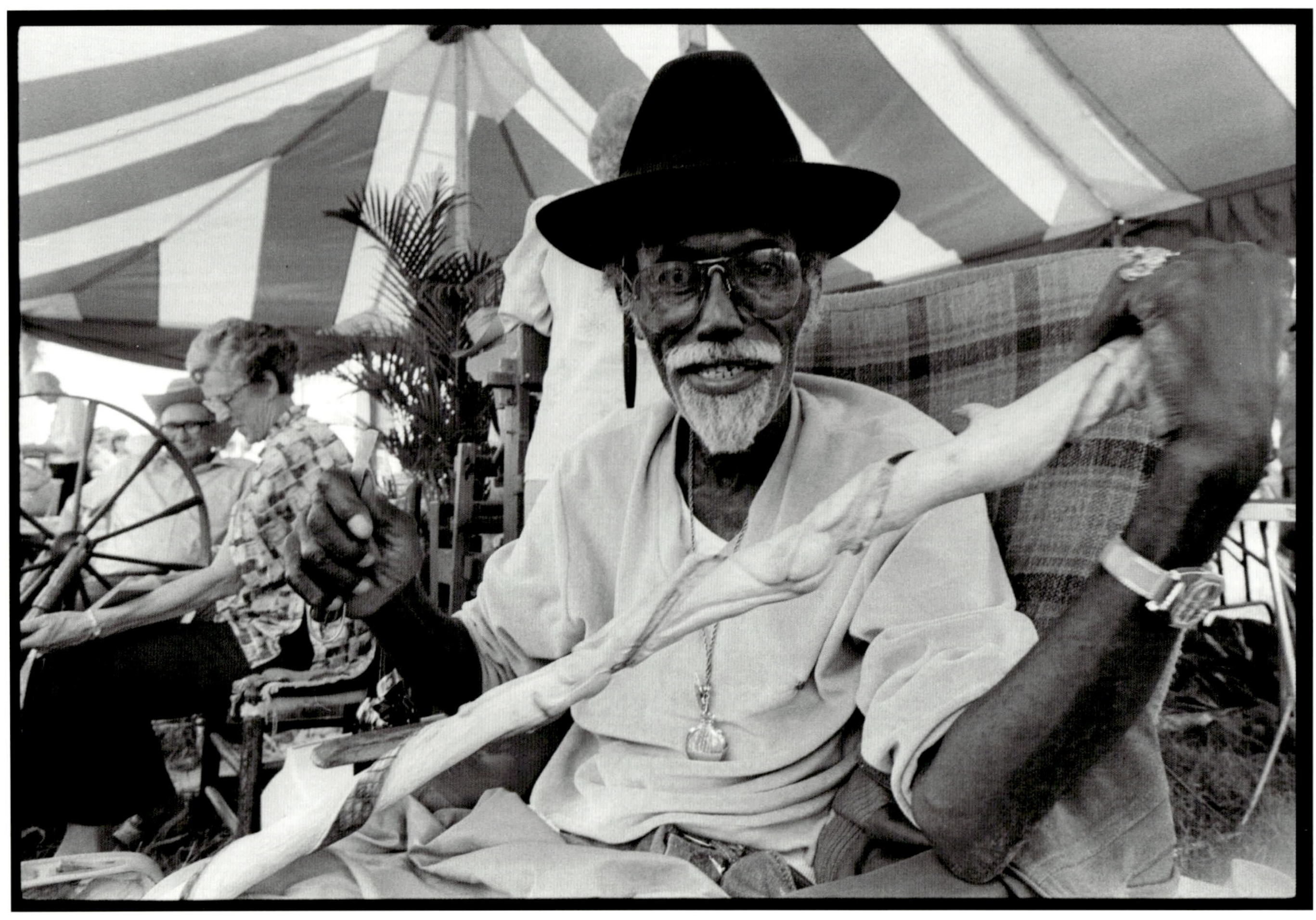

**HUGH "DADDY BOY" WILLIAMS, WOODCARVER** | JAZZ FEST, NEW ORLEANS; 1981

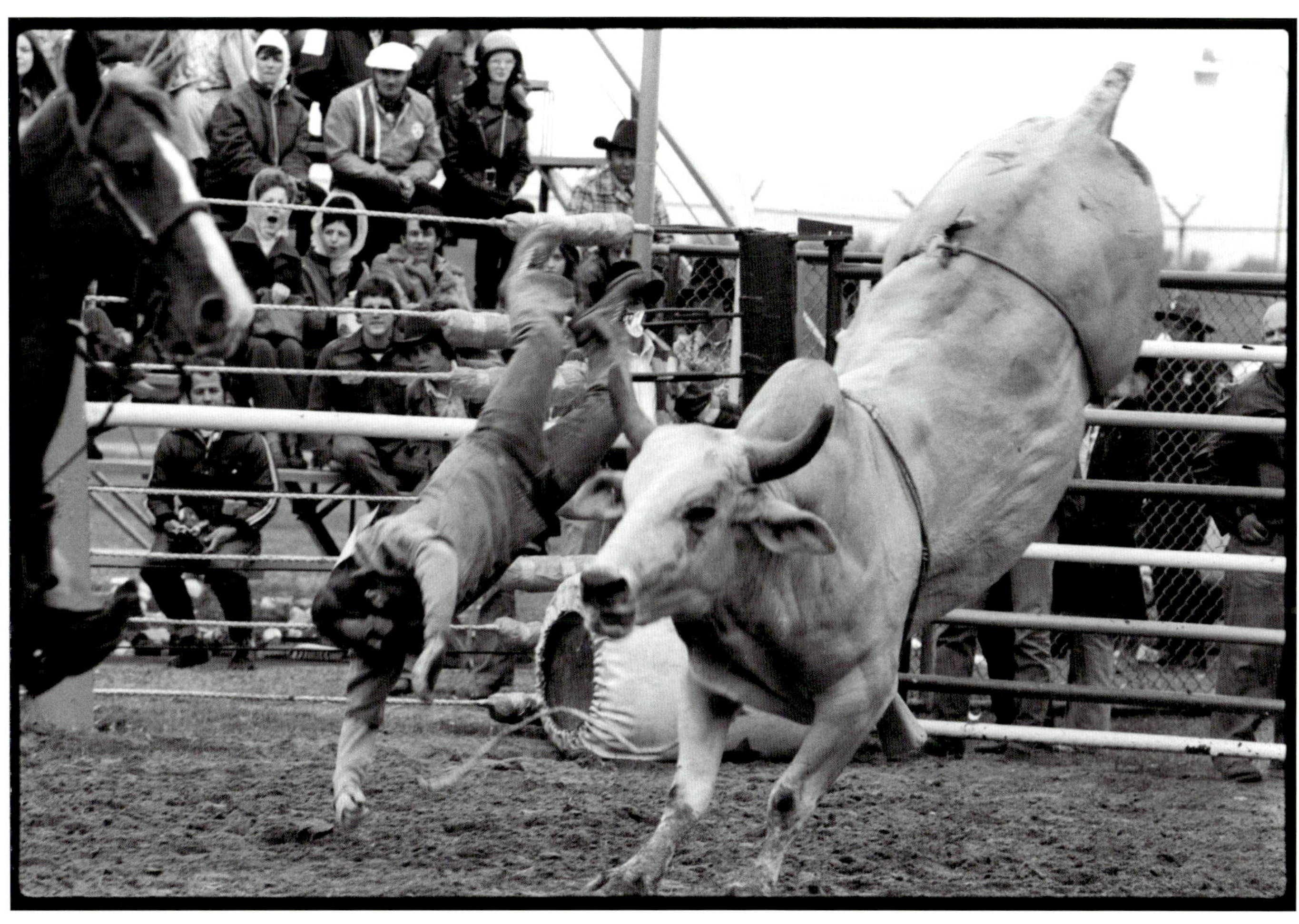

PRISON RODEO, LOUISIANA STATE PENITENTIARY | ANGOLA, LOUISIANA; 1975

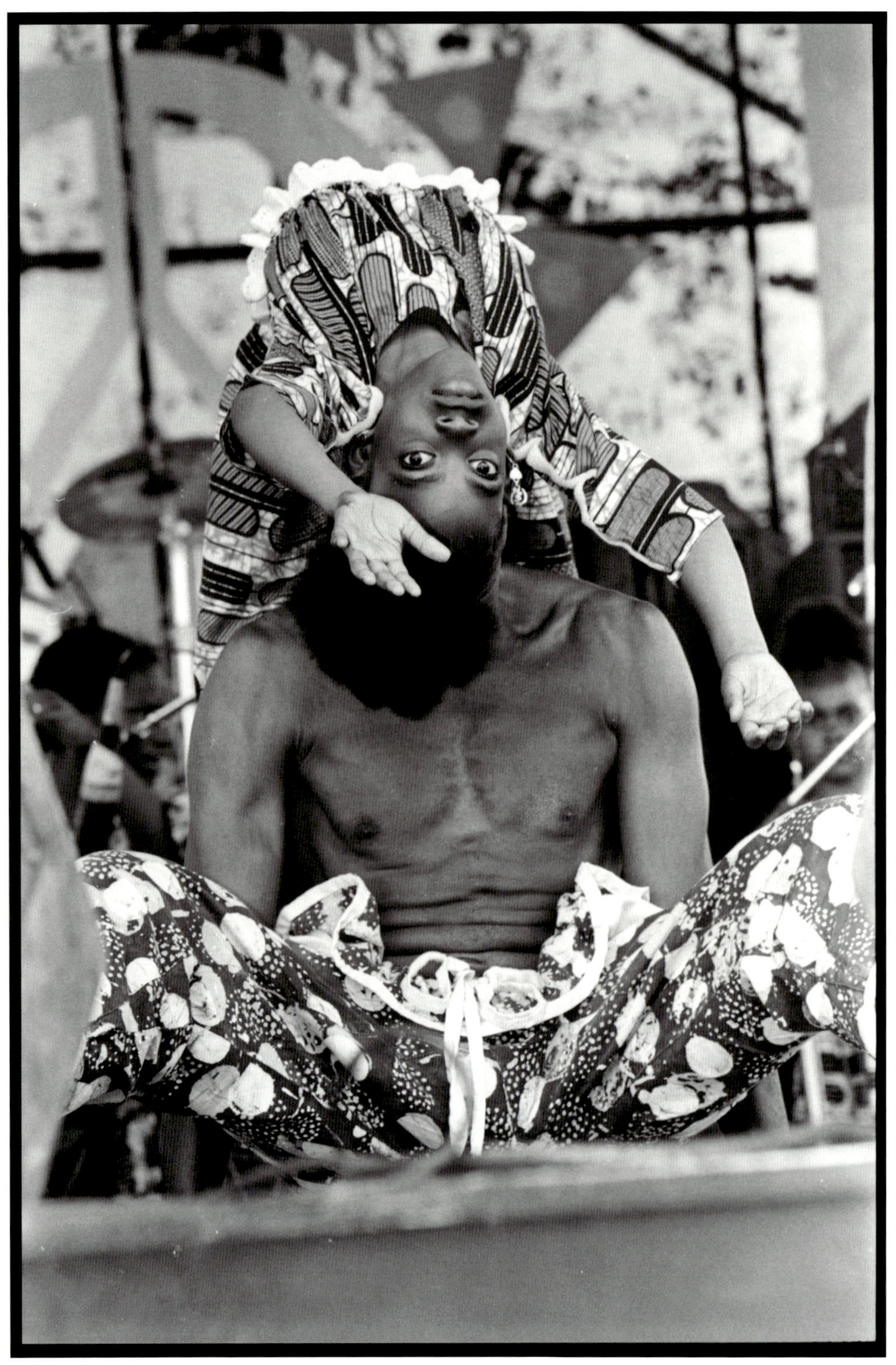

**BACKSTAGE** | JAZZ FEST, NEW ORLEANS; 1993

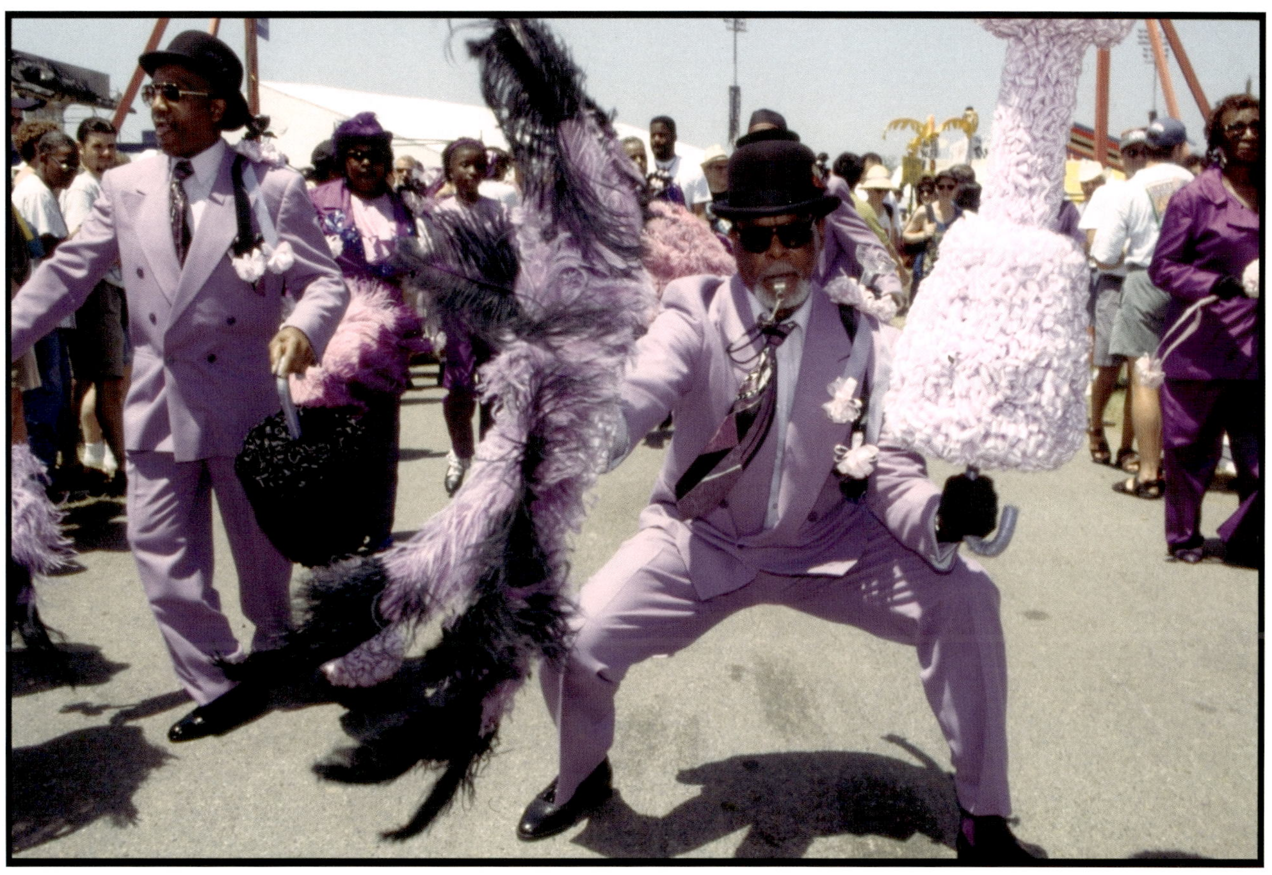

**SECOND LINE PARADE** | JAZZ FEST, NEW ORLEANS; 1996

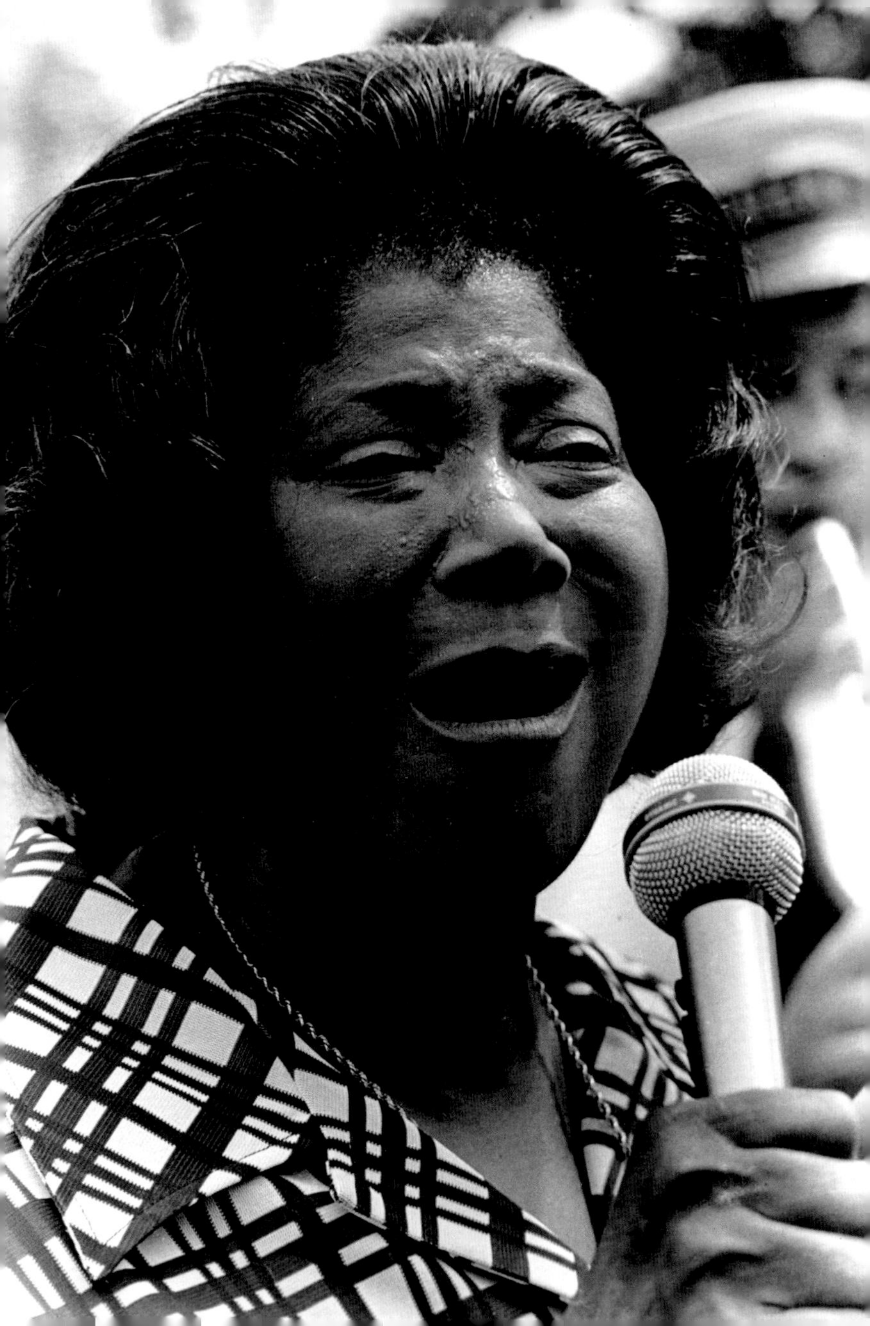

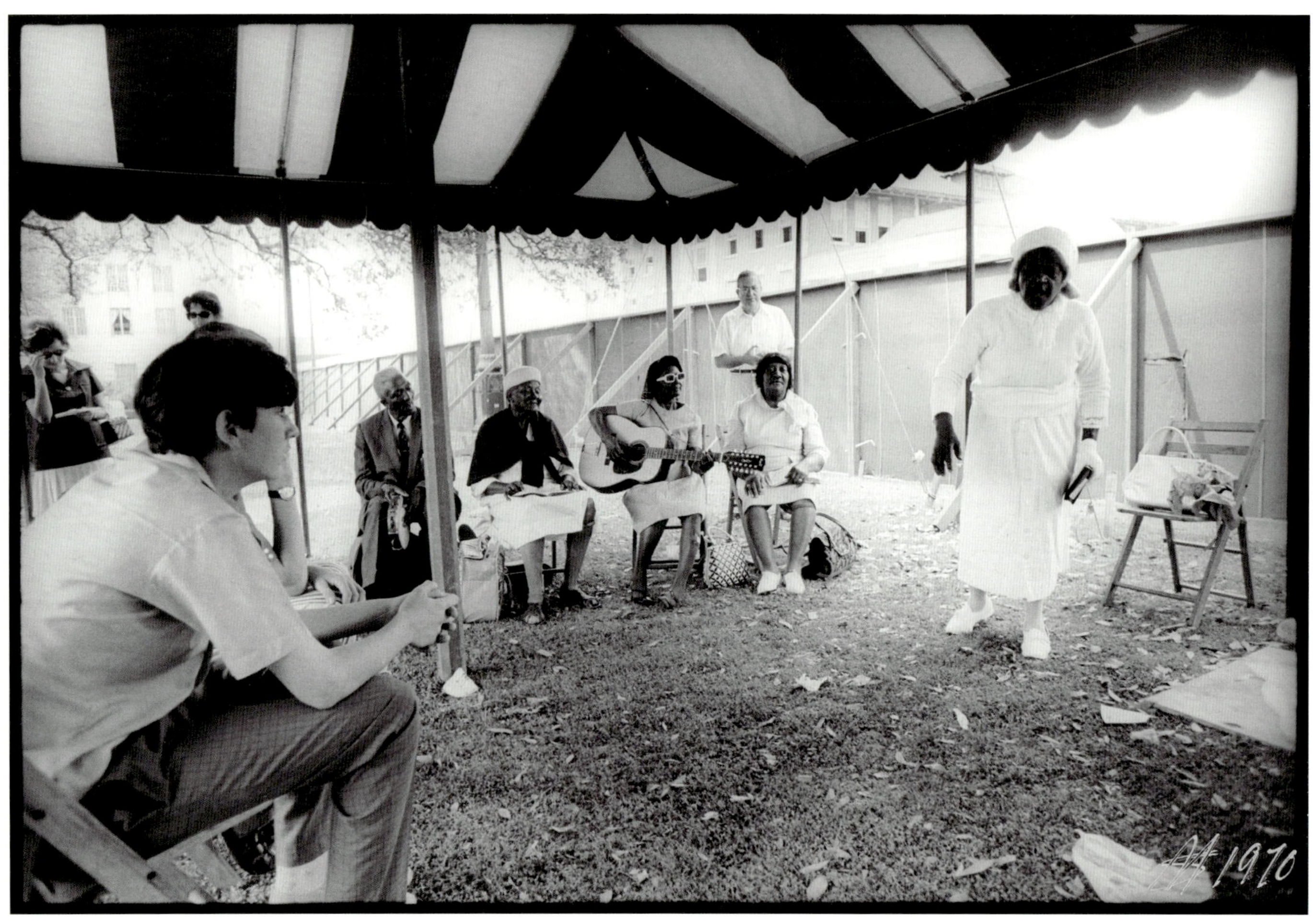


**SISTER GERTRUDE MORGAN** | 1970

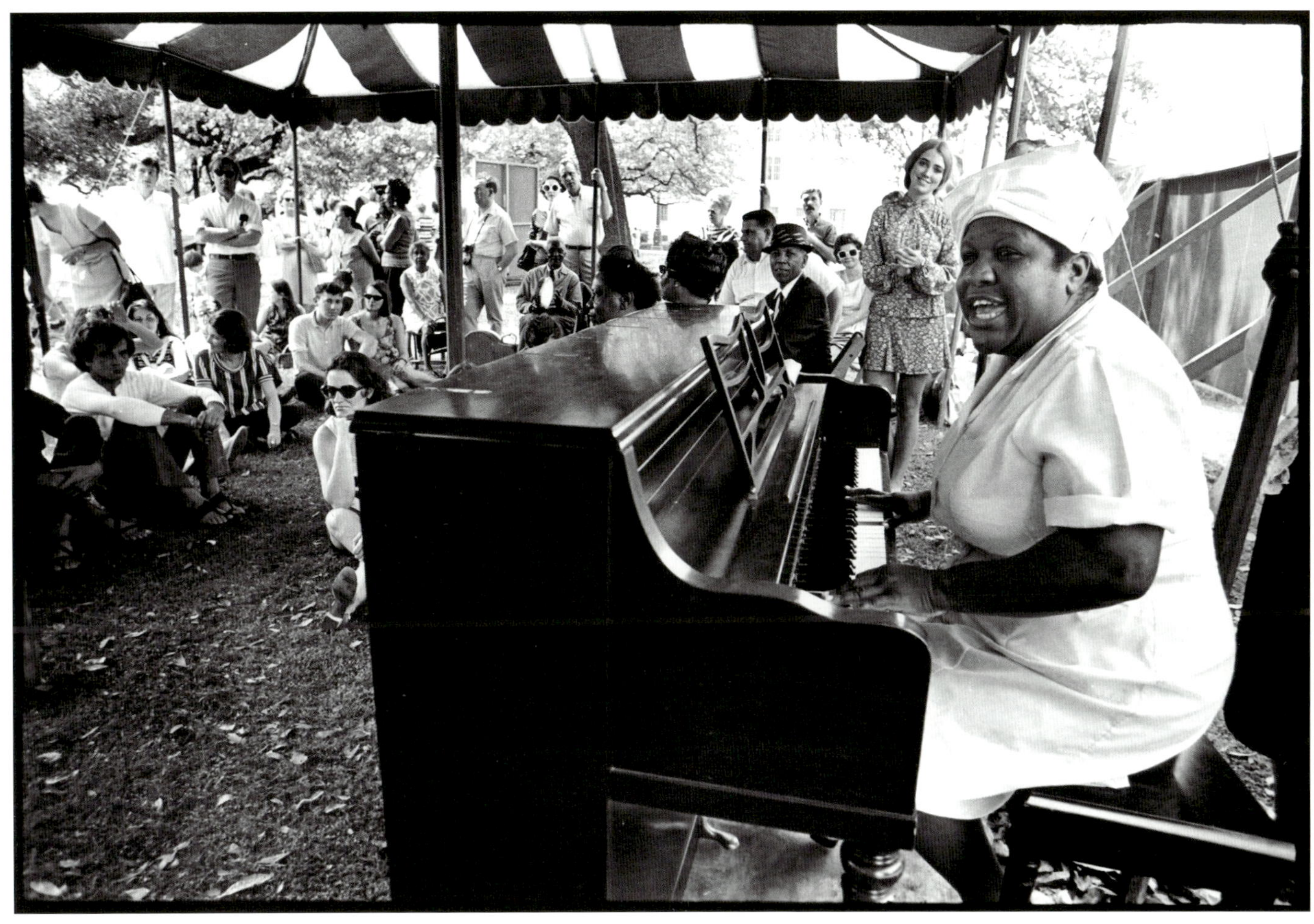

ALICE MAY VICTOR IN THE GOSPEL TENT | 1970

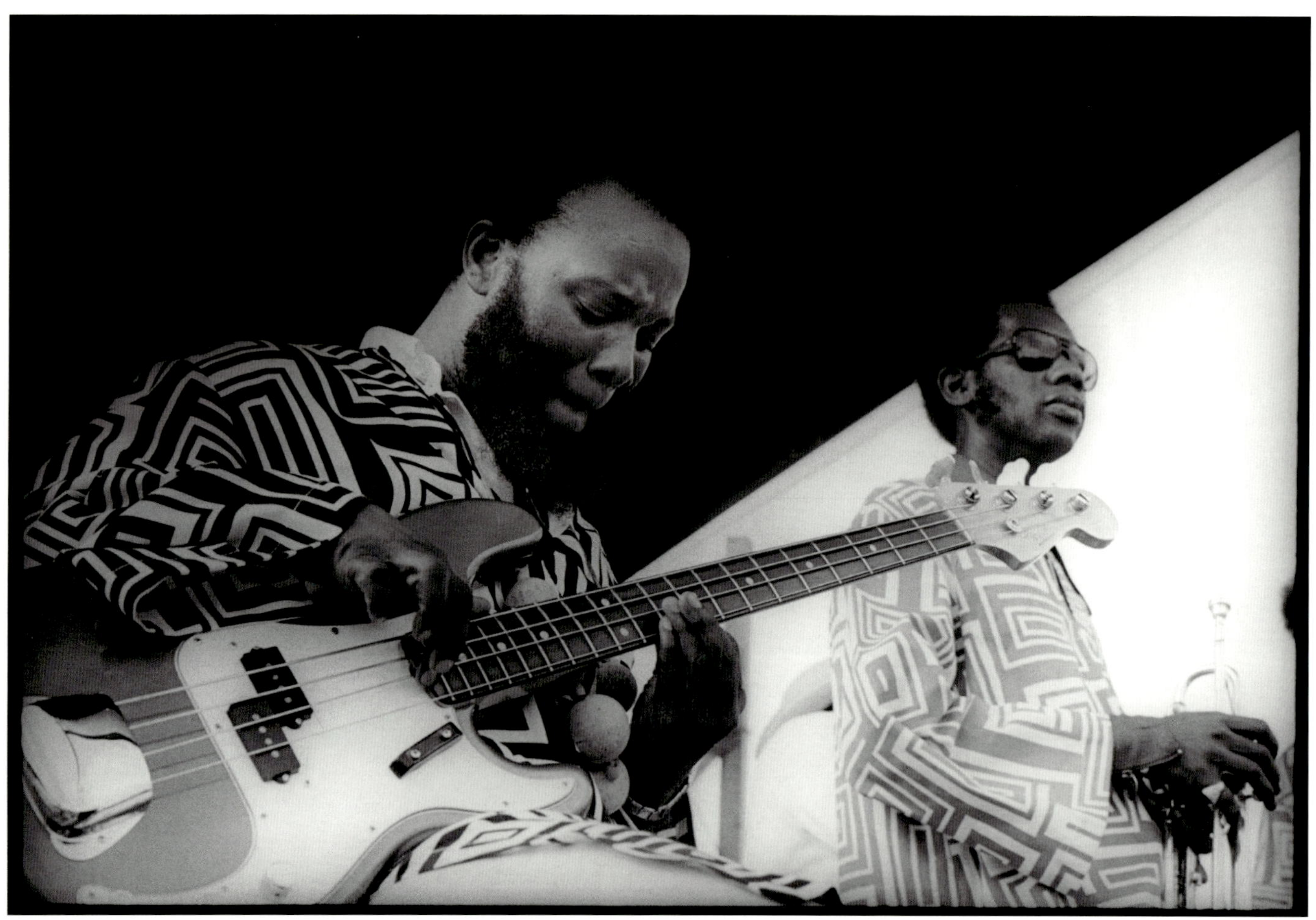

WALTER PAYTON & PERCY JONES | 1972

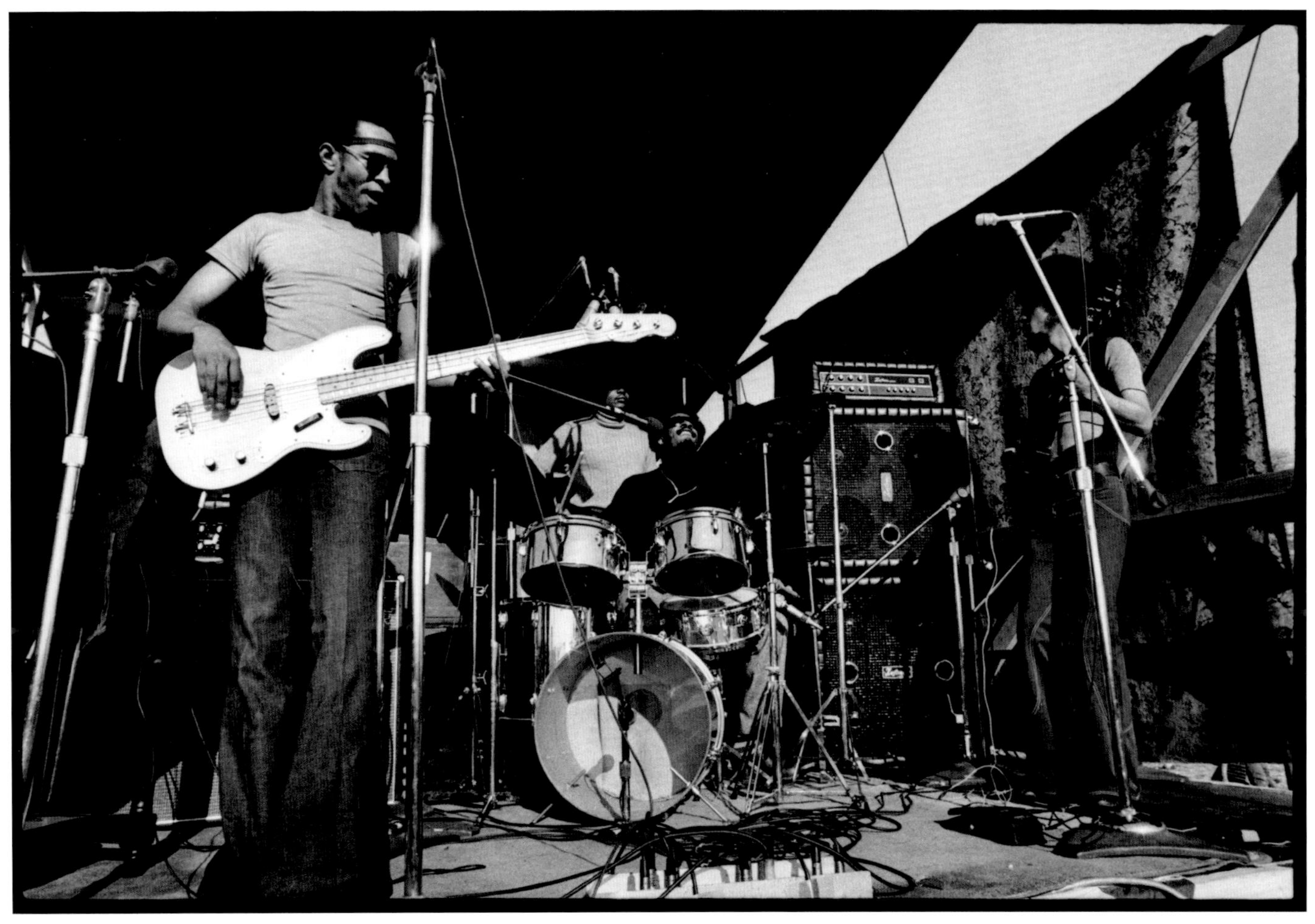

GEORGE PORTER, STEVIE WONDER, AND ZIGABOO MODELISTE | 1973

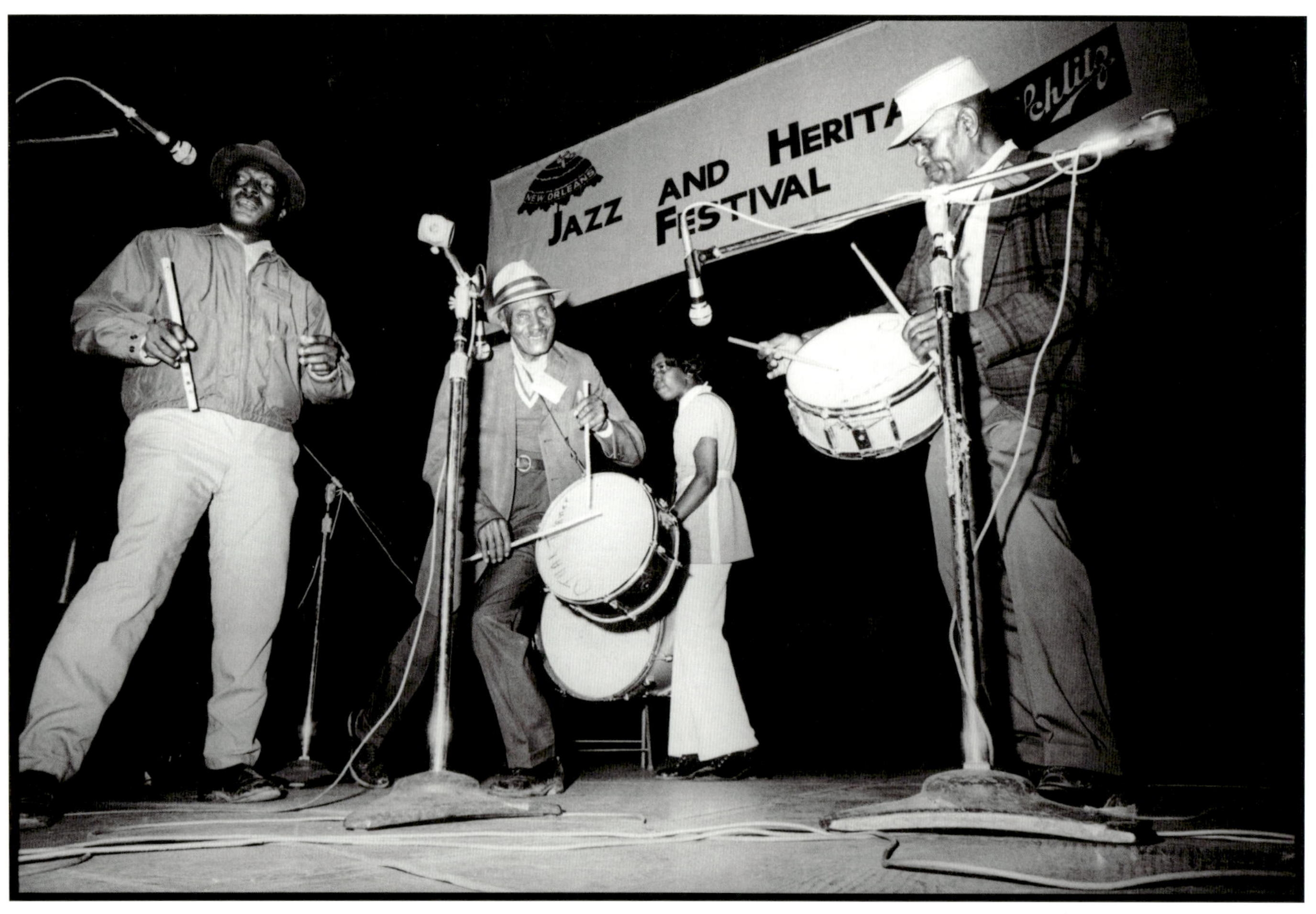


COMO FIFE & DRUM CORPS (LEFT TO RIGHT: NAPOLEON STRICKLAND, R.L. BOYCE, BERNICE TURNER, AND OTHA TURNER) | 1973

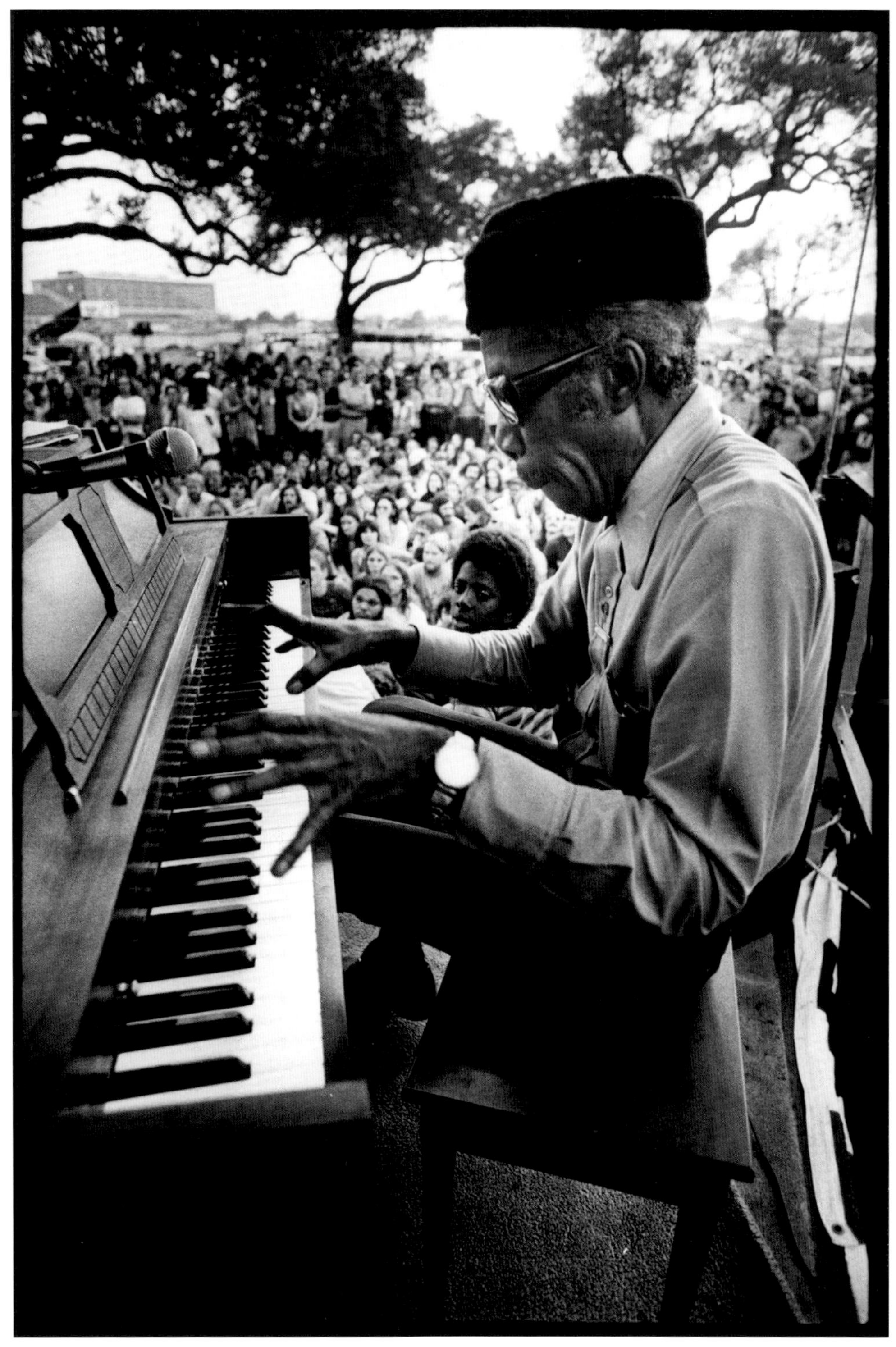

PROFESSOR LONGHAIR | 1973

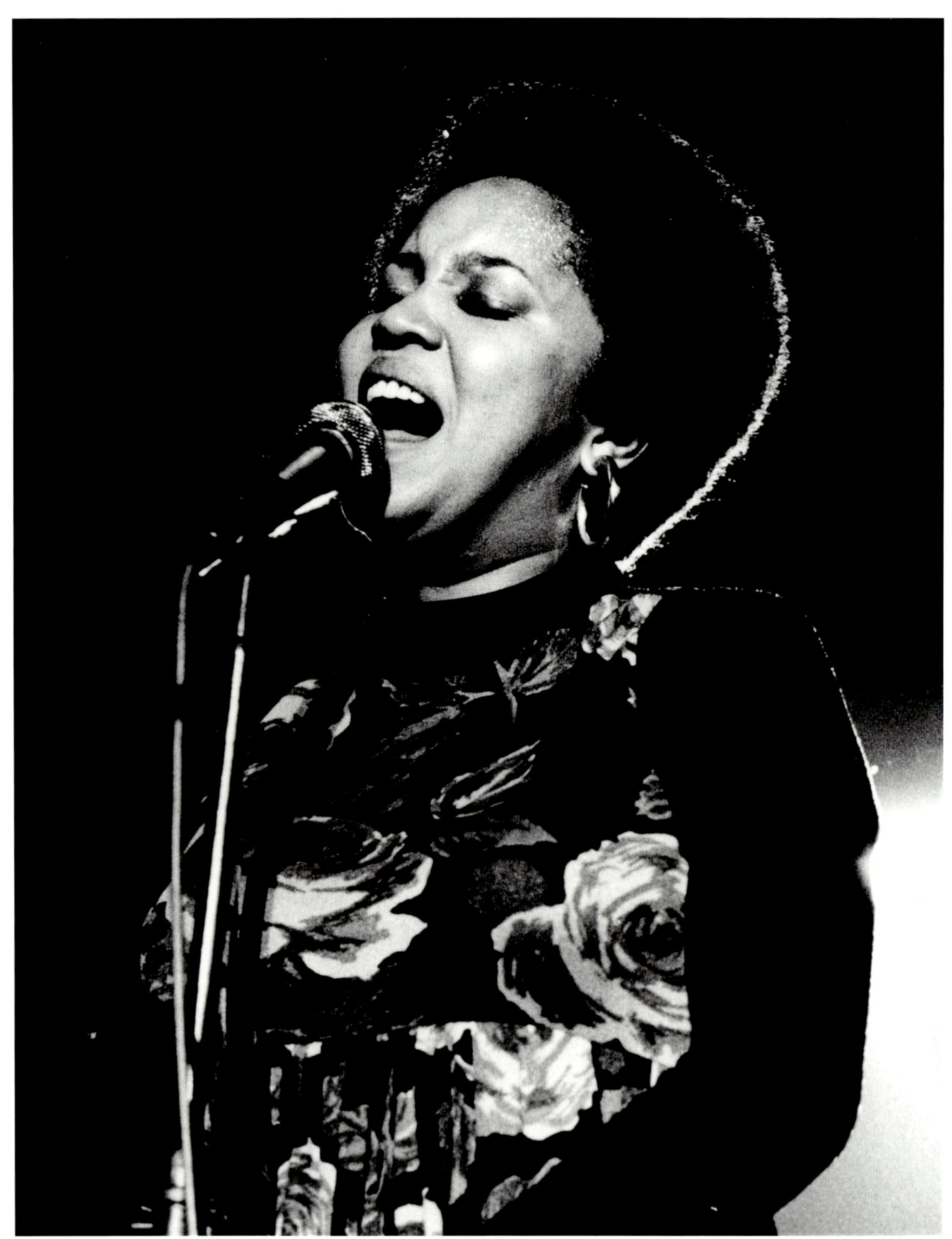

**MAVIS STAPLES** (DETAIL) | 1973

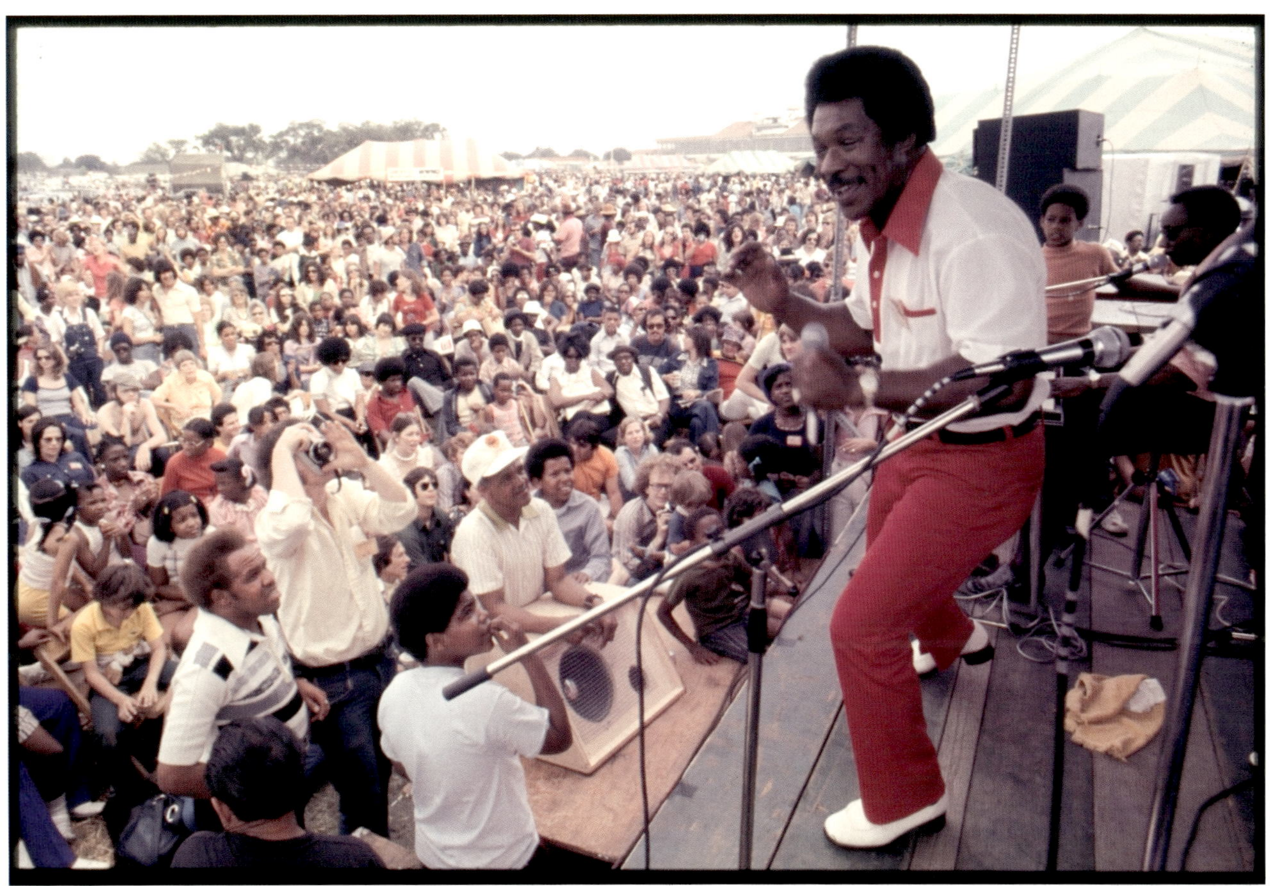

BENNY SPELLMAN | 1974

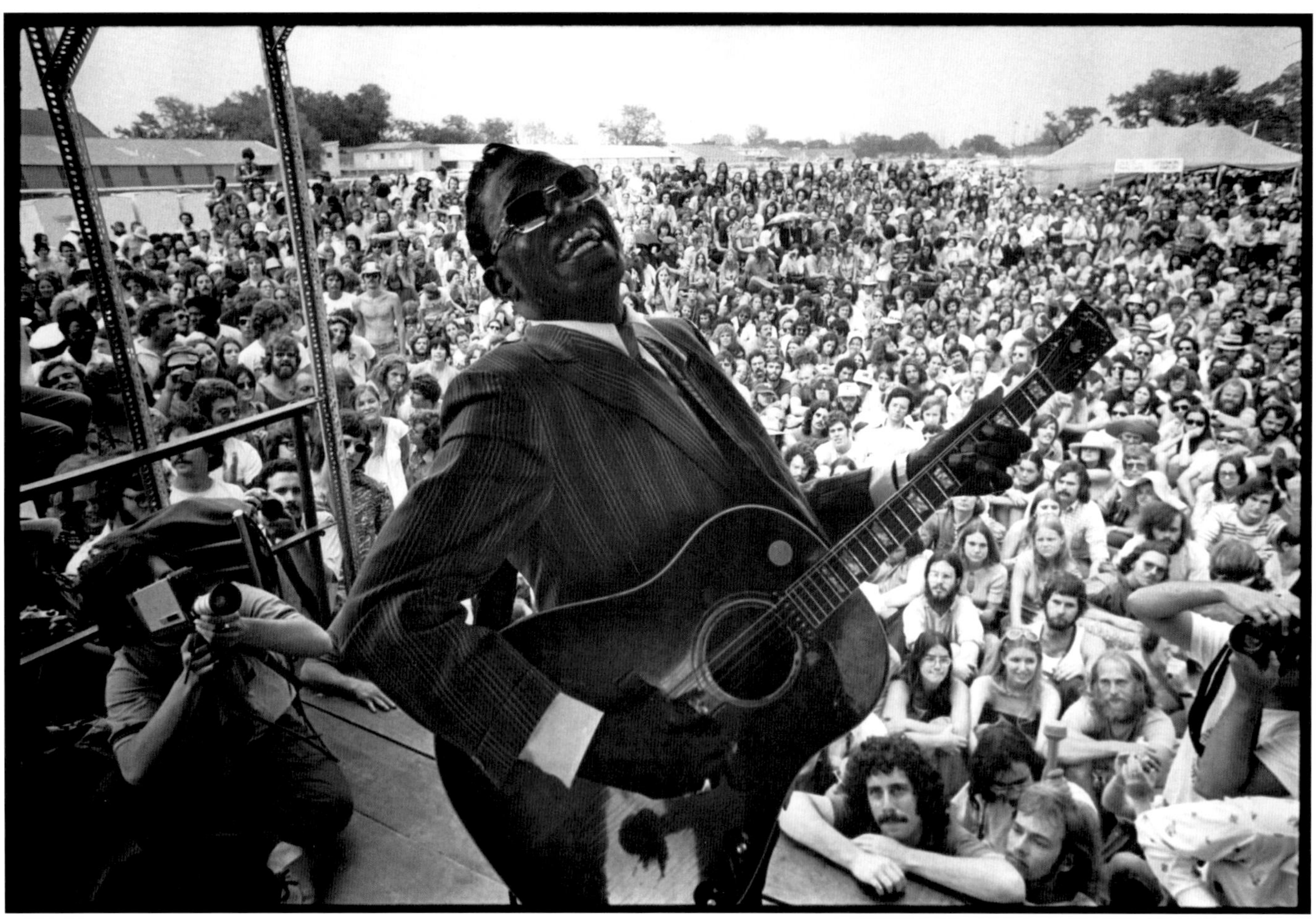

LIGHTNIN' HOPKINS | 1974

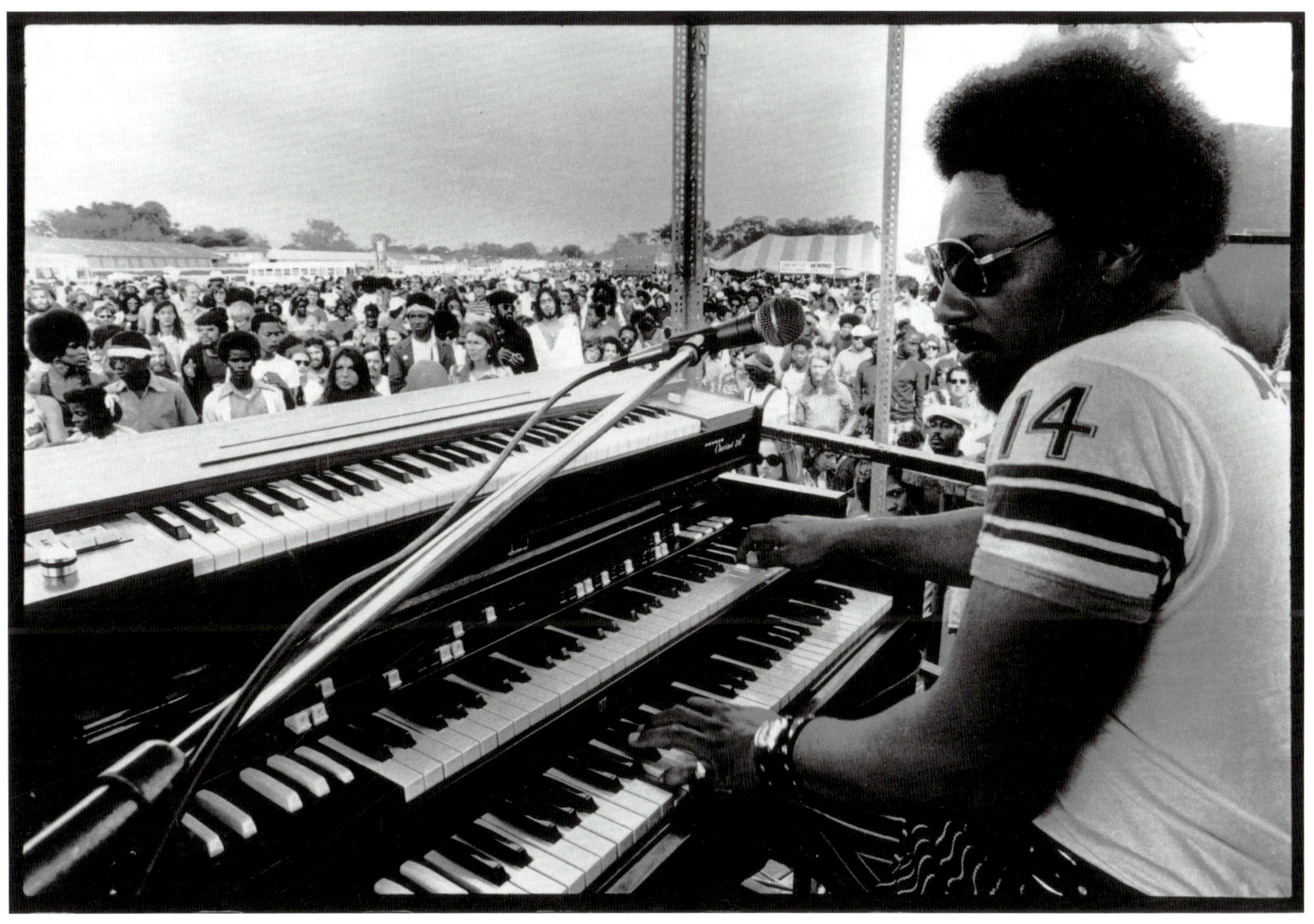


ART NEVILLE WITH THE METERS | 1974

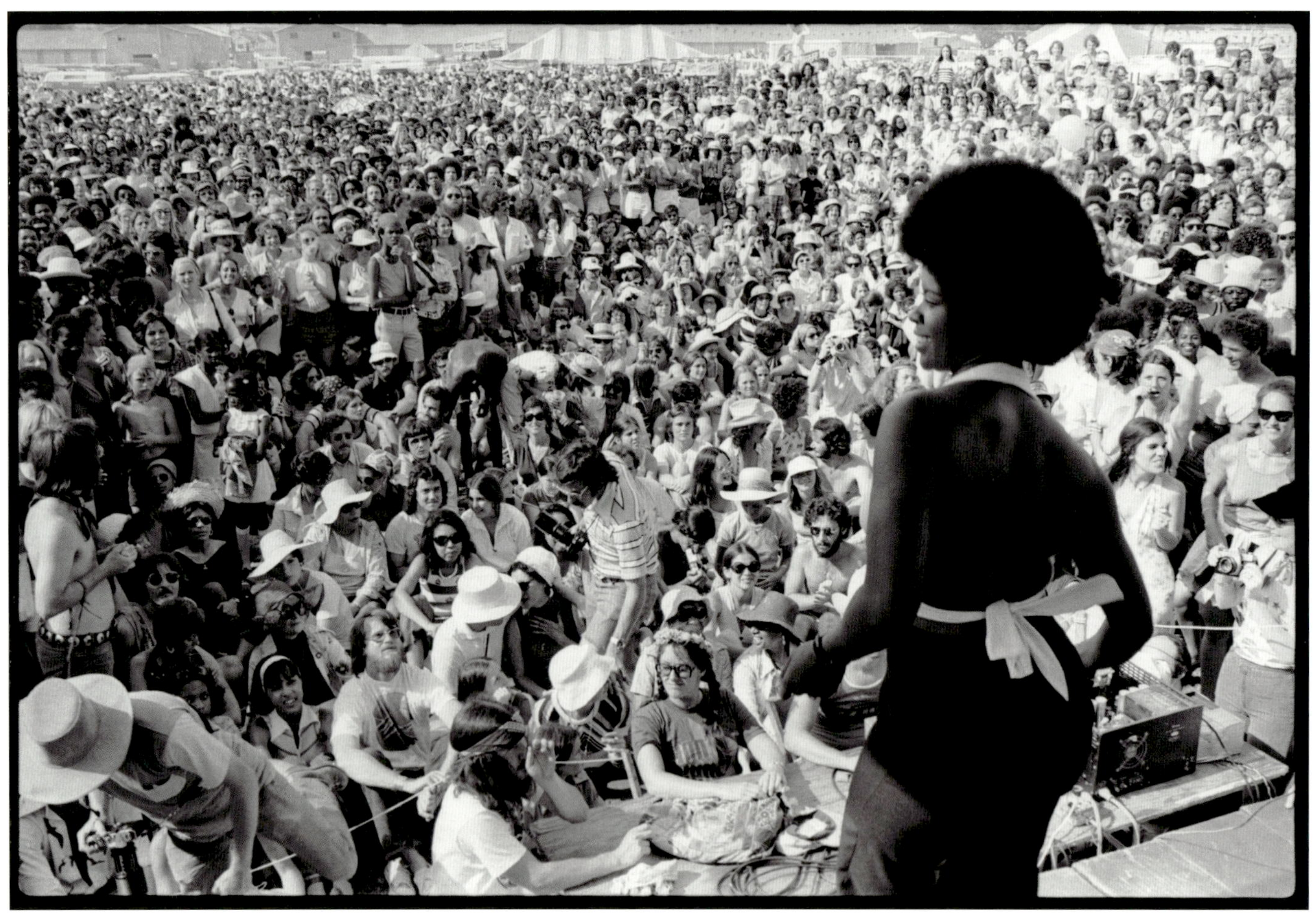

**IRMA THOMAS** | 1975

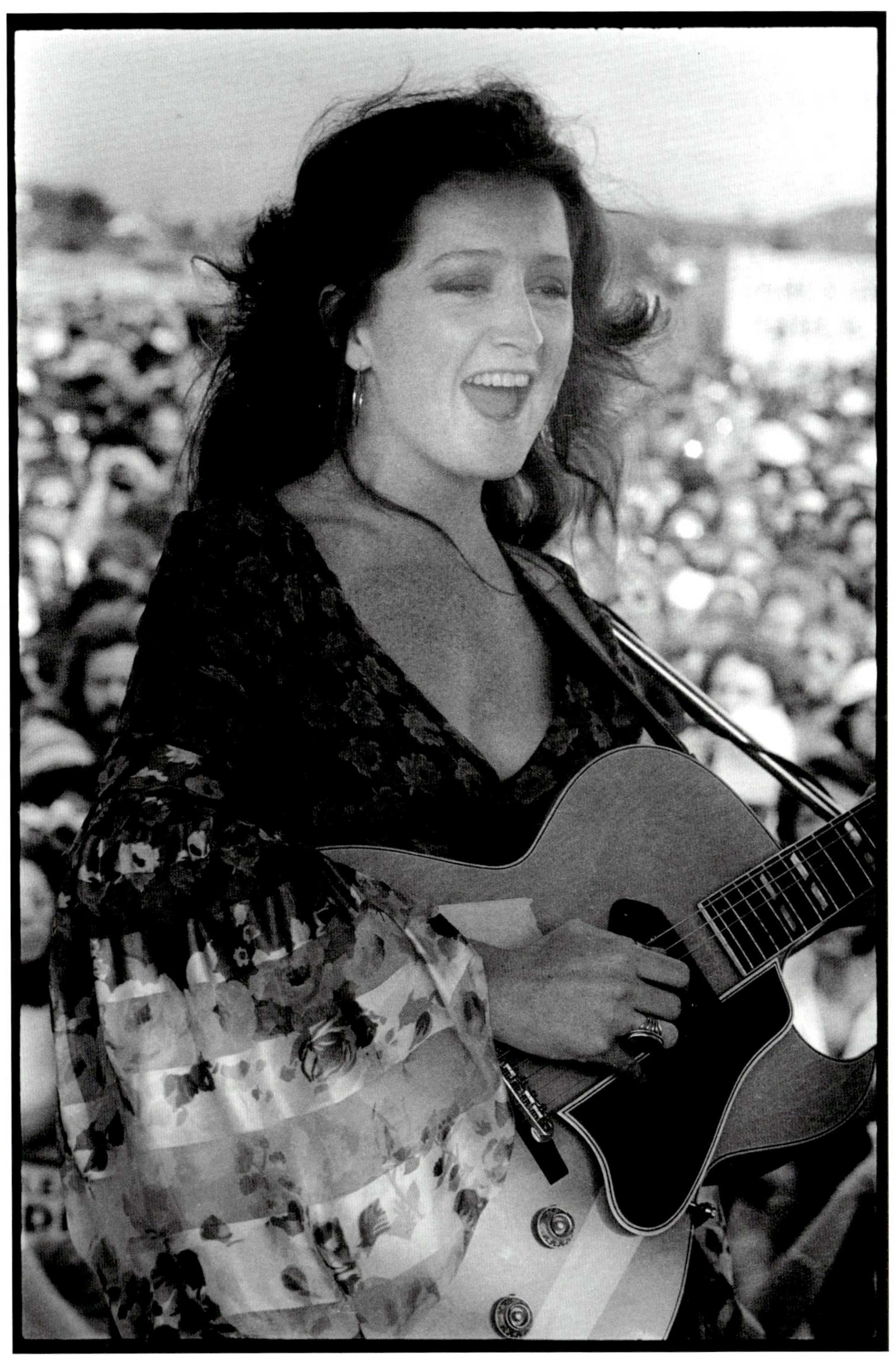

**BONNIE RAITT** | 1977

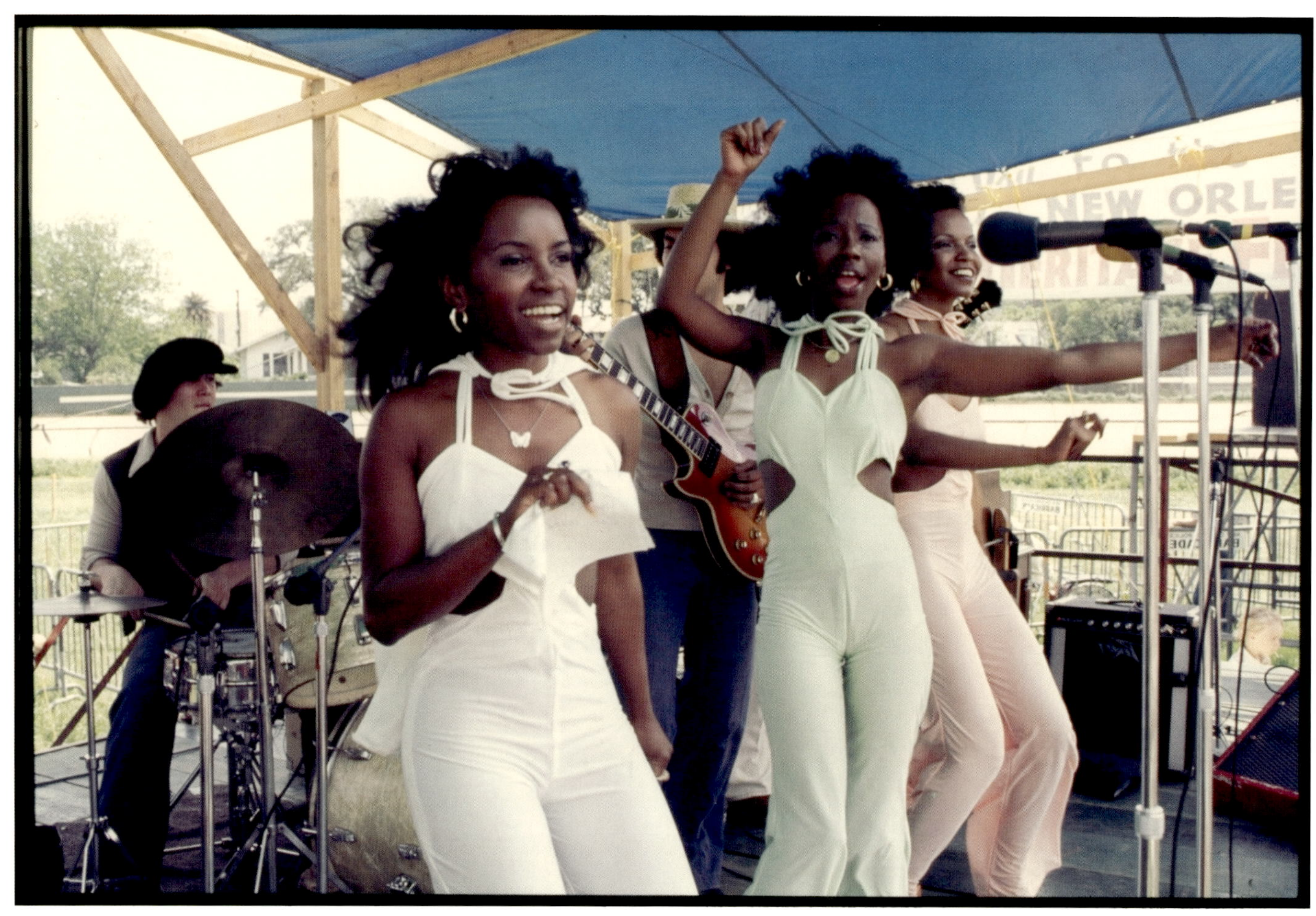

**THE DIXIE CUPS** (LEFT TO RIGHT: ROSA LEE HAWKINS, JOANNE KENNEDY, AND BARBARA HAWKINS) | 1977

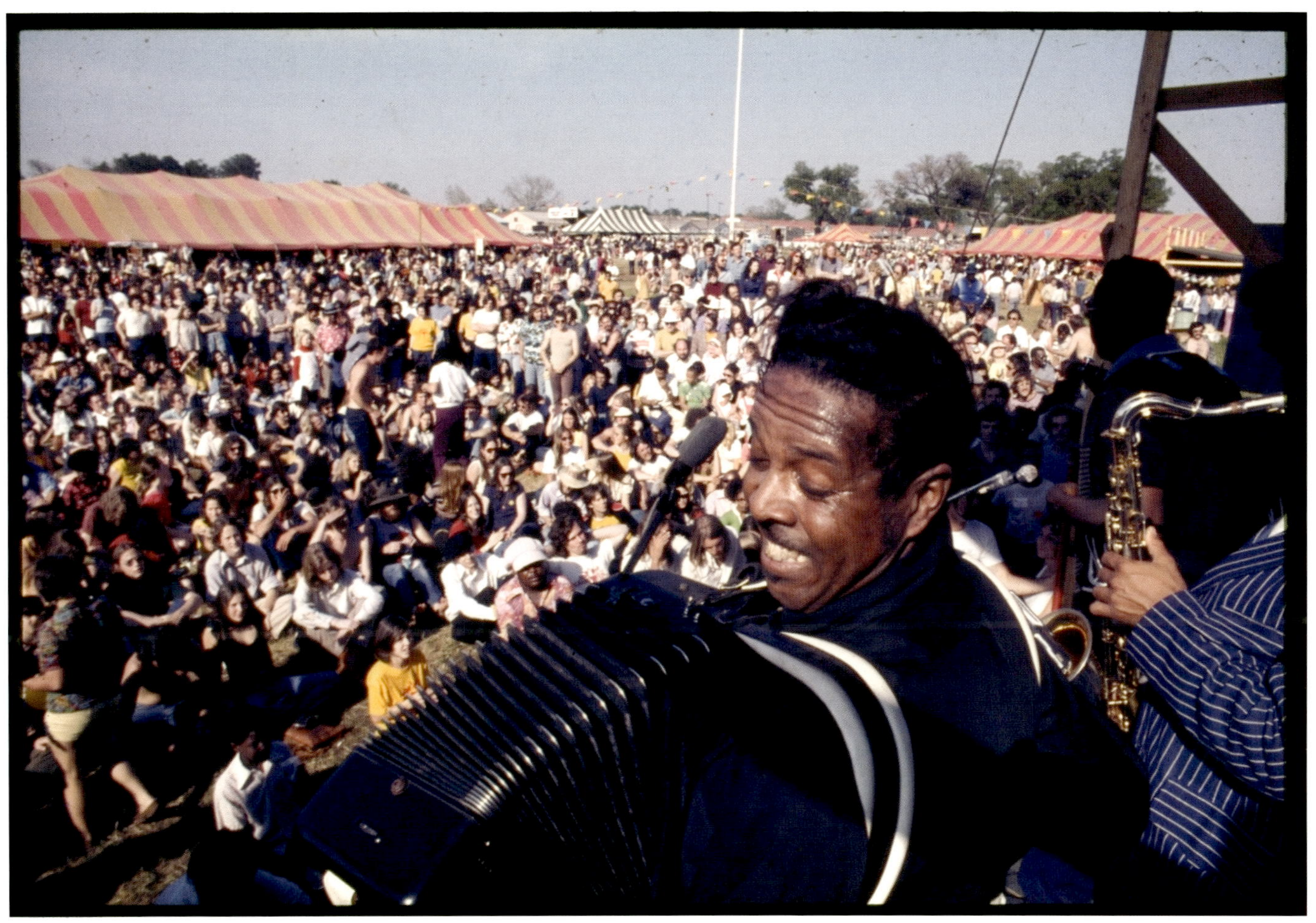

CLIFTON CHENIER | 1978

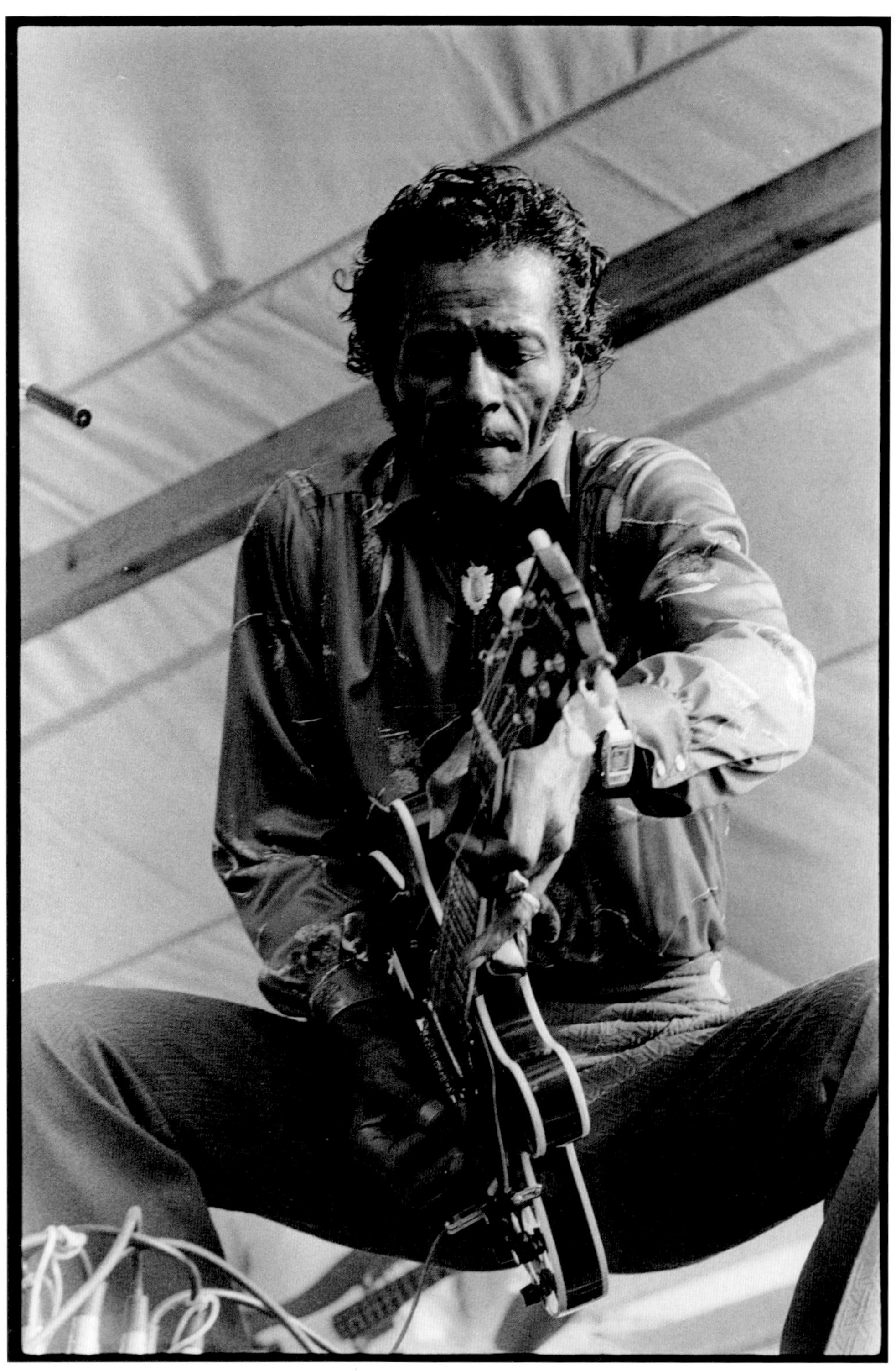

CHUCK BERRY | 1982

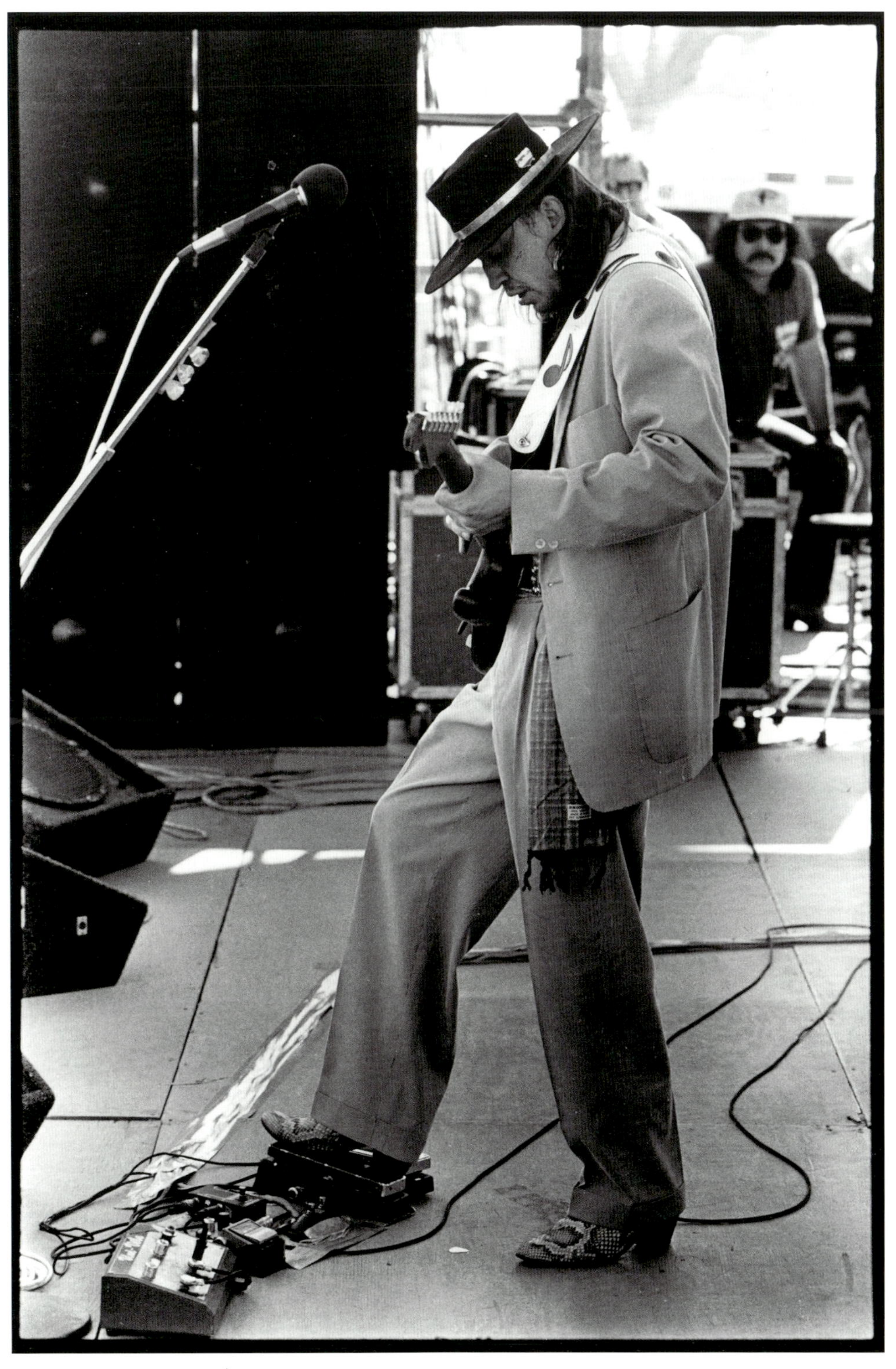

**STEVIE RAY VAUGHAN** | 1986

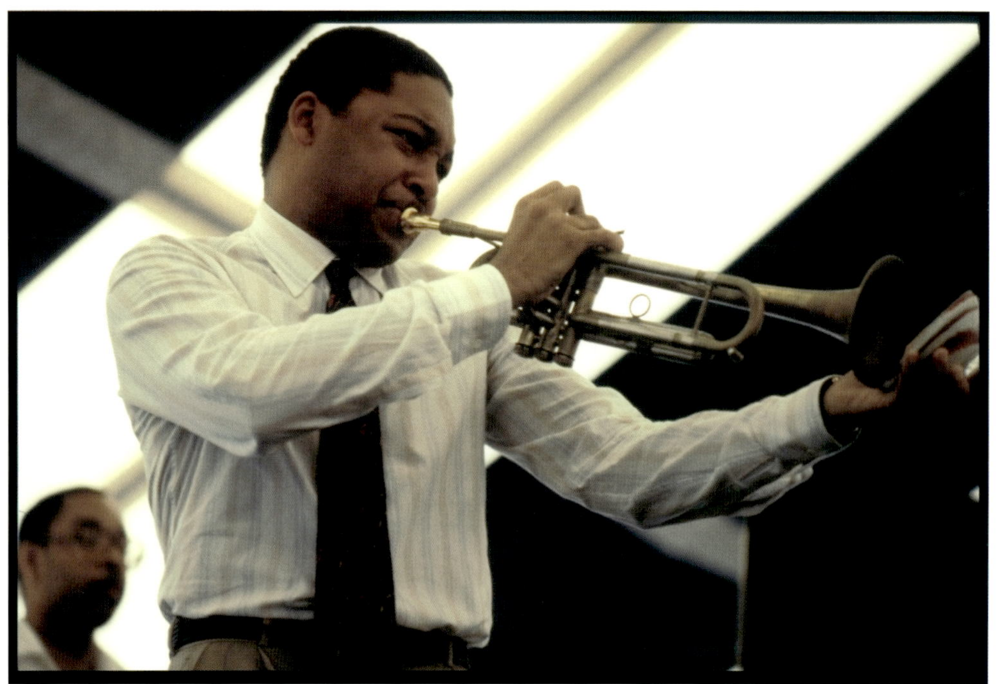

WYNTON MARSALIS | 1989

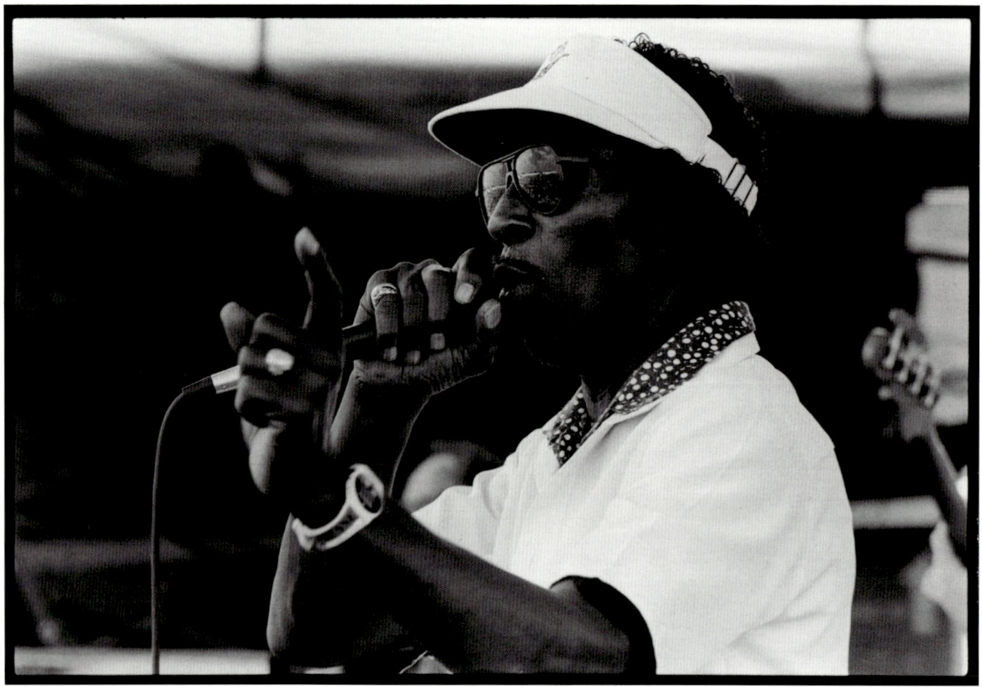

JOHNNY ADAMS | 1990

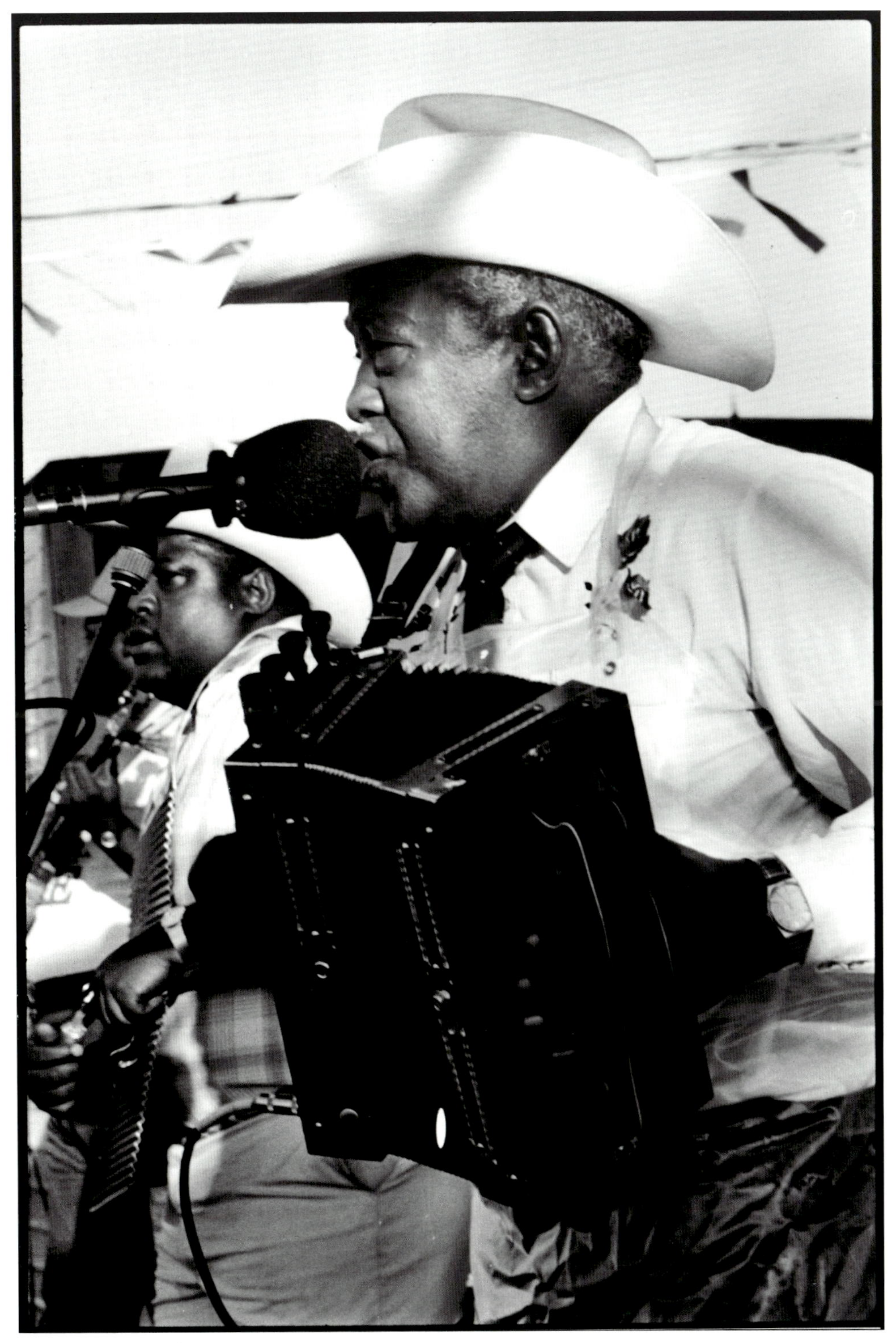

BOOZOO CHAVIS | 1990

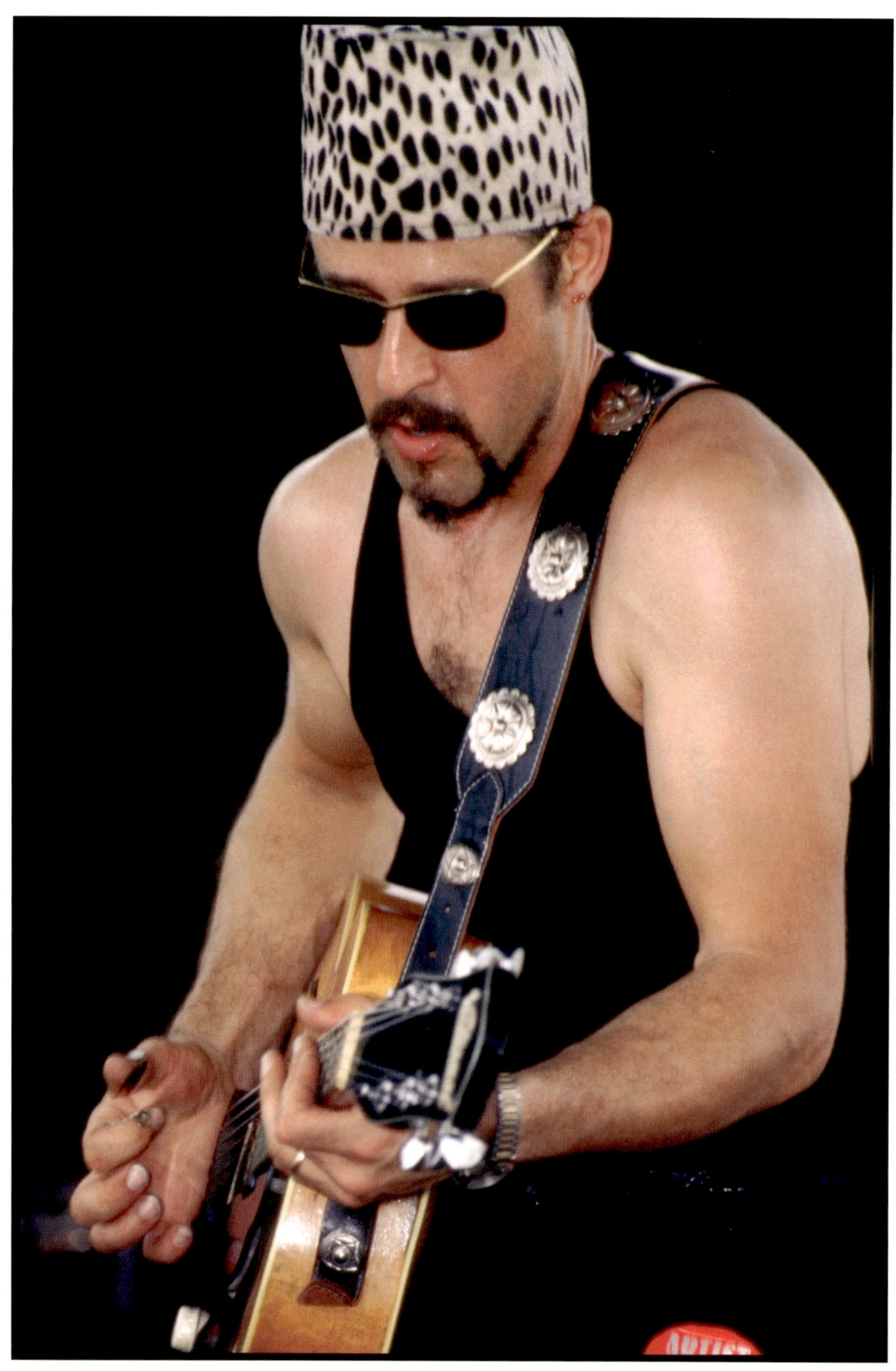

**JOHN MOONEY** | 1991

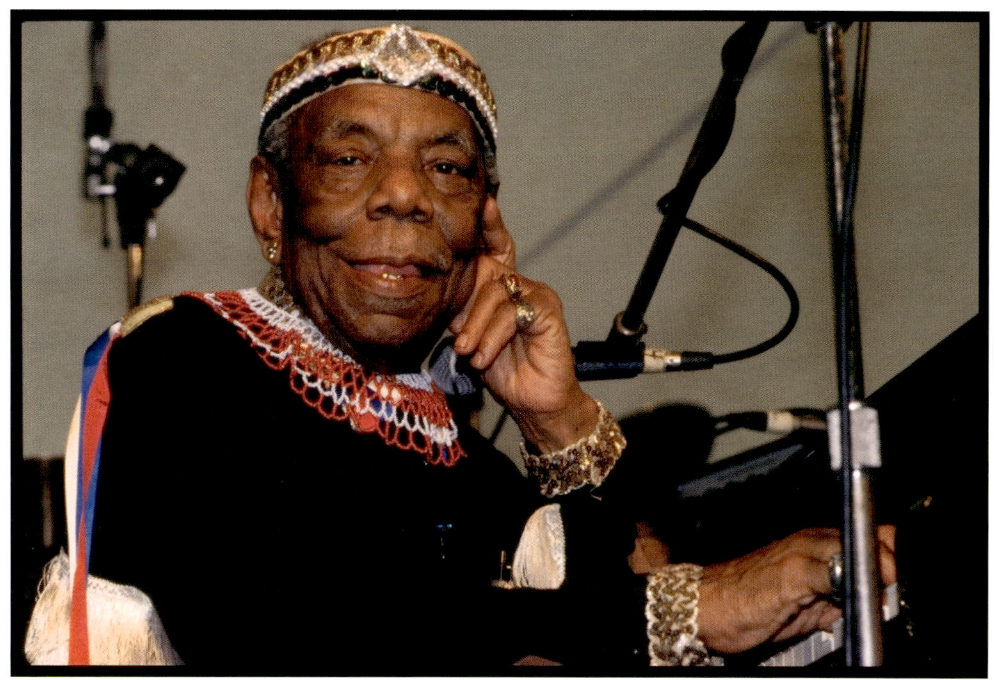

CHAMPION JACK DUPREE | 1991

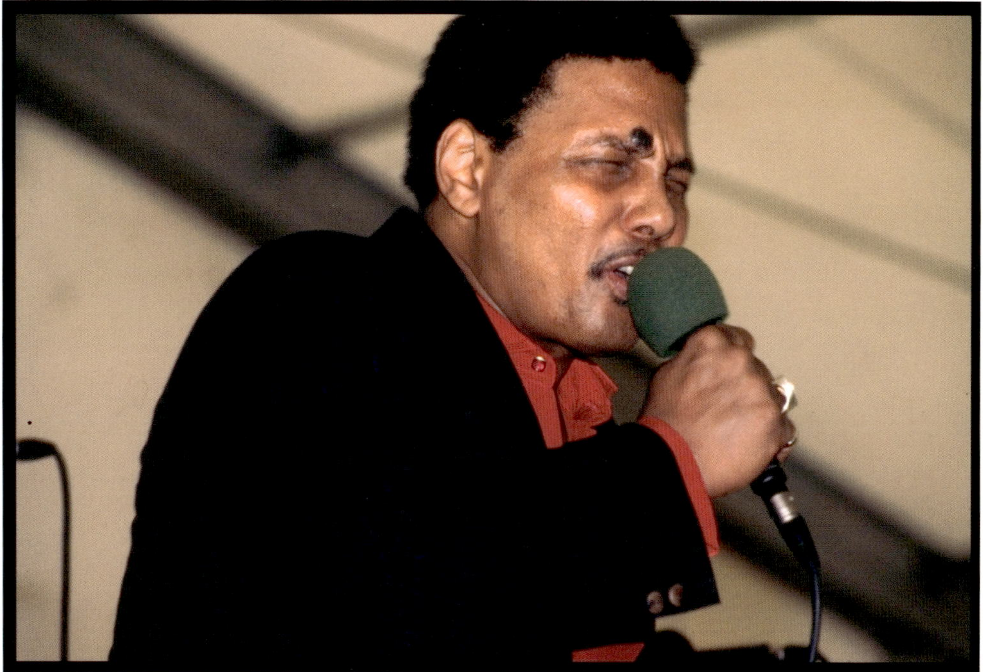

AARON NEVILLE | 1991

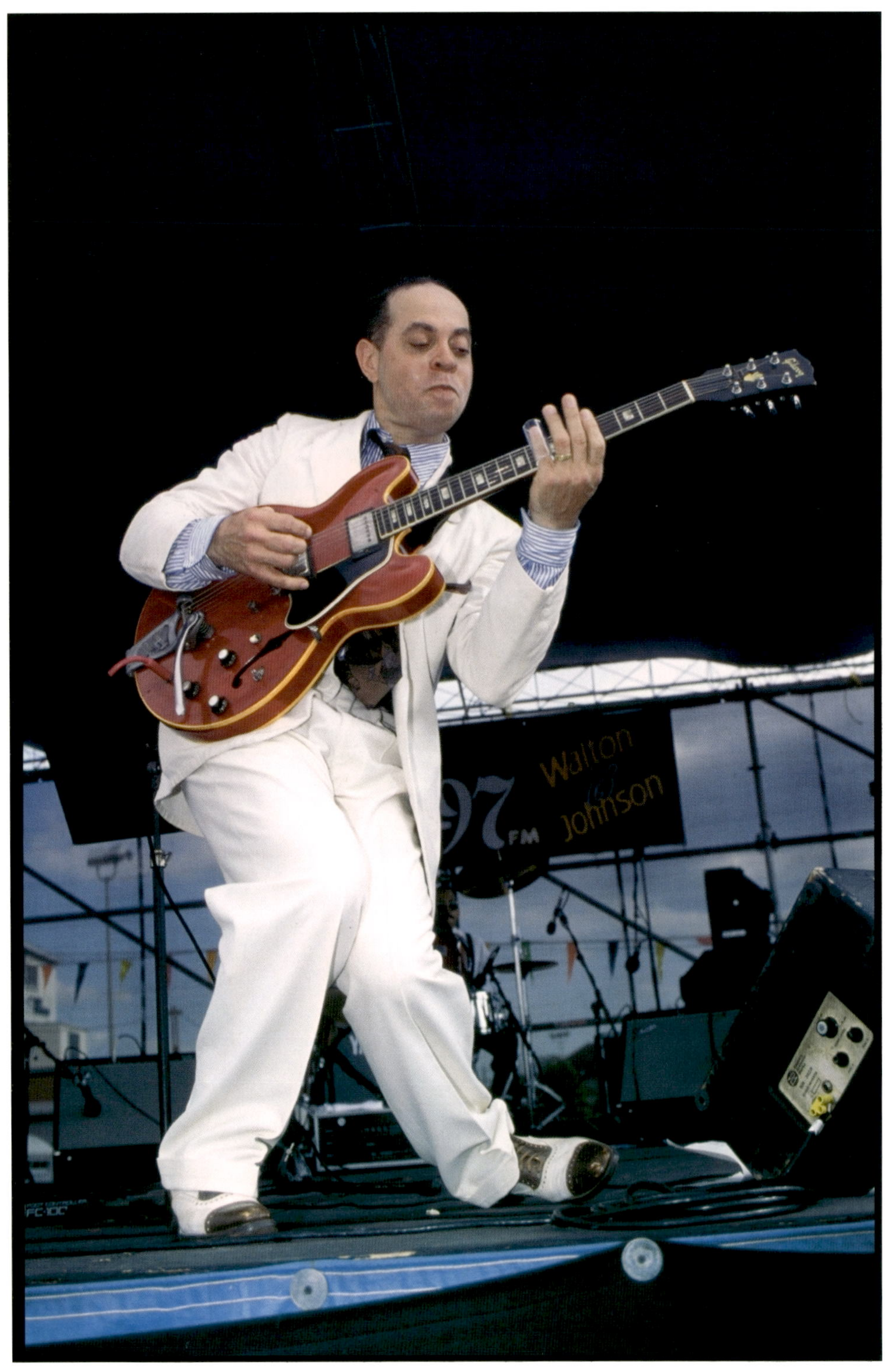


**"DEACON JOHN" MOORE** | 1992

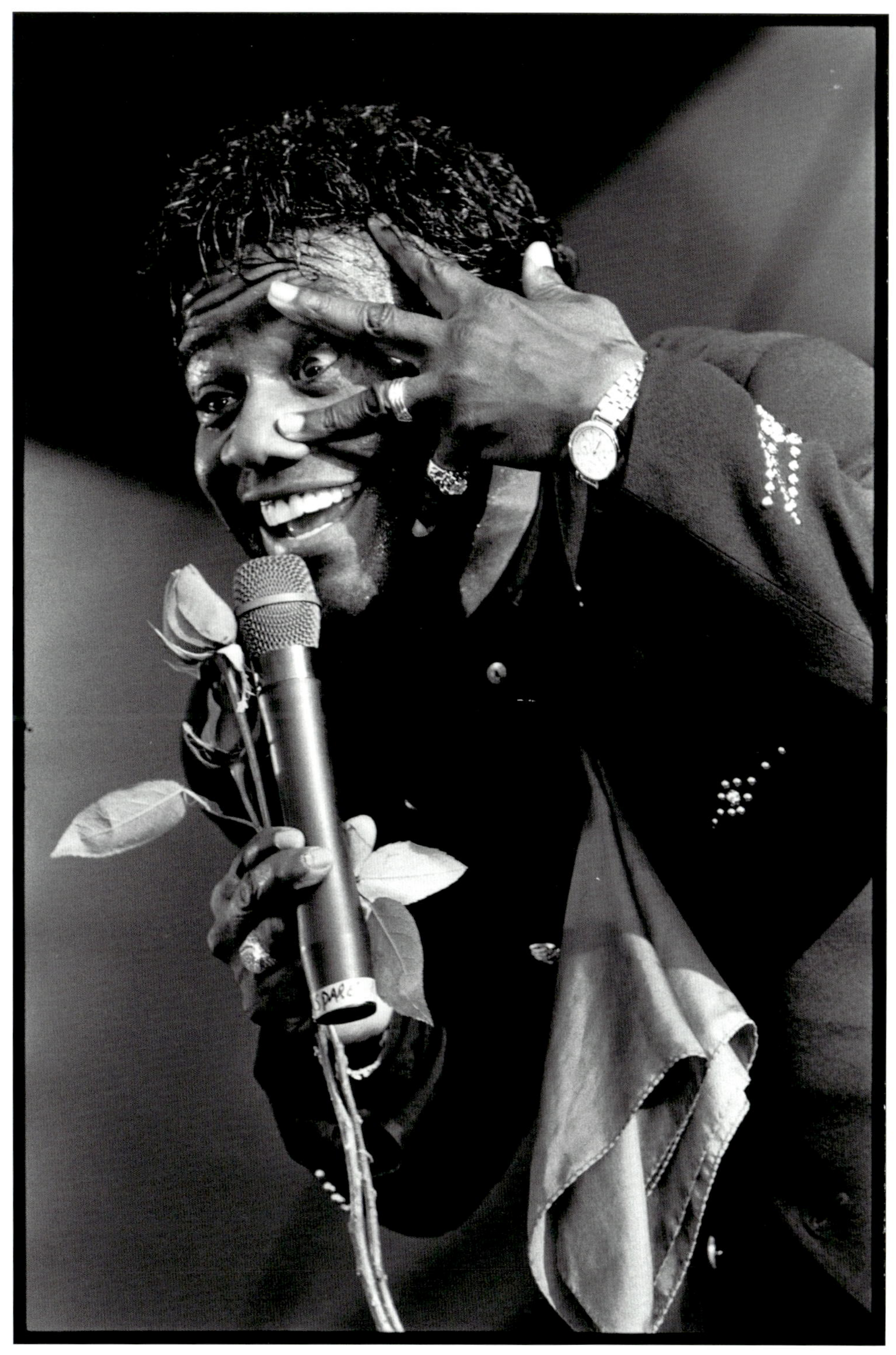

AL GREEN | 1995

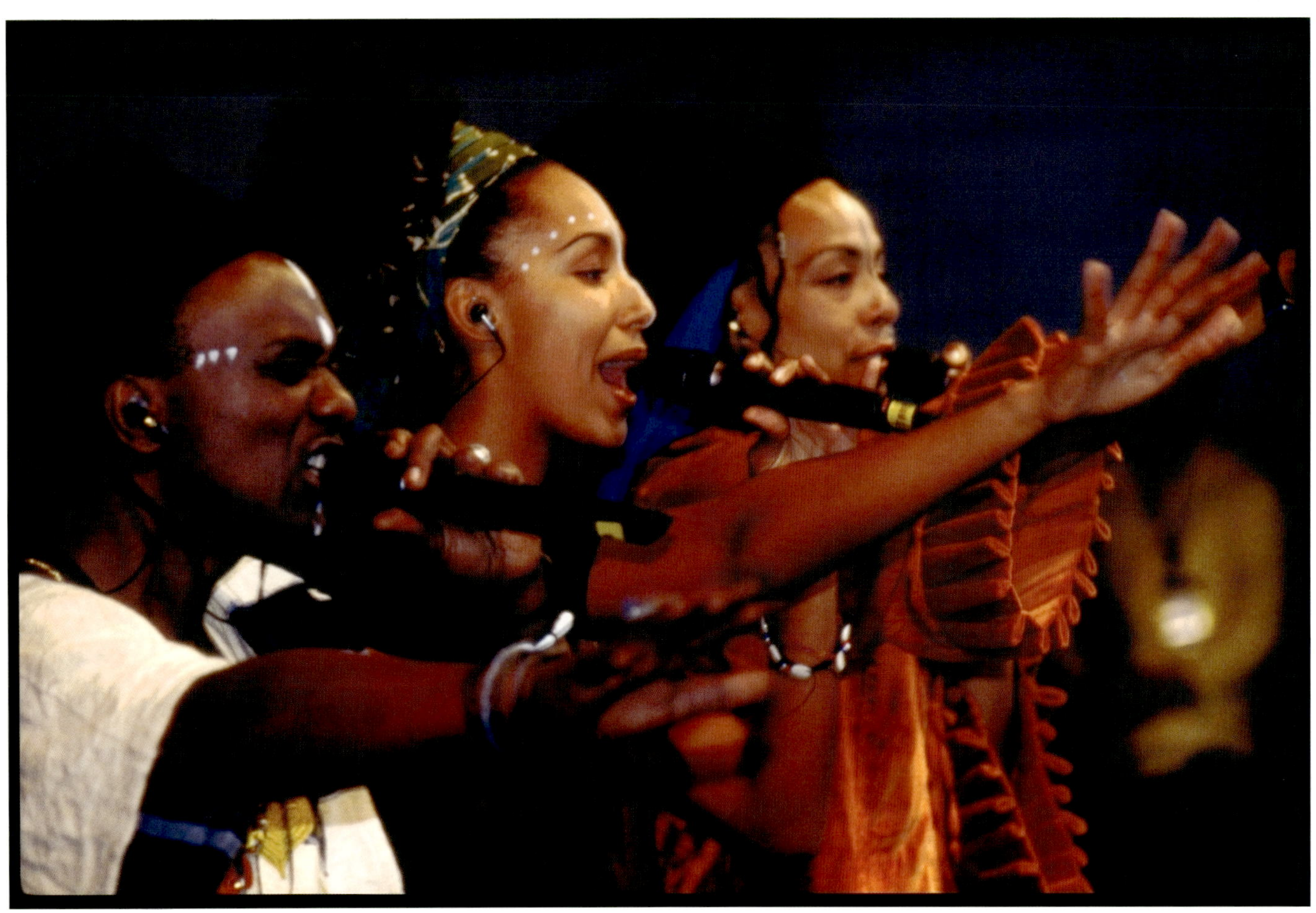

**ZAP MAMA** | 1997

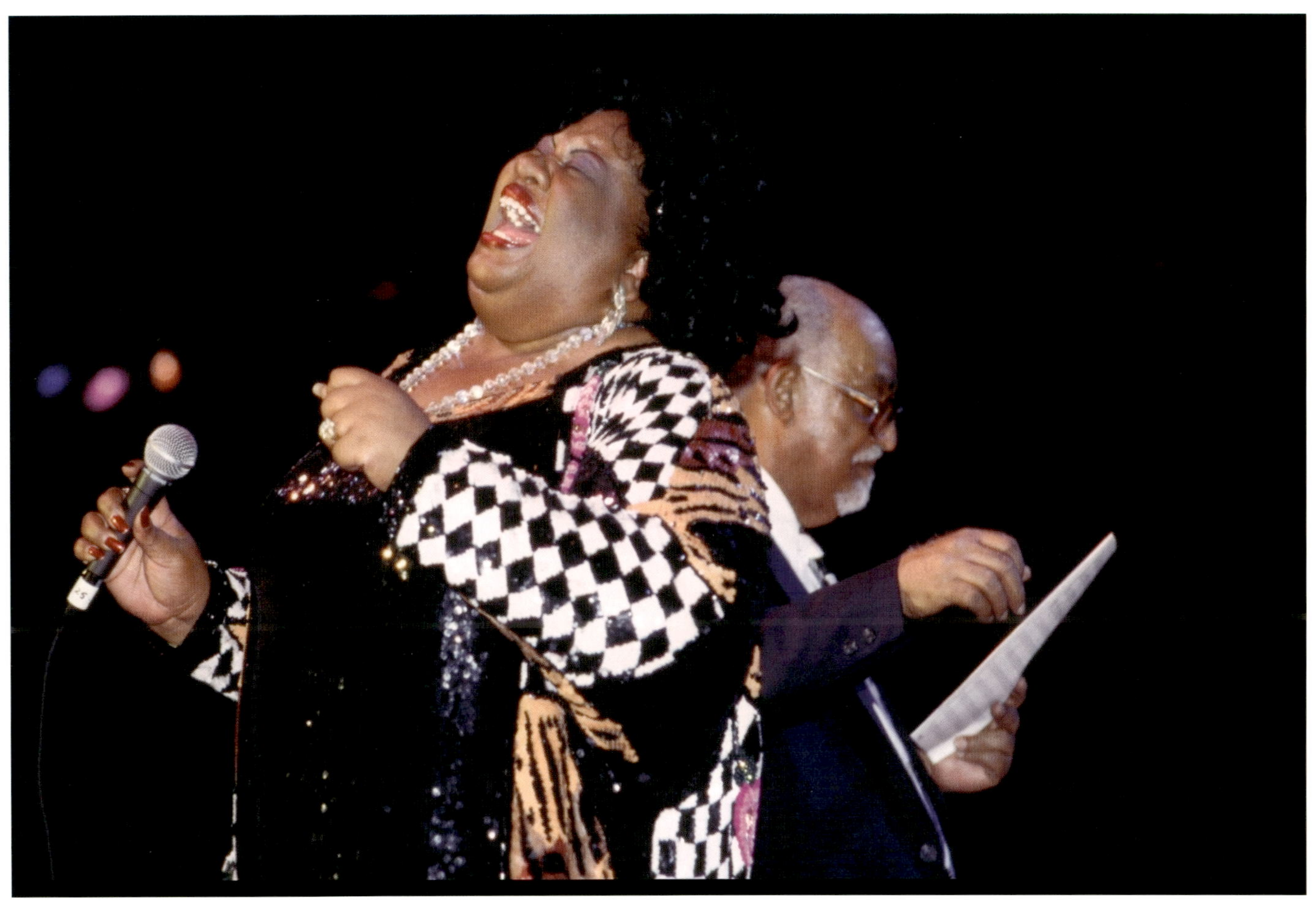

MARVA WRIGHT & WARDELL QUEZERGUE | 1997

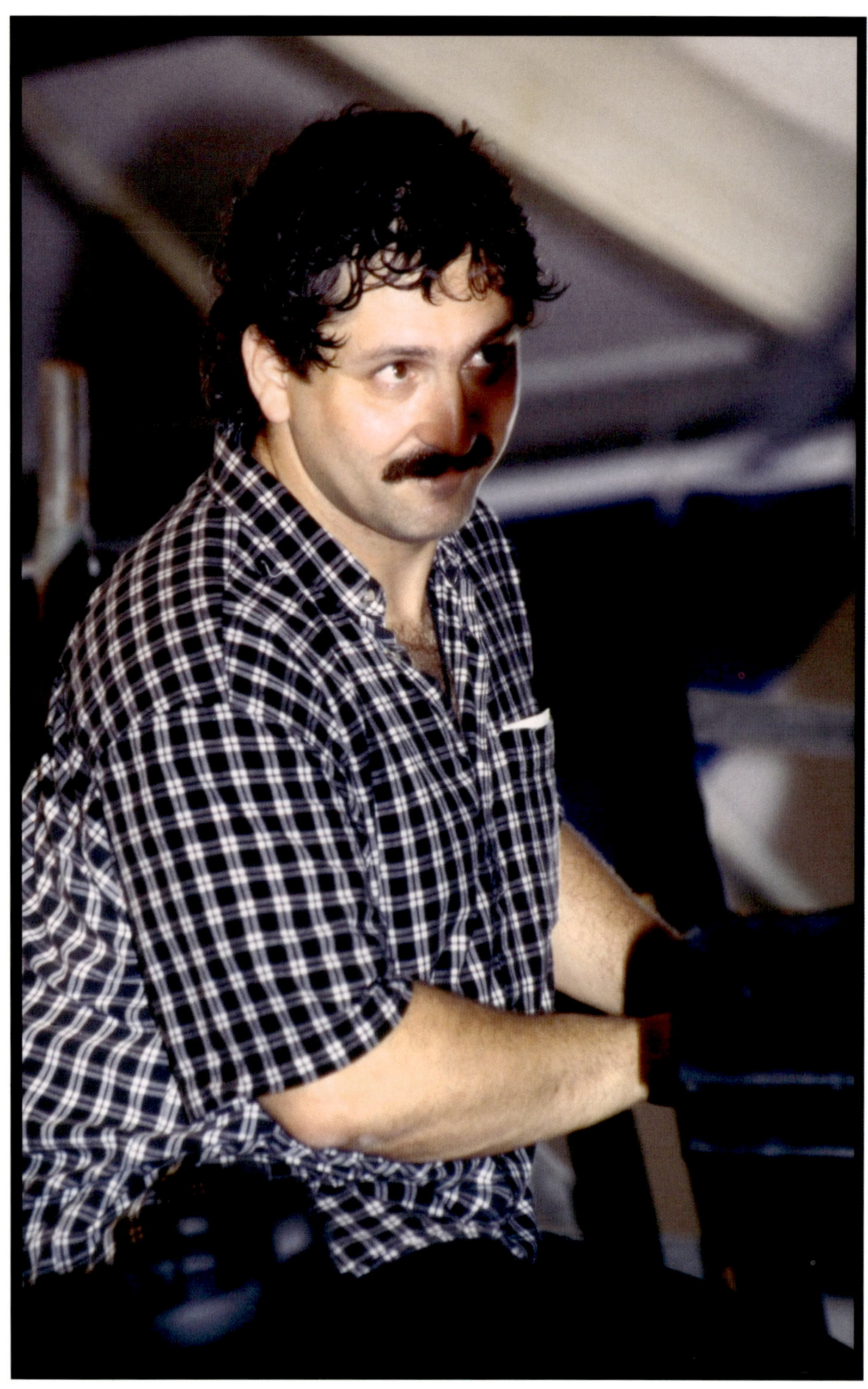

**DAVID TORKANOWSKY** | 1997

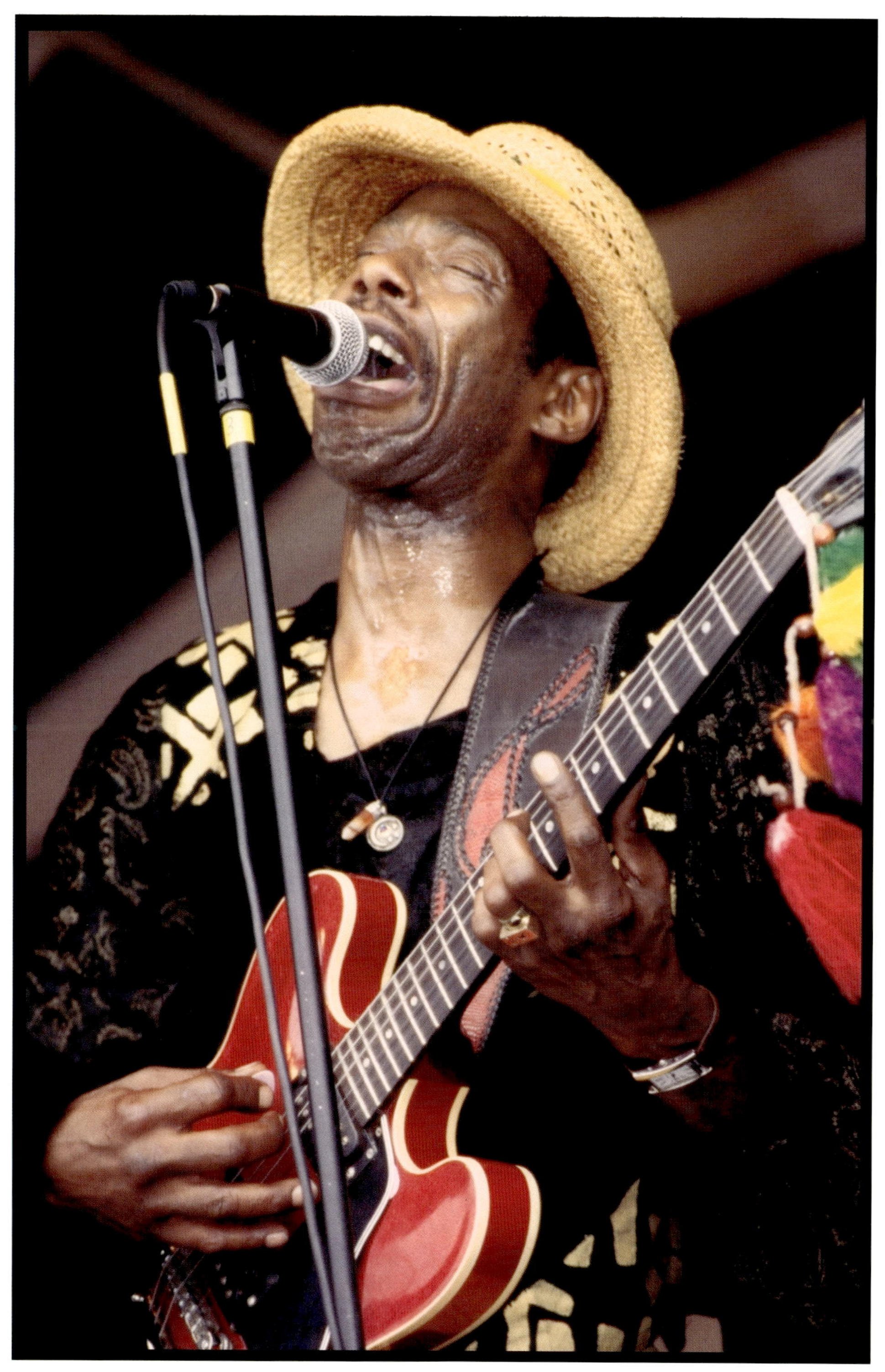

WALTER "WOLFMAN" WASHINGTON | 1997

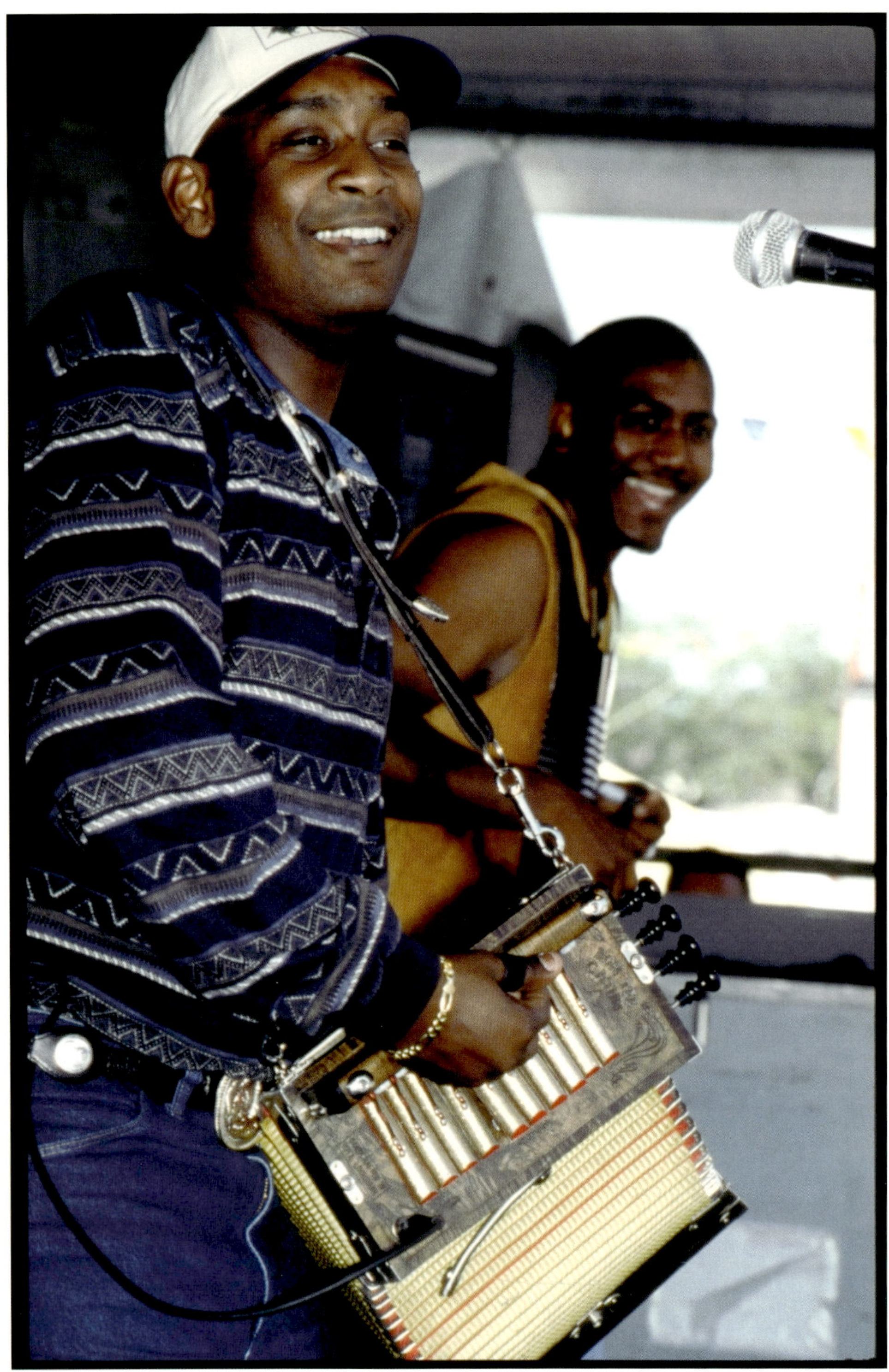

**GENO DELAFOSE** | 1998

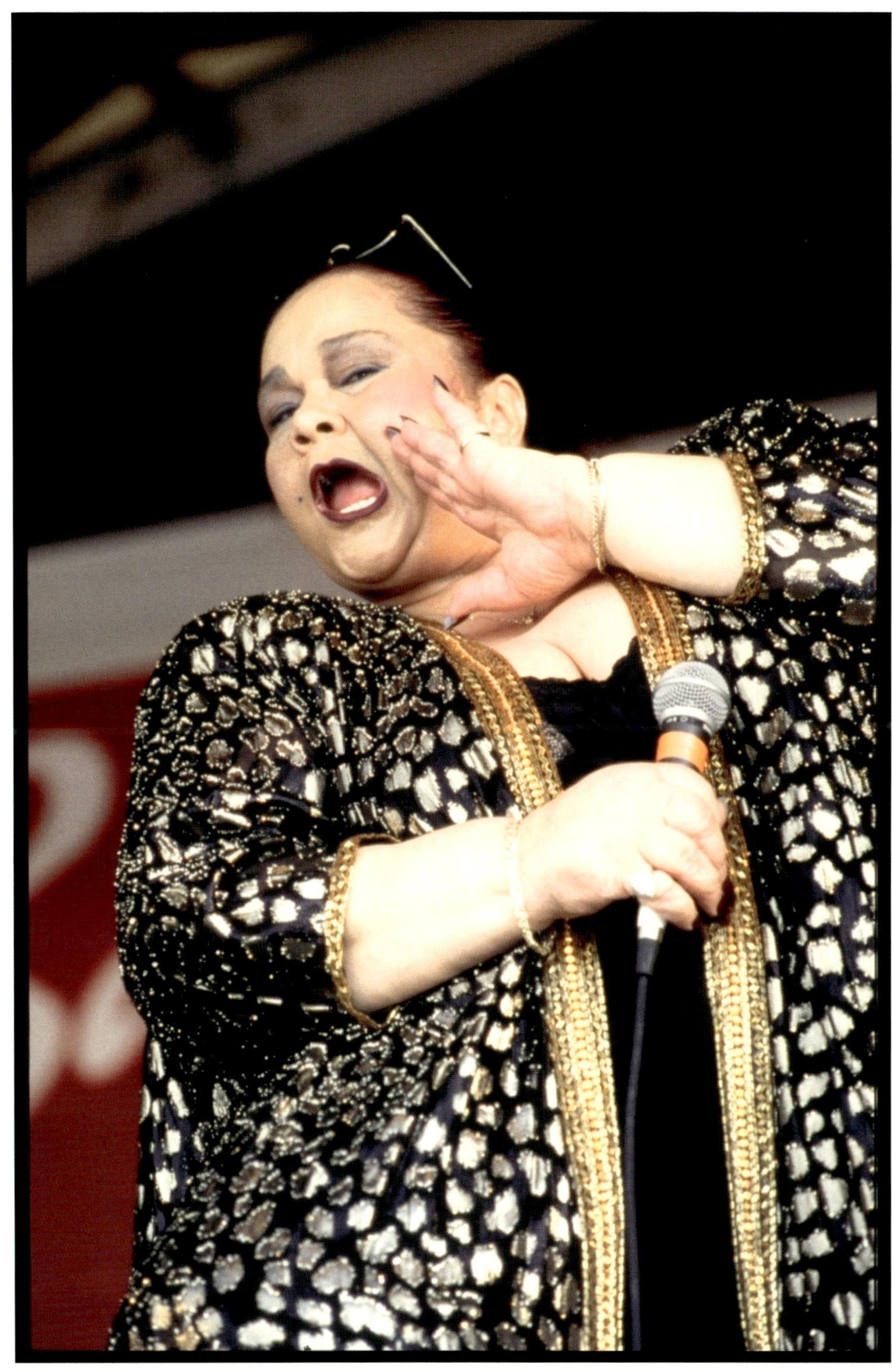

ETTA JAMES | 1998

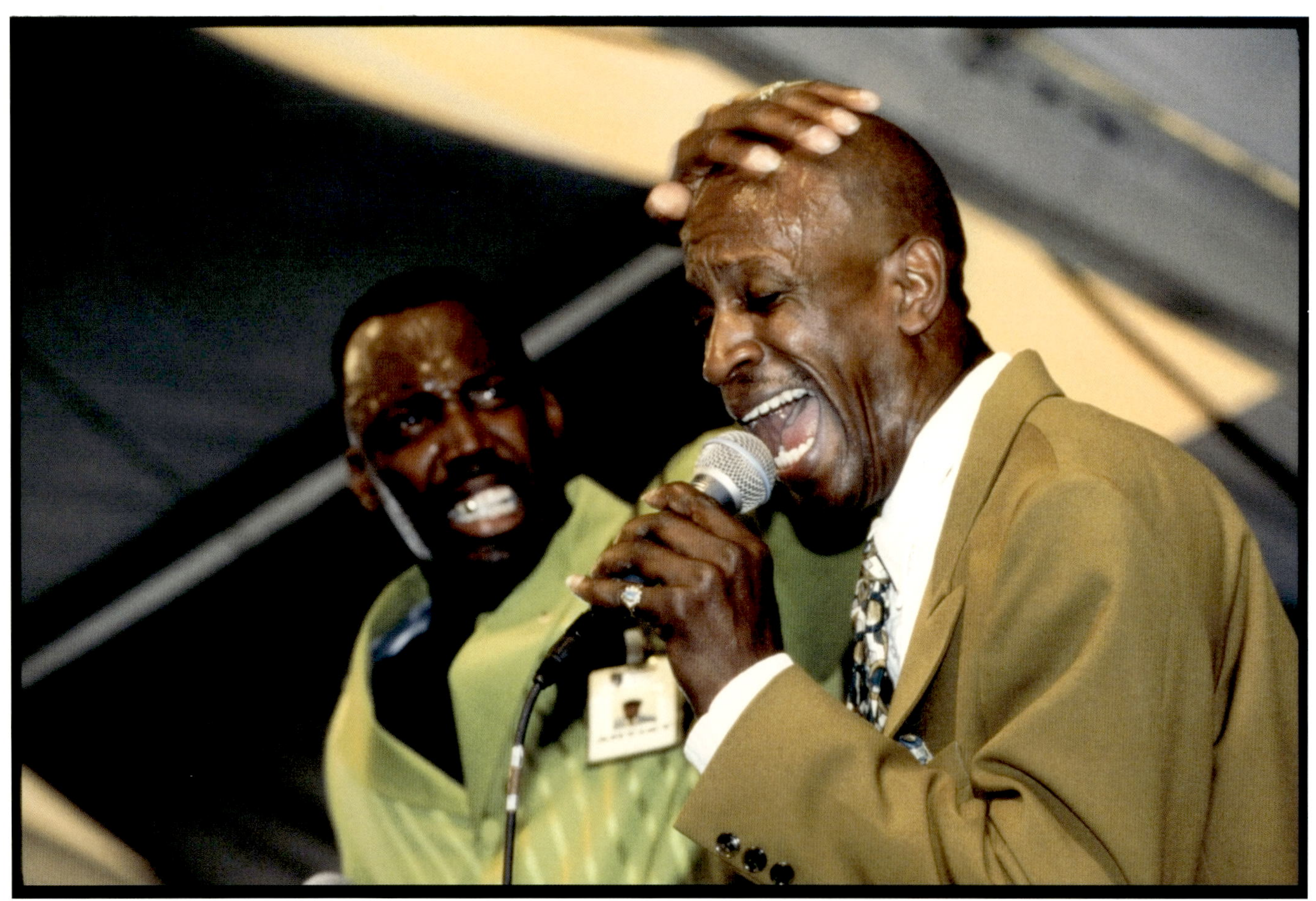

MIGHTY CHARIOTS OF FIRE | 1998

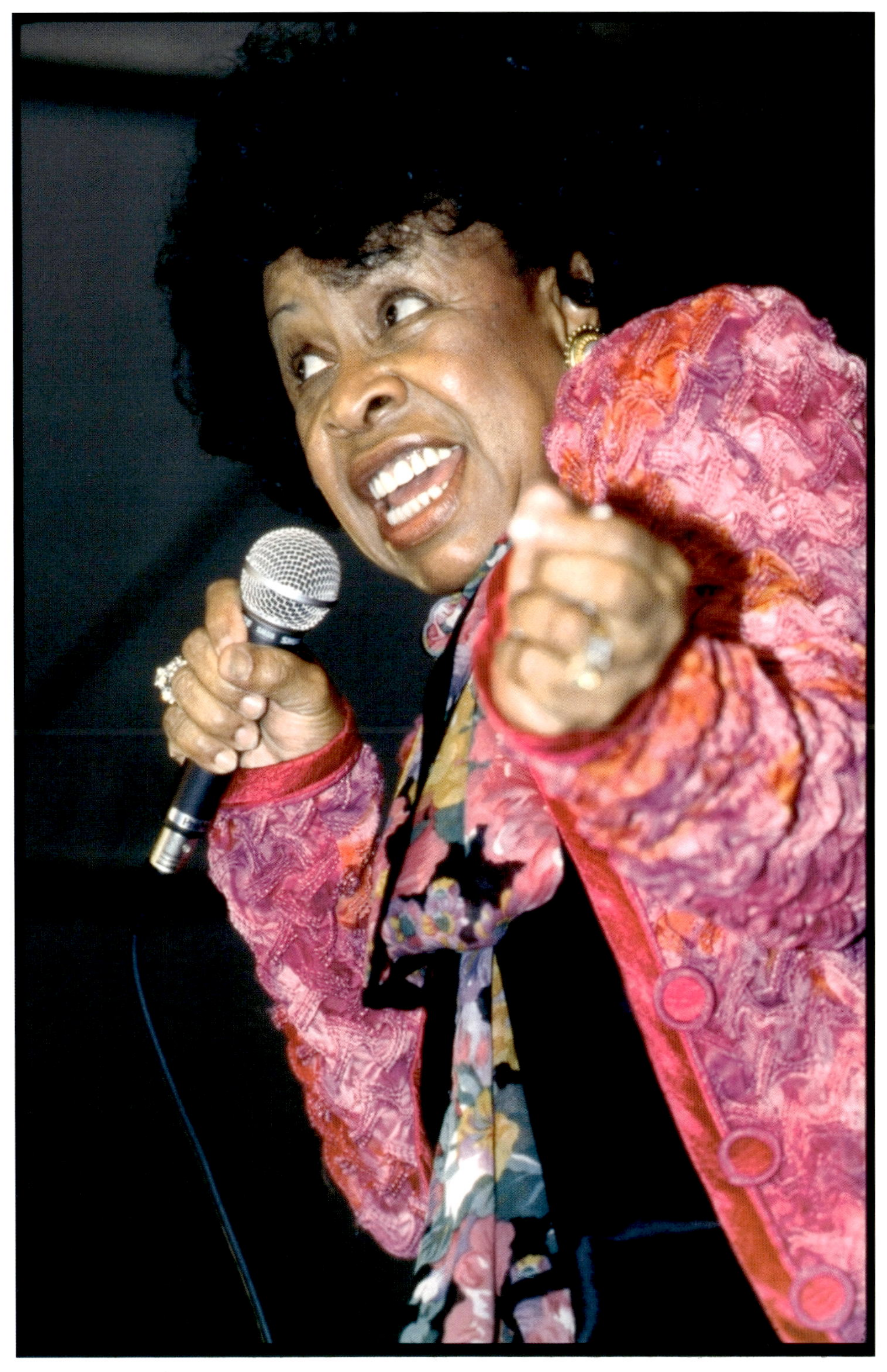

**BETTY CARTER** | 1998

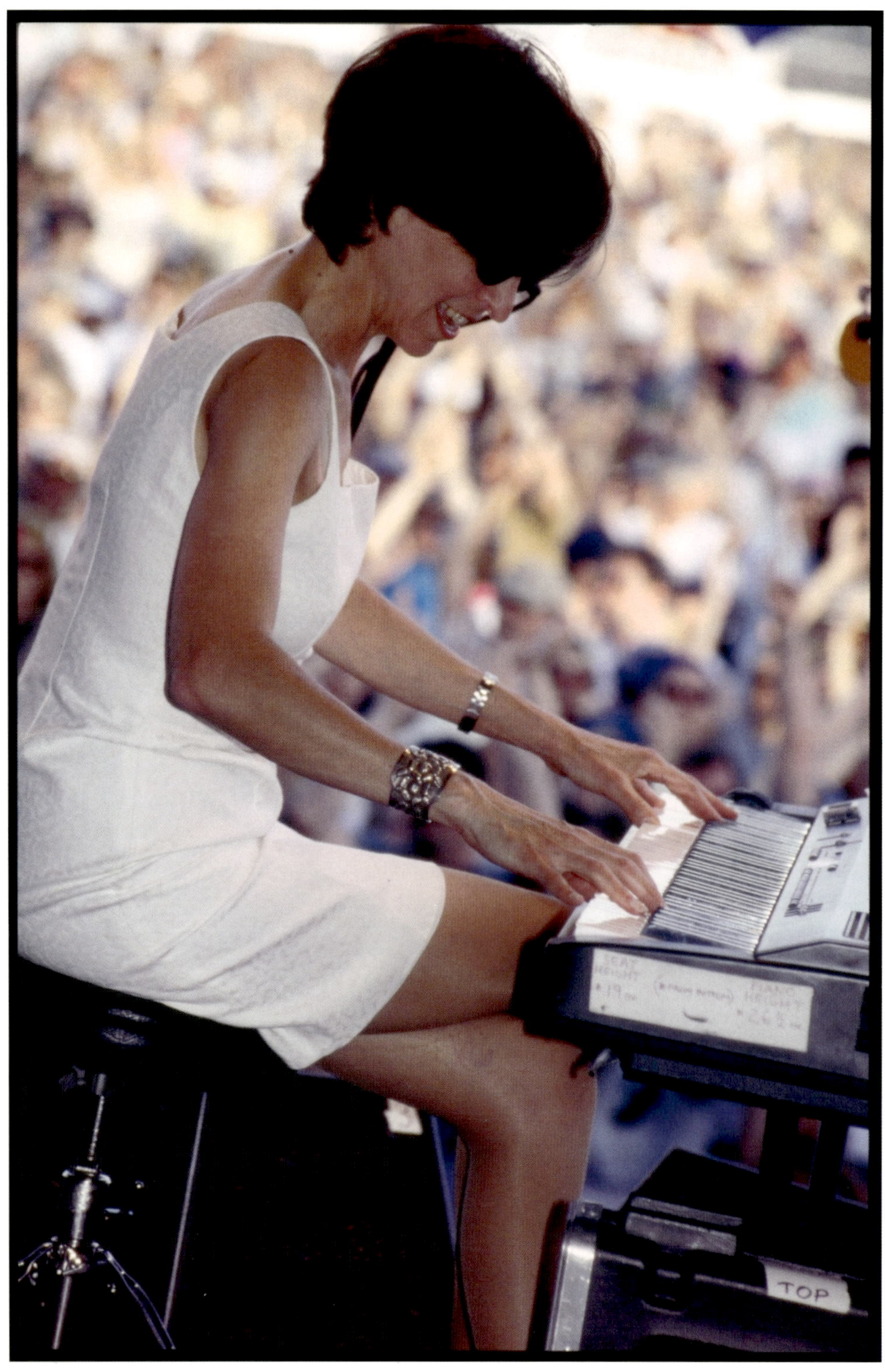


**MARCIA BALL** | 1999

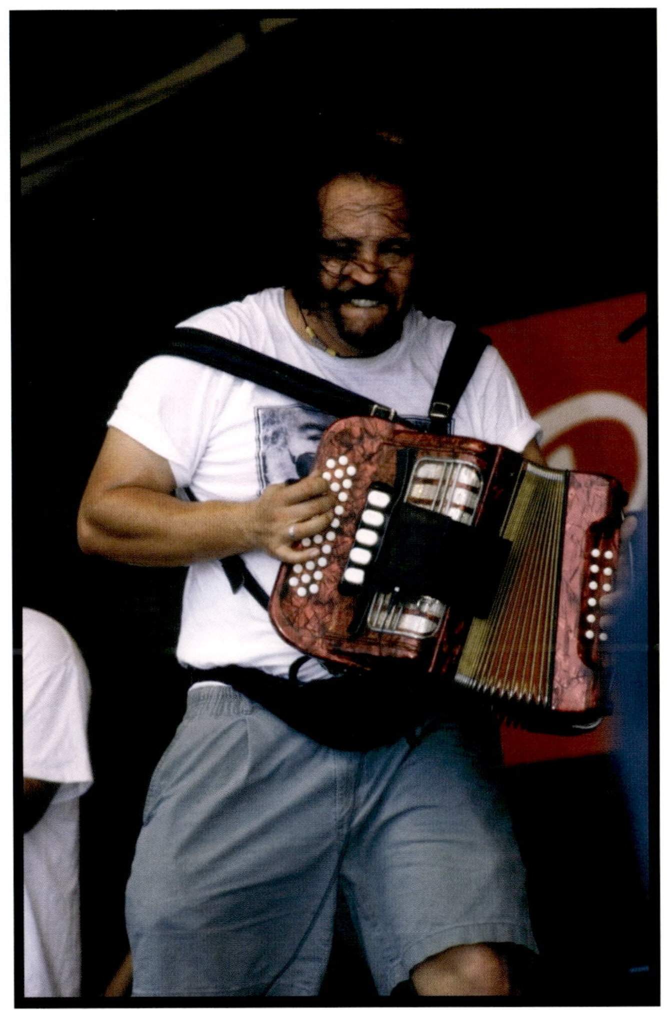

TERRANCE SIMIEN | 1999

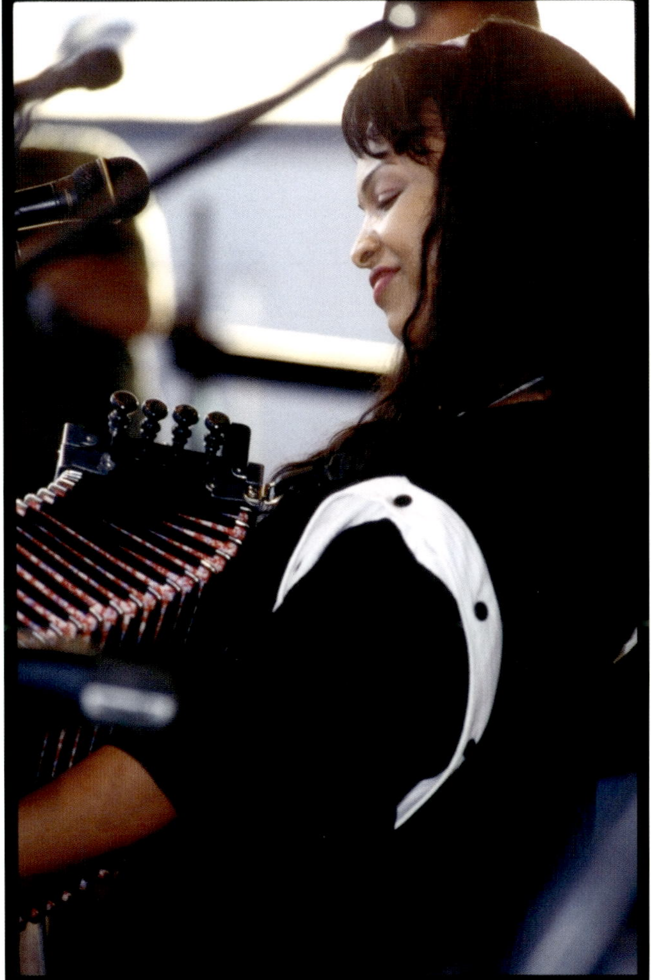

ROSIE LEDET | 1999

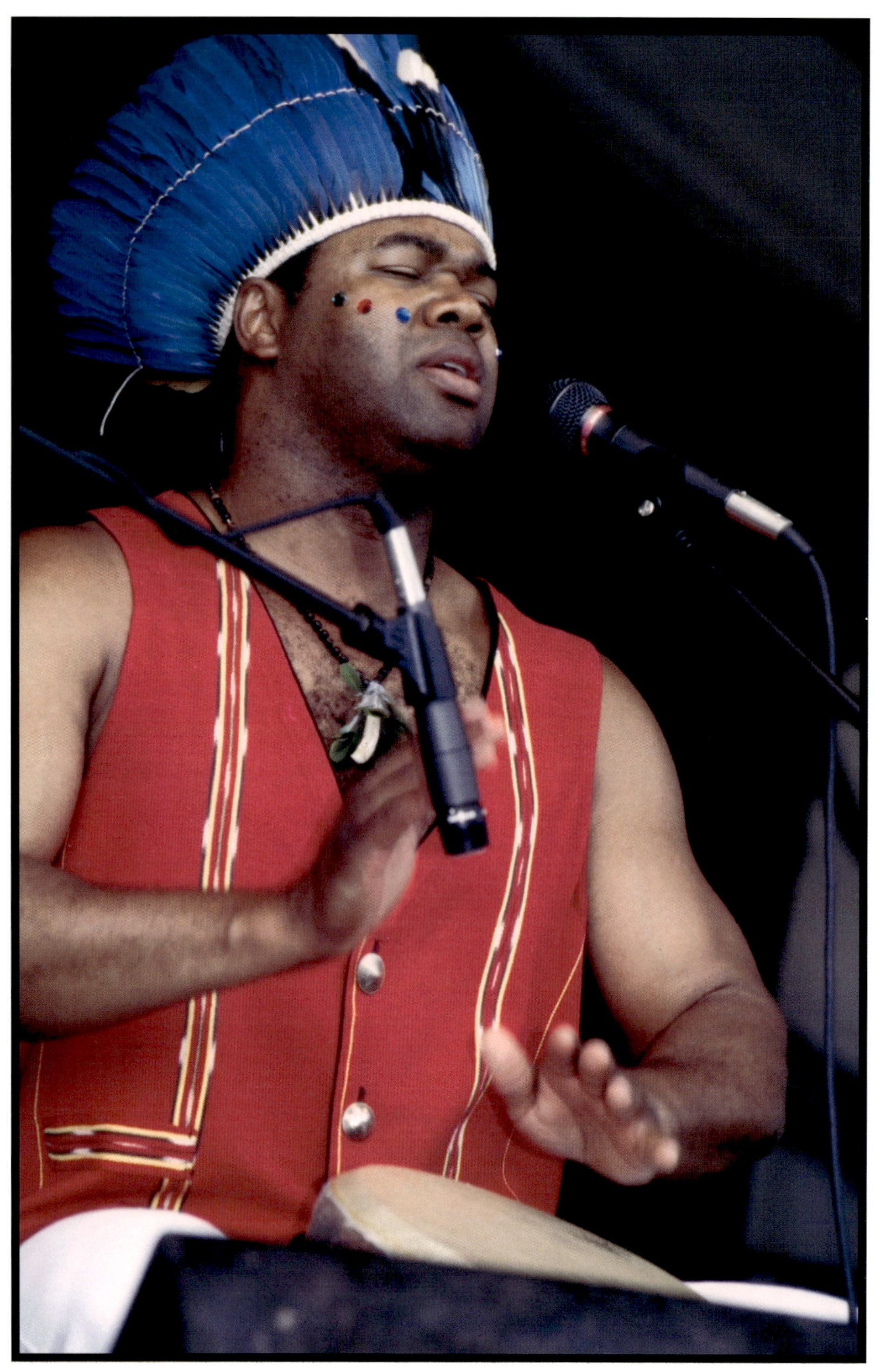

SUNPIE BARNES | 2000

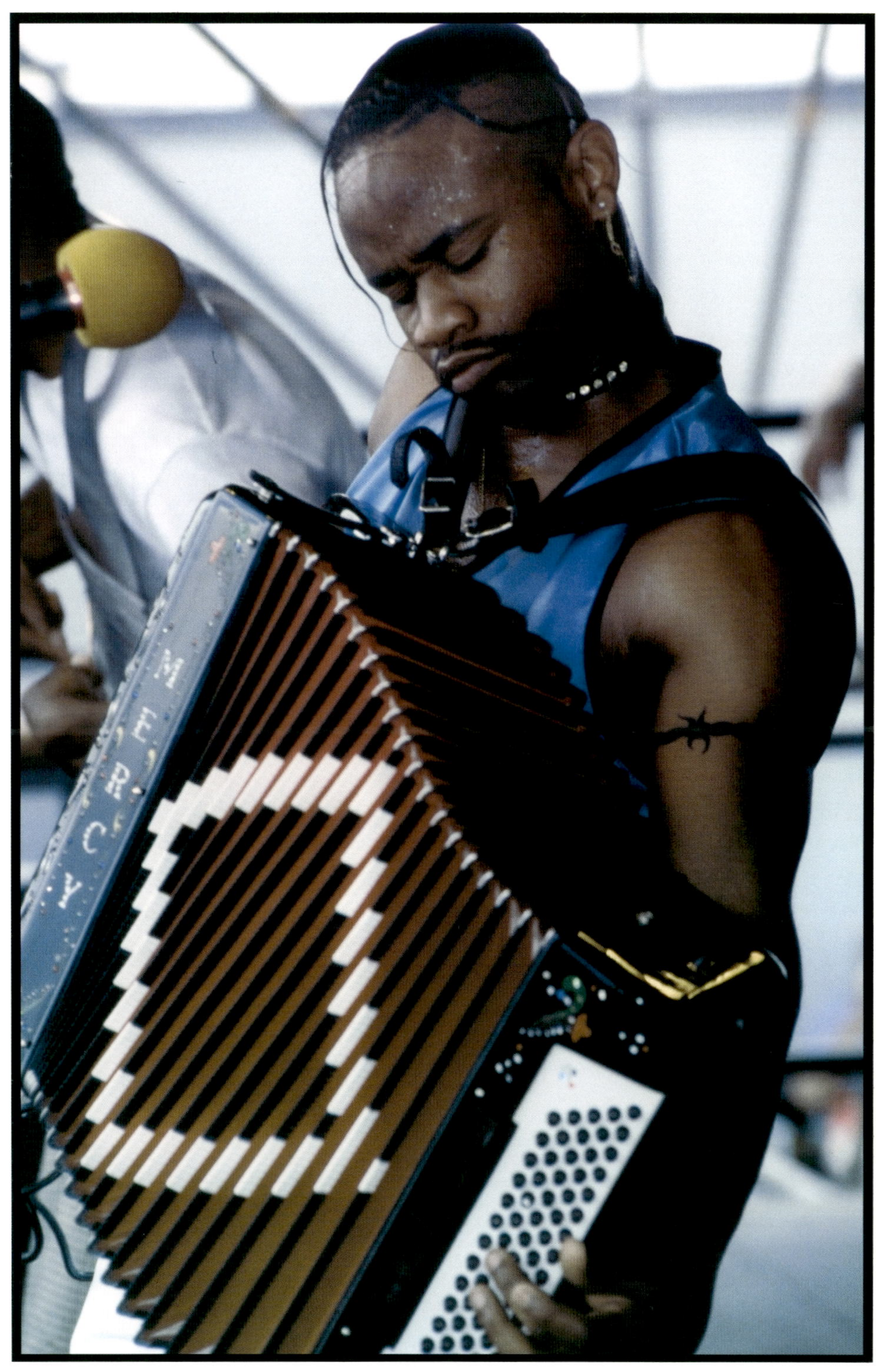


DWAYNE DOPSIE | 2000

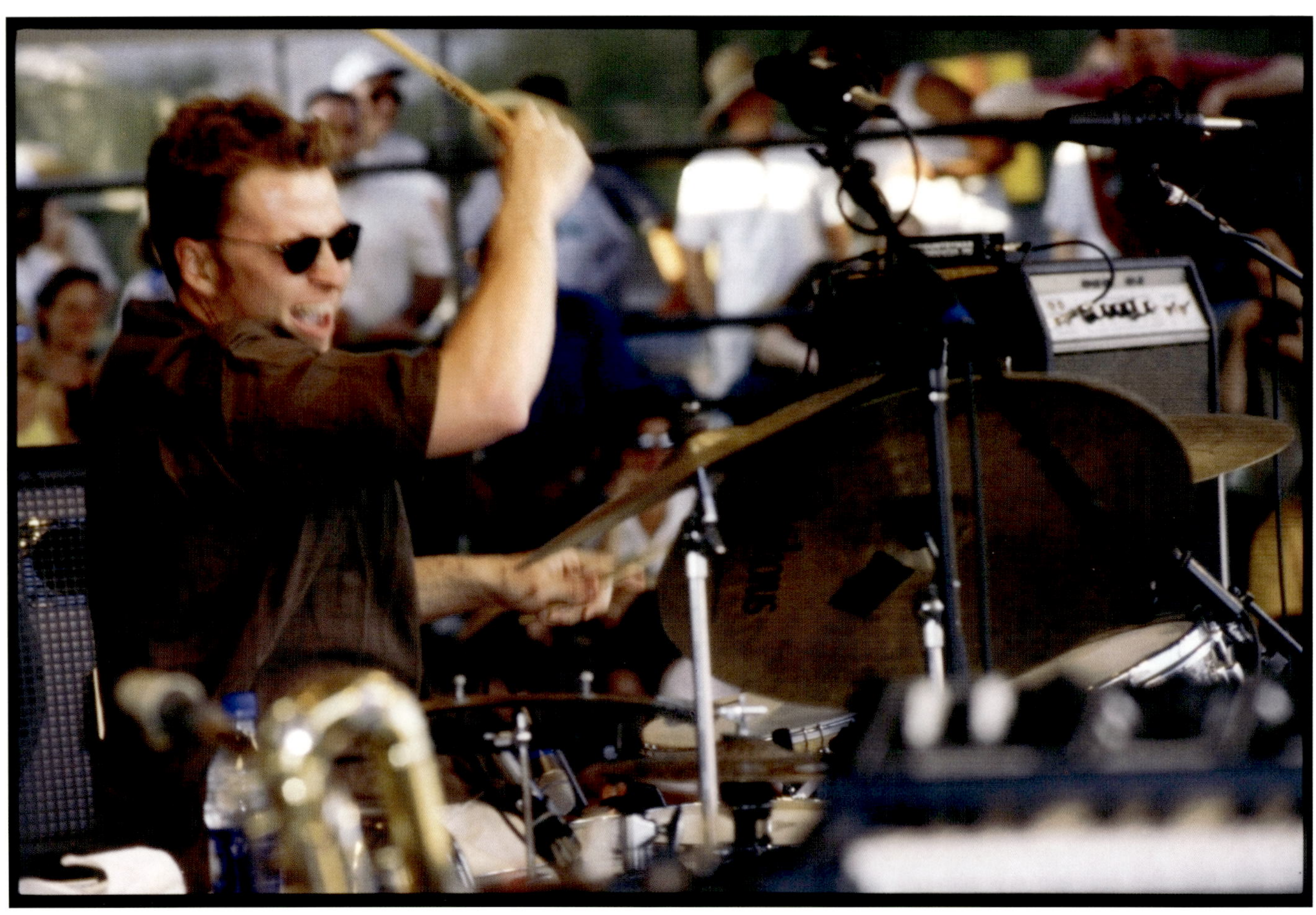

STANTON MOORE | 2000

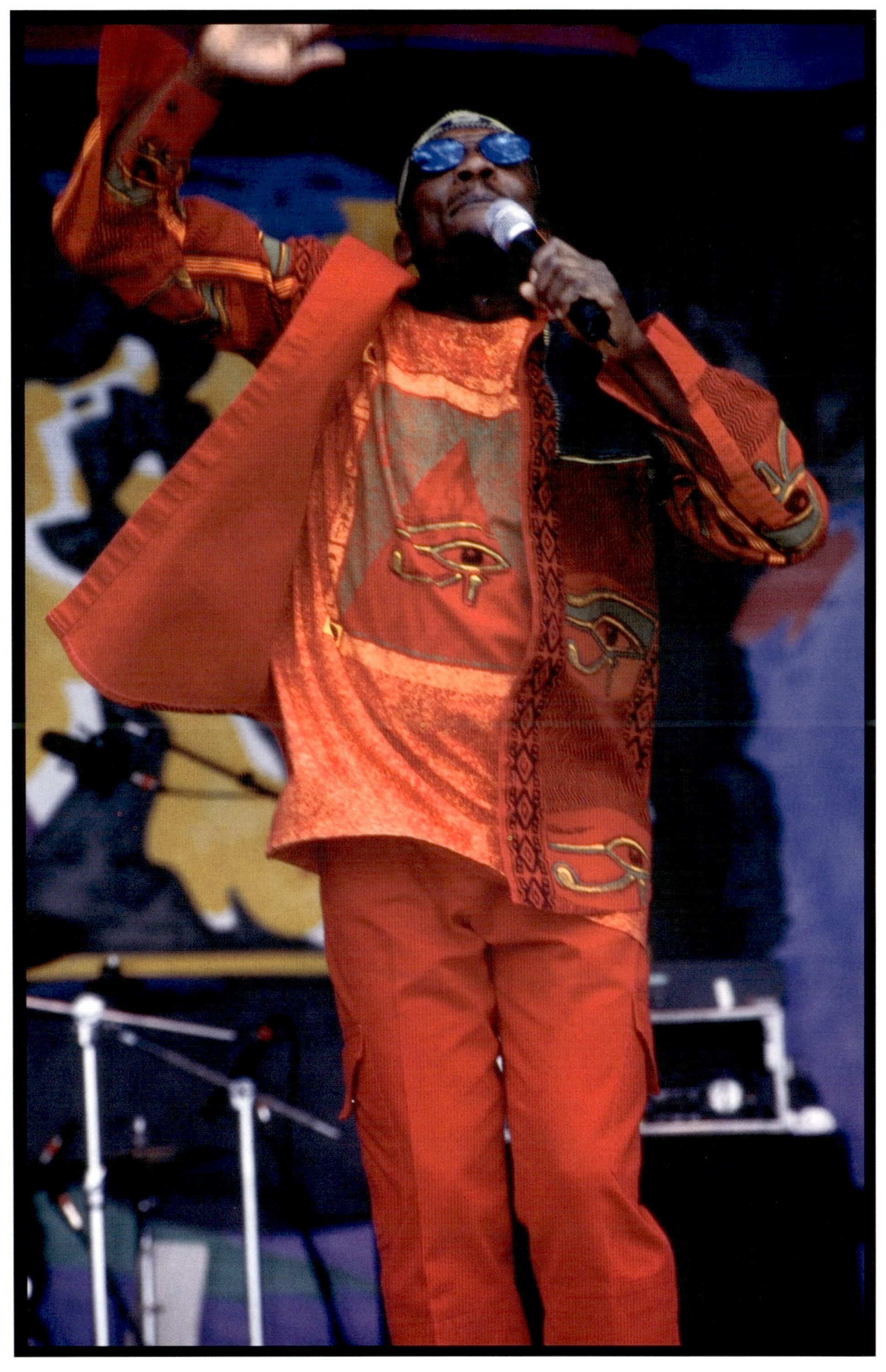

JIMMY CLIFF | 2000

## MICHAEL PROCTOR SMITH: AN ABBREVIATED CHRONOLOGY

Mike Smith was born in New Orleans on June 15, 1937. Some thirty years later, while working as a staff photographer at the Hogan Jazz Archive at Tulane University, he began the work which ultimately earned him recognition as someone who recorded aspects of New Orleans's culture with both artistry and understanding. And unlike many who labor in their chosen fields for love more than recognition or remuneration, Smith's contributions were recognized throughout his career. The following chronology highlights some of the key accomplishments in a life that ended September 26, 2008.

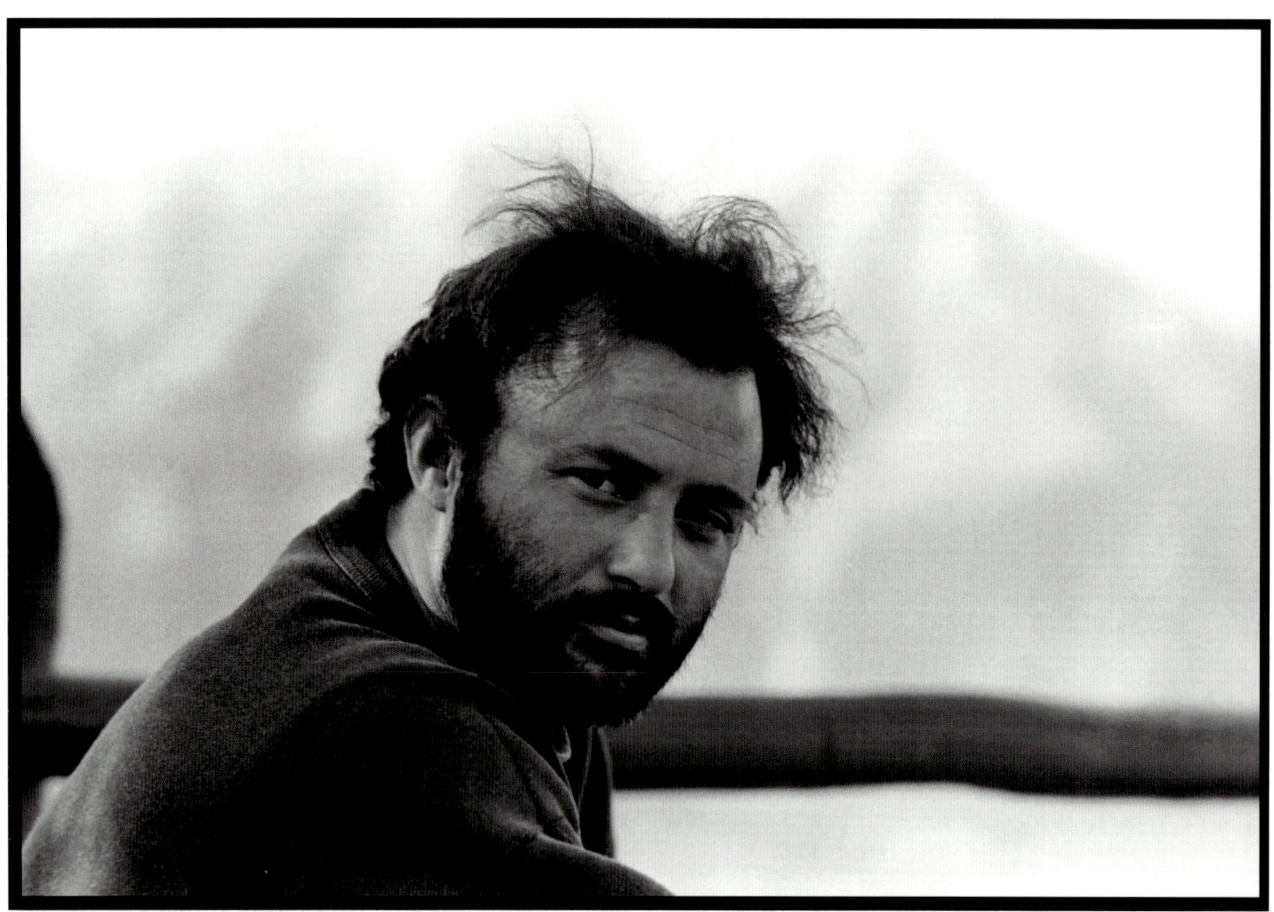

**SELF-PORTRAIT** | 1968

## EXHIBITIONS*

| | |
|---|---|
| 1968 | Listening Eye Gallery, New Orleans |
| 1972 | *Offbeat Moods of the City: A Candid Study of the Social and Cultural Environment in Urban New Orleans*, New Orleans Public Library |
| 1973 | *Images of Concern* (group exhibition), New Orleans Museum of Art |
| 1974 | Photo Exchange Gallery, New Orleans |
| 1975 | Biennial Exhibition (group exhibition), New Orleans Museum of Art |
| 1976 | *Journey into a Spiritual World*, International Center of Photography (ICP), New York<br>Fine Arts Gallery, Louisiana Tech University, Ruston, Louisiana |
| 1978 | Galería de la Raza and Museum of Modern Art, San Francisco |
| 1983 | *Spirit World*, Louisiana State Museum, New Orleans |
| 1984 | Louisiana World Exposition (group exhibition), New Orleans |
| 1986–1987 | *Spirit World*, Amsterdam, West Africa, and the Caribbean |
| 1988 | North Sea Jazz Festival, the Netherlands |
| 1990 | *A Joyful Noise*, East and West Germany |
| 1992 | Smithsonian Institution's National Museum of American History, Washington, DC |
| 1999 | Retrospective, Contemporary Arts Center, New Orleans<br>*Restoring Cultural Links for the Next Millennium*, Havana, Cuba |
| 2001 | Photo Exchange II Gallery, New Orleans<br>Columbia University, New York |
| 2005–2007 | *Before the Storm, or Vor der Sturm: The Soul of New Orleans*, Munich, Roth, and Nürnberg, Germany; Salzburg and Innsbruck, Austria |
| 2007 | *Moments in Time: New Orleans at the Crossroads* (group exhibition presented by the New Orleans Photo Alliance), New Orleans Academy of Fine Arts, New Orleans<br>14th annual Dixie Festival of Tarragona, Catalonia, Spain |

## PUBLICATIONS & FILMS

| | |
|---|---|
| 1977 | Principal consultant, field production coordinator, still photographer for *Always for Pleasure,* a film by documentarian Les Blank (released 1978) |
| 1982 | Consultant, field production coordinator, still photographer for *Jazz Parades: Feet Don't Fail Me Now,* a film produced by Alan Lomax for the Association for Cultural Equity, Hunter College, New York (released 1990) |
| 1984 | *Spirit World: Pattern in the Expressive Folk Culture of Afro-American New Orleans*, New Orleans: New Orleans Urban Folklife Society<br>Still photographer on location in Cuba, *Routes of Rhythm with Harry Belafonte*, produced by Howard Dratch and Eugene Rosow with the support of the Ford Foundation (released 1990) |
| 1988 | Consultant, field production coordinator, still photographer for *National Geographic: On Assignment,* "Battle of the Big Chiefs," a National Geographic production |
| 1990 | *A Joyful Noise: A Celebration of New Orleans Music*, with commentary by Alan Govenar, Dallas: Taylor Publishing Co. |
| 1991 | *New Orleans Jazz Fest: A Pictorial History*, Gretna, LA: Pelican Publishing Co. |
| 1997 | *Jazz Fest Memories*, with Allison Miner, Gretna, LA: Pelican Publishing Co.<br>Still photographer on location in China, *All in This Tea*, produced by Les Blank and Gina Leibrecht (released 2007) |

***All exhibitions were one-man shows unless otherwise noted.**

## JAZZ & FOLK FESTIVAL PHOTOGRAPHY

| | |
|---|---|
| 1970-2004 | New Orleans Jazz & Heritage Festival |
| 1990-1995 | Lowell (Massachusetts) Jazz Festival |
| 1994 | 56th National Folk Festival, Chattanooga, Tennessee |
| 1995-1996 | Nice (France) Jazz Festival |

## AWARDS, GRANTS & HONORS

| | |
|---|---|
| 1973 | Photographer's Fellowship, National Endowment for the Arts |
| 1975 | Photographer's Fellowship, National Endowment for the Arts<br>New Orleans Ethnic Music Research Project Grant, National Endowment for the Humanities Grant, Louisiana Endowment for the Humanities |
| 1983 | Grant, Louisiana Endowment for the Humanities |
| 1993 | Special Humanities Award, Louisiana Endowment for the Humanities<br>Photographs acquired by the Bibliothèque nationale de France, Paris, and the Metropolitan Museum of Art, New York |
| 2001 | Invited lecture, Columbia University, New York<br>Photographs acquired by the Louisiana State Museum, New Orleans<br>Lifetime Achievement Award, Louisiana Endowment for the Humanities<br>Music Photographer of the Year, *OffBeat* magazine |
| 2003 | Keeping the History Alive Award, Estate of Danny Barker |
| 2004 | Mayor's Arts Award, Arts Council of New Orleans<br>Clarence John Laughlin Lifetime Achievement Award, American Society of Media Photographers, New Orleans/Gulf South Chapter |
| 2005 | NOMA Delgado Society Lifetime Achievement for Louisiana Artists Award, New Orleans Museum of Art |
| 2007 | Michael P. Smith Archive acquired by The Historic New Orleans Collection |

## COMMUNITY INVOLVEMENT & TEACHING

| | |
|---|---|
| 1968 | Founding member, Listening Eye Gallery & Jazz Workshop, New Orleans |
| 1974 | Photographer's assistant to Clarence John Laughlin, Ansel Adams Summer Workshop, Yosemite, California |
| 1977 | Founding member and board member (1977–1984), Summa 2-4-U, managing board of Tipitina's Social and Pleasure Club |
| 1977–1981 | Consultant and photo documentarian, Jean Lafitte National Park and Preserve |
| 1979 | Task Force on Arts Policy, Office of the Mayor of New Orleans |
| 1980 | Advisory board member, Nora Blatch Educational Communications Foundation (WWOZ-FM community radio) |
| 1981 | Benefit organizer, fund for the families of deceased musicians Walter Daniel Lastie and Henry Roeland Byrd |
| 1984 | Summer workshop faculty, International Center of Photography, New York |
| 1992 | Research associate and board member, Midlo Center for New Orleans Studies, University of New Orleans |
| 1999 | Photographer and civic and cultural delegate to Cuba, Cuban Studies Institute, Tulane University, New Orleans |

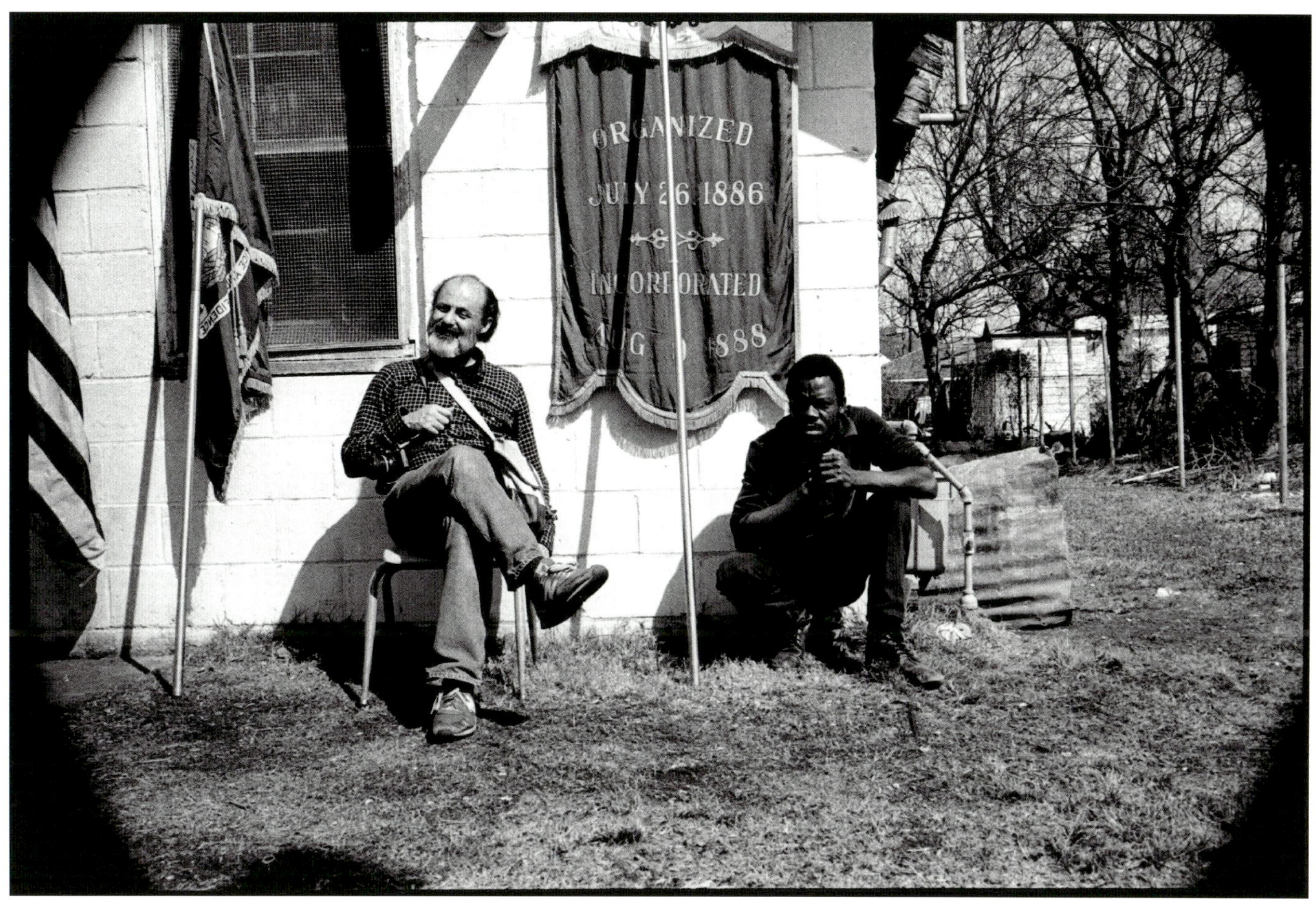


**MICHAEL P. SMITH & AN UNIDENTIFIED CLUB MEMBER** BY JULES CAHN | 1979

# ACKNOWLEDGMENTS

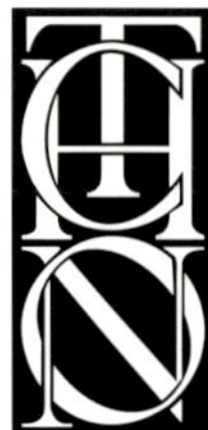

**The Historic New Orleans Collection**

BOARD OF DIRECTORS
**Mrs. William K. Christovich,** CHAIRMAN
**Charles Snyder,** PRESIDENT
**John Kallenborn,** VICE PRESIDENT
**Fred M. Smith,** SECRETARY
**John E. Walker,** IMMEDIATE PAST PRESIDENT
**Drew Jardine**
**Hunter Pierson Jr.**
**Alexandra Stafford**

**Priscilla Lawrence**
EXECUTIVE DIRECTOR

**John H. Lawrence**
DIRECTOR OF MUSEUM PROGRAMS

**Warren J. Woods**
COLLECTIONS MANAGER/EXHIBITIONS COORDINATOR

**John H. Lawrence and Jude Solomon**
EXHIBITION CURATORS

**Lisa Brown, Melissa Carrier, Mary Lou Eichhorn, Daniel Hammer, Brian Lavigne, Amanda McFillen, and Sally Stassi**
EXHIBITION RESEARCH

**Terry Weldon**
HEAD PREPARATOR/EXHIBITION DESIGNER

**Scott Ratterree**
PREPARATOR

**Larry Falgoust, Douglas Stallmer, and Tony Rodgers**
INSTALLATION ASSISTANTS

**Steve Sweet**
GRAPHICS, INTERNET, AND INTERACTIVE

**Erin Greenwald and Jessica Dorman**
EDITORS

**Teresa Devlin and Anne Robichaux**
MARKETING

**Viola Berman, Maclyn Hickey, Anna Hilderbrandt, and Goldie Lanaux**
REGISTRATION

**Keely Merritt, Teresa Kirkland, and Melissa Carrier**
PHOTOGRAPHY

**Susan R. Laudeman and Eddy Parker**
EDUCATIONAL OUTREACH

**Alison Cody**
CATALOGUE DESIGN

SPECIAL THANKS TO
**Karen Snyder and Leslie Blackshear Smith**

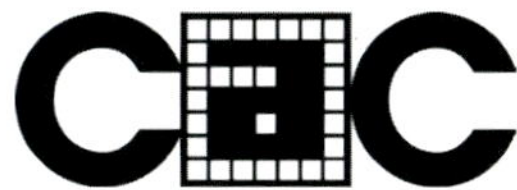

**Contemporary Arts Center, New Orleans**

**Dan Cameron**
DIRECTOR OF VISUAL ARTS AND EXHIBITION CURATOR

**Claire Tancons**
ASSOCIATE CURATOR

**Johnny King**
EXHIBITIONS MANAGER

**Jason Berry**
CONTRIBUTING WRITER

**Jay Weigel**
EXECUTIVE DIRECTOR

**Glenn Gruber**
DEPUTY DIRECTOR FOR OPERATIONS

**Merit Shalett**
DEPUTY DIRECTOR FOR DEVELOPMENT AND SPECIAL PROGRAMS

**Marie Lamb**
DIRECTOR OF EDUCATION

**Melissa Weber**
MARKETING AND PUBLIC RELATIONS

*Twenty-Five Jazz Fests* at the Contemporary Arts Center, New Orleans, is funded under a grant from the Louisiana Endowment for the Humanities, the state affiliate of the National Endowment for the Humanities. The opinions expressed in this program do not necessarily represent the views of either the Louisiana Endowment for the Humanities or the National Endowment for the Humanities.

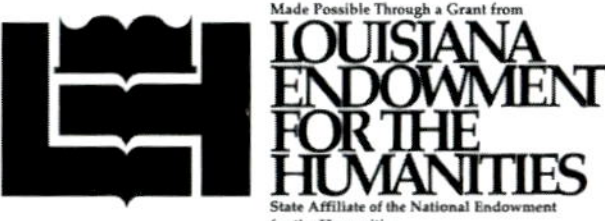


The exhibition is also made possible by the New Orleans Jazz & Heritage Festival and Foundation, Inc.

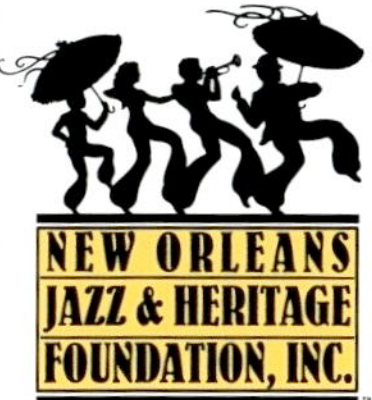

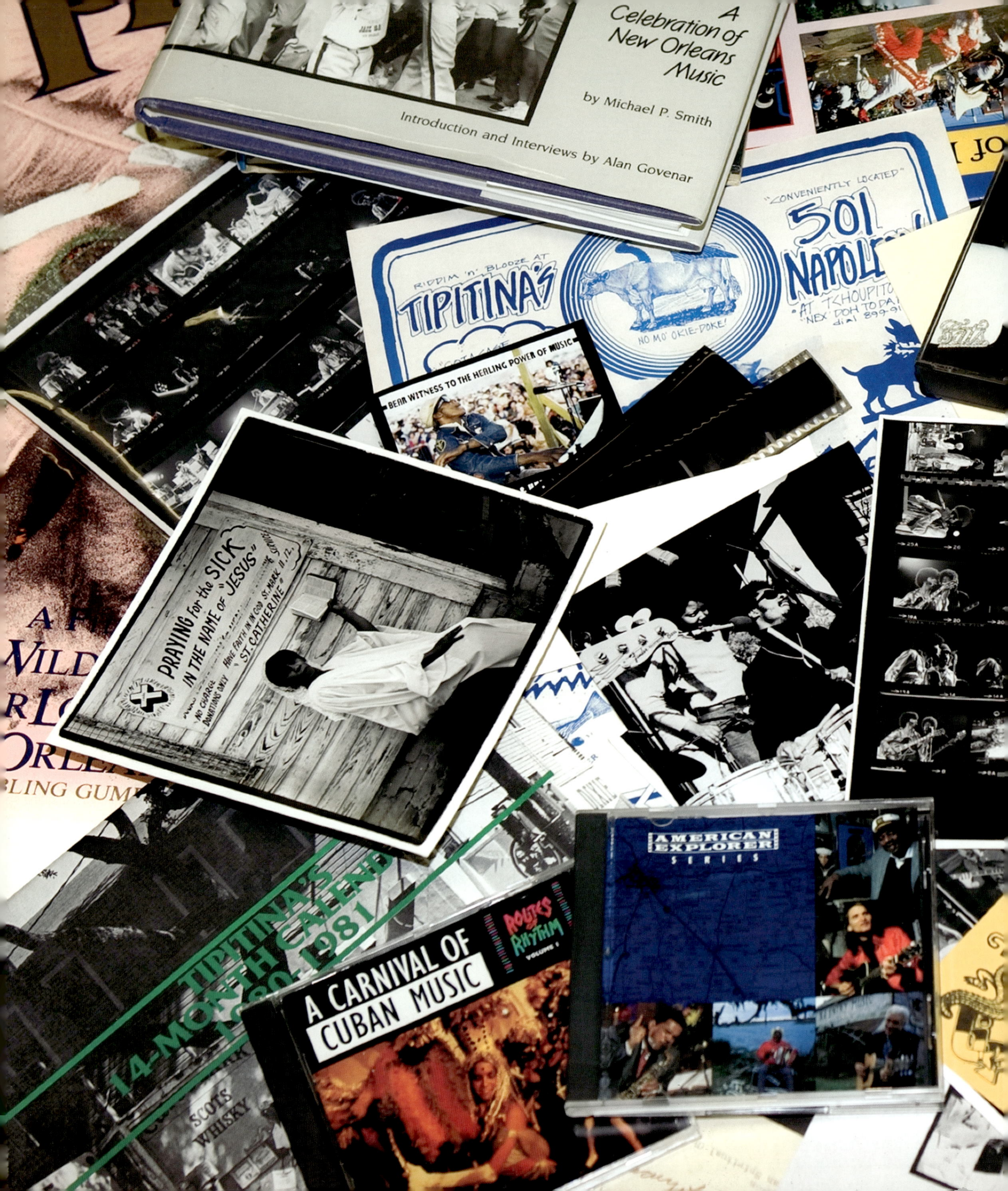
A Celebration of New Orleans Music
by Michael P. Smith
Introduction and Interviews by Alan Govenar
Riddim 'n' Blooze at
TIPITINA'S
"Conveniently Located"
No Mo' Okie-Doke!
BEAR WITNESS TO THE HEALING POWER OF MUSIC
PRAYING for the SICK
IN THE NAME OF "JESUS"
NO CHARGE
DONATIONS ONLY
HAVE FAITH IN GOD ST. MARK 11.12.
"ST. CATHERINE"
TIPITINA'S
A CARNIVAL OF CUBAN MUSIC
ROUTES OF RHYTHM
AMERICAN EXPLORER SERIES
SCOTS WHISKY